Dr. Delicious

MEMOIRS OF A LIFE IN CANLIT

Robert Lecker

Véhicule Press

Published with the generous assistance of The Canada Council for
the Arts, the Book Publishing Industry Development Program of the
Department of Canadian Heritage and the Société de développement des
entreprises culturelles du Québec (SODEC).

Cover design: David Drummond
Set in Adobe Minion by Simon Garamond
Printed by Marquis Book Printing Inc.

LIBRARY AND ARCHIVES CANADA CATALOGUING IN PUBLICATION

Lecker, Robert, 1951-
Dr. Delicious : memoirs of a life in CanLit / Robert Lecker.
Includes index.

ISBN 1-55065-210-9

1. Lecker, Robert, 1951-. 2. Canadian literature (English)—Publishing—
Canada—History—20th century. 3. Publishers and publishing—Canada—
History—20th century. 4. Publishers and publishing—Canada—Biography.
5. College teachers—Canada—Biography. I. Title.

Z483.L43A3 2006   070.5'092   C2005-907141-9

Published by Véhicule Press, Montréal, Québec, Canada
www.vehiculepress.com

Distribution in Canada by LitDistCo
orders@litdistco.ca

Distribution in U.S. by Independent Publishers Group
www.ipgbook.com

Printed in Canada on 100% post-consumer recycled paper.

DR. DELICIOUS

To Bruce —
with best wishes,

[signature]

March 24/06 —

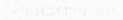

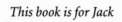

This book is for Jack

Acknowledgements

I would like to thank the following people who offered insightful comments, assisted me in my research, and stopped me from embarrassing myself too much: Graham Carr, Michael Darling, Jack David, Allan Hepburn, Don McLeod, Apollonia Steele and the Special Collections and Archive Division of the University of Calgary Library, Carolyne Van Der Meer, and Sarah Waisvisz. I am particularly grateful to Simon Dardick and Nancy Marrelli of Véhicule Press; their faith in the book means a great deal to me. Most of all, I want to thank Mary Williams, for hanging out with Dr. Delicious, and for helping out Professor Lecker in more ways than can ever be told.

Contents

INTRODUCTION

We were in Mexico, talking about Mexican family names. Then I started making up stories about our own name. We came from a long line of Russian nobility. Our ancestors were Romanian fur traders who crossed the ocean in huge ships, questing for Canadian pelts. My great-great-grandfather owned a shoe shop in Ukraine and was the local millionaire. We were potato farmers in nineteenth-century New Brunswick before opening a beauty parlour and weight loss clinic in Montreal. I had no idea. My daughter Claire, nine at the time, got into the ancestral fantasy. "Maybe there's a Lecker flag," she mused. "I haven't seen it," I said, "but you could always make one up." She hesitated a few seconds and then said, "I would put the family motto on the flag." I asked her what that motto might be. "I set my foot upon my enemies," she said, remembering the inscription on a shield depicted in a story she was reading. I wondered what I'd done to make her think of Leckers that way, stomping on their foes. Then I told her what our name really meant. More than a decade ago I had a student who came from Germany. One day after class she approached me with a question:

"Do you know what your name means in German?"
"No, what?"
"Lecker. It means delicious. You are Dr. Delicious."
I liked that title. Dr. Delicious. Canadian literature was being taught by a delicious doctor. I began to reconceive myself. Then, a few years after that, a South African student came to my office:

"Do you know what your name means in Afrikaans?"
"No, what?"
"Lekker." (She rolled the "r.") "It means nice. Especially for food. *That wors is lekker.*"

I was nice. I was delicious. I imagined myself as a tasty treat. Once you start to imagine yourself in a different way, anything is possible.

9

The idea of being Dr. Delicious instead of plain old Professor Lecker made me think about the kind of writing I would have done if I was really the tasty version of myself. Professor Lecker would be reluctant to tell stories about his own life. He would resist the temptation to make his life in Canadian literature personal. He would not gossip. He would write scholarly articles and books that no one would read. But Dr. Delicious would lead a completely different life. He would delight in his classroom experiences. He would take liberties with his life story. He would talk about the ups and downs of being a Canadian publisher. He could bring in music, painting, hypochondria, malt whisky, deranged students, government grants, questionable authors, bank debt, termite infestations, a teaching stint in Brazil, lawsuits, the pleasures of hot sauce. He would write about his passions, his failures, how the whole business of CanLit drove him crazy, lost him sleep, drove him on.

These are my memoirs of a life in CanLit. It's what I've been doing for more than 30 years. My whole professional life. I've done it as a professor in front of thousands of students who have changed the way I see this country's fiction, poetry, and literary criticism. I've done it as a publisher with a company that put out more books on Canadian literature than any other press, and paid a hefty price for doing so. My teaching life and my publishing life were always intertwined. The business end of publishing allowed me to see how literary taste and value were inseparable from the material end of things. In the beginning I believed, however naively, that literary reputations were simply a function of inherent quality. Good authors would rise to the top. But as the publishing venture expanded, I realized that literary value is also a function of the kinds of federal and provincial grants that are available to publishers, that it is dependent on the kind of money a publisher can put into promoting a book, that publishing literary criticism can be good when library budgets are good and bad when they are cut. I discovered that in Canada, selling 1,000 copies of a novel is not too shabby. I found out, to my dismay, how few people really read literary criticism. And yet there are all these professors around, writing articles and books that almost no one will read, getting grants to travel and give papers at conference sessions attended by a handful of people who are largely unfamiliar with the subject at hand. You look around the room at those sessions and you see the restlessness, the glaze in people's eyes. They don't want to be there. It's just no fun. They are there because a friend is giving a paper and needs some bodies in the room, so it doesn't look like this is all for nought. Well, it isn't all for nought. Some good ideas do come out of those papers from time to time, and they give people a sense of belonging to a community. But even the best papers are written for such a specialized audience that the literate public can have little interest in them. Most of the profs write tedious criticism that is not engaging and fun to read. Their prose is safe and boring, or it's filled with alienating buzzwords, the badge of their profession. They created a private club, closed to the public. But even within the club the members seem to have little interest in reading what the other members write.

I certainly participated in this club. For years I researched and published criticism that I thought people would read. Then, one summer, I spent three months writing a critical article on the first anthology of Canadian literature to include short fiction—Albert Durrant Watson and Lorne Pierce's *Our Canadian Literature*. It involved an enormous amount of research, but I was proud of the result. Watson was an eccentric kook who practised theosophy. He believed that he was visited by spirits who informed his editorial choices. How weird was that? A Methodist minister, Pierce saw religious value in converting people to his Canadian literary cause. So one of the groundbreaking Canadian literary anthologies was put together by an evangelical minister and a seance-seeking physician whose odd values and habits proved to be a formative influence in determining the kind of Canadian literature that came to be studied by students across the country. Their anthology was released during the crucial period of national self-redefinition following World War I—a period marked by the massive labour unrest that culminated in the Winnipeg General Strike. It struck me that their literary interests provided a key to some of the values that showed up throughout Canadian criticism, which was often evangelically nationalist, perhaps a displaced expression of the link between Methodism and the conversion experience that characterized Watson and Pierce's editorial work.

When I was writing that article I was influenced by a number of theorists who were drawn to the importance of historicizing literary works, by which they mean explaining how a work originated in the context of the social, cultural, political, and economic forces of the day. I spent all kinds of time historicizing the Watson and Pierce anthology. I brought in the Canadian theosophical movement, its impact on the Group of Seven, the Winnipeg General Strike, labour poetry, the force of Methodism. I knew the essay was rich in its range of association. Finally, I had done something different. I submitted it to one of the better-known Canadian scholarly journals. About six months later it was in print. I was sure that a few people would pick up on it, maybe even write me a little note. But the silence was deafening. I never received a single comment on that essay. I have never even seen it mentioned in a footnote. It was as if it had never existed. I spent months writing it. Something had to change.

To be frank, the publishing business had already made me cynical. I had been co-editing the critical journal *Essays on Canadian Writing* since 1975. We pursued Canadian criticism with a passion, even though it seemed clear that few of the articles we published reached a very wide audience. Without federal and provincial subsidies the journal would have folded after a few years. It is still being published, but only because it keeps getting funded. At some point, however, one has to ask whether all that funding really changed things. How would the field of Canadian literature be different today if *ECW* and other journals like it had never been published? Fewer Canadian literature profs would have tenure, but would that necessarily be a bad thing? The same question could be asked of a publishing program devoted to Canadian criticism. Why do it? From 1979 until the mid-1990s ECW Press published more books about Canadian literature than any other publishing company. I suppose the cumulative effect was to alter the critical landscape in some way, but if you stand back and try to assess whether all that activity really achieved its end—which was to broaden and encourage the study of Canadian literature—you would have to say it didn't. In the last decade there have been far fewer books published on Canadian writing than there were in the 1980s. Why? Because the companies that did devote their resources to Canadian criticism realized that it could never be sustained without government funding. And, more often than not, that funding was such a pain to get that it was easier simply to pursue other projects. In addition, publishers came to understand just how small the audience is for Canadian criticism. Why put time and resources into a venture that promises so little in the way of profit? As a result, we have entered a period of exhaustion. The really good critics have retreated as the publishing venues available to them have disappeared or been cut back.

In my case, a continuing investment in Canadian literature ended up taking me in strange directions that originally had nothing to do with my life as a professor. As I pursued those new directions I discovered that my new interests could be brought back to CanLit. During the 1990s, as the government money dried up and library budgets were cut, ECW began to focus on more commercial book projects and to publish real trade titles that were not dependent on the limited scholarly market and red-tape-entangled scholarly grants. There were books on television shows, popular culture, rock music, Canadian art, politics, travel, food, sports. I purchased some Canadian paintings. I got interested in the music my students were buying. In one of the courses I taught—an introduction to Canadian literature that enrolled about 250 students—I started each lecture by playing a Canadian song. The students brought in their discs. Wide Mouth Mason. Tragically Hip. Billy Talent. k.d. lang. Bran Van 3000. Alanis Morissette. Barenaked Ladies. Johnny Favourite. Hot Hot Heat. Ashley MacIsaac. Ron Sexsmith (ugh). I taught Michael Turner's *Hard Core Logo* and learned about Canadian punk rock. I taught Jane Urquhart's *The Underpainter* and showed slides of Tony Scherman's amazing encaustic paintings, palimpsests of narrative wax. I screened films of Leonard Cohen performing at Carnegie Hall in New York, flanked by sexy backup singers. The power was still there. I felt a lump in my throat when he remembered his encounter with Janis Joplin at the Chelsea Hotel. I asked the whole class what CD I should listen to if I listened to only one. The response was virtually unanimous: *Further Down the Spiral* by Nine Inch Nails.

OK, so it wasn't Canadian. I got into Trent Reznor's brilliant abstractions. I tried to imagine a lecture in which I would play the CD that contained five versions of his song, "The Perfect Drug," in order to demonstrate how different readings of a single text could unfold by playing on a central motif. When teaching Michael Ondaatje's "Tin Roof," I tried to explain why modern art was so suspicious of language, why so many writers were tortured about the fact that they were condemned to use language. I took a class down Sherbrooke Street and showed them the huge all-black canvas by Claude Tousignant at the Montreal Museum of Fine Arts. Is it possible to create a work of art that does not mean anything at all? Why did the museum pay so much for that pure black work? I could relate that to Ondaatje's *The Collected Works of Billy the Kid*. Why did Ondaatje begin the book with a blank page in a black frame, inviting us to complete the picture? Why was Phyllis Webb so obsessed with iambic pentameter?

When I tried to present these questions, or to bring in all kinds of outside material that might or might not work, I began to feel reinvigorated by the subject matter. But the real problem was that even if I admitted alternative media to these classes in Canadian literature, I was still dealing with writers and works that I had been teaching for years. To get out of that rut, I tried to bring in writers whom I didn't know— writers whose books had received very little in the way of extended critical commentary, so there wasn't much of a safety net when it came to teaching those works. Lynn Crosbie's amazing *Paul's Case*. Gil Courte-manche's *A Sunday at the Pool in Kigali* (so good I taught it in translation). The brilliant short stories of Lisa Moore. Then there was the final rut—my own critical voice. It wasn't as if I'd been writing the same way for years. I was aware of my prose and had been trying not to fall back on conventional academic forms of discourse. I tried to achieve a more conversational tone, to vary my sentence pacing and structure. When I gave conference papers I took even more risks. Once, I used an expletive in one of those papers, just to see how that would feel. The bottom line, however, was that I kept myself out of the writing. That's what I had been taught to do. I wasn't a creative writer after all. I had no business being confessional, or trying out various rhetorical devices normally considered the property of novelists and poets.

Then, gradually, I decided to break out. Take some risks. Tell some stories. But what stories could I tell? My students are always asking me whether I write poetry or fiction. Nope, I just write criticism, I say. Then I began to think about how strange it was to be a professor and a publisher. You got older and more decrepit, but every year the students stayed the same age, as if they were frozen in time. You walked into a class in September, looked around, and almost everyone was 19 years old. Over the years, you watched the changes in their tastes in clothing and music and movies and sex, but their basic bodies remained the same—forever young. You remembered when they had paper clips in their noses and half of their head shaved bare. Now they had tongue studs and rings hanging from their eyebrows. You remembered when they were heterosexual. You remembered their bodies before tattoos. You remembered the look on the women's faces the day Russell Smith came to class. How they believed they were immortal, most of them. Every year new students would show up in my office with impossible questions. Should I get an abortion? Why are so many Canadian protagonists called David? My boyfriend left me, what should I do? My father was killed in 9/11. I'm an alcoholic. My mother is in jail, can you help me raise bail? Can you explain phenomenology? Will you sign my passport application? Did you really impersonate a woman in an Internet chat room? Why do you listen to Linkin Park? I have no money. I am HIV positive. I have to quit school. Can I have the number of that woman who was in your office before me? My computer ate my disk. Is Yann Martel married? Can I have an extension?

A constant parade of energy, discovery, questions, desperation. I realized that the profession I had chosen made me incredibly fortunate.

Every year the university would bring me hundreds of new students, each with a story to tell. I never knew what would happen next. Year after year they put me in a classroom with those students and said do what you think is best. They never checked. Over the years I came to understand the heaviness of that responsibility, as well as the opportunity it offered for constant personal renewal, not to mention all kinds of fun. Meanwhile, the publishing business churned on. Book upon book about Canadian authors. The ever-increasing company debt, supported by heavier and heavier personal guarantees. Hatching schemes to get grants, private money, royalties, anything to keep us afloat. Dealing with the full professors who didn't want their writing touched. Dealing with the printers who were threatening to sue. Getting e-mails from loony authors who wanted to write celebrity biographies of people I had never heard of. Having a wonderful time at the University of Virginia helping an author do research on the Dave Matthews Band. Finally, in my last year with ECW, publishing a book called *WrestleCrap: The Very Worst of Pro Wrestling*. .

It started with Canadian literature and ended up there. Well, not really, because even though I left ECW Press soon after the pro wrestling book appeared I was reminded that the Canadian literature part of my life is still very much intact. I received an invitation to deliver a paper at a conference in New Zealand. A student stopped by my office to ask a question about Alice Munro. The university had recently acquired John Metcalf's library. Would I attend a reception? Then I received a memo, asking what courses I would like to teach next year. Let me see. How about a course on the Canadian long poem, a crazy course based on five big poems I've never read? Maybe I could get some of those poets to visit the class. Sounds like it could get interesting. Sounds like fun. Let go, Professor Lecker. Dr. Delicious is ready to roll.

CHAPTER ONE

When I graduated from Wagar High School in 1969 I knew nothing about Canadian literature. Looking back, I find this amazing. After all, I was living in Montreal, a bilingual city that was home to some of Canada's best-known writers—Hugh MacLennan, Norman Levine, Leonard Cohen, John Newlove, Irving Layton, F. R. Scott, Louis Dudek, and Mordecai Richler. My parents had hung out on rue St. Urbain, keeping company with Duddy Kravitz. Another group of authors—Hugh Hood, John Metcalf, Clark Blaise, Ray Smith, and Ray Fraser—formed an innovative group called the Montreal Story Teller Fiction Performance Group, informally known as the Montreal Story Tellers. They were determined to read at high schools throughout the city and to challenge existing notions about Canadian literature. Apparently they met with considerable success but they were never seen at Wagar, where I do not recall encountering a single Canadian writer in the four years it took me to get out of the place. Still, when it came to Canadian literature, Montreal at that time was the place to be.

Clearly the high school's teachers and administrators had little interest in promoting Canadian poetry or fiction. True, there was an option called "North American Literature" that included a few Canadian writers, but there was no sense that Canadian literature was a living, breathing thing, with real writers just around the corner. While I studied the French Revolution and the American Revolution in my history class, I had no idea that the Quiet Revolution in Quebec was about to reach a boiling point, and certainly no idea about how the discussion of Canadian writing could have any impact on the seismic shift that would soon engulf Quebec and Canada. One year after I graduated there were soldiers in the streets of Montreal and bombs exploding in mailboxes. The separatists were beating their drums, Hubert Aquin and others were deeply involved in writing for the separatist cause, Pierre Vallières was issuing a call to arms in *Nègres blancs d'Amériques*, Scott Symons was dreaming about combat in *Place d'Armes*, the war in Vietnam was sending thousands of draft dodgers to Canada, and thinkers across the country were becoming increasingly preoccupied with the relation between literature, identity, and nation. Who were we? Where was here? How did we write, and why?

Among literary scholars, a preoccupation with these questions had been building for years, catalysed by the introduction of the New Canadian Library series in 1955, and by the whole support system for the publication of literary criticism that developed in conjunction with the proliferation of NCL titles between 1957 and the Centennial a decade later. By the time I entered high school there were dozens of those NCL classics around, lots of critics commenting on them, and a strong group of English-Canadian writers in Quebec who were producing wonderful short stories, novels, poetry, and criticism. A complex network of associations joined those writers to wider currents in Canadian literature outside the province. The first modern history of Canadian literature, released in 1965, tried to make sense of those currents, while Northrop Frye, in his conclusion to the *Literary History of Canada*, developed his ideas about the garrison mentality as a central theme in Canadian literature, a highly influential concept that would inform (and deform) the study of Canadian literature for years to come. Yet, at least at Wagar High School, we remained blissfully unaware of these forces, largely, I suspect, because the teachers had no fundamental interest in Canadian literature, or were woefully out of date in their ideas about current Canadian writing.

Did they ever read the writers who lived in their city and whose work was reviewed in the local papers week after week? No. Better to make us study "Stopping by Woods on a Snowy Evening" than some of Layton's new poems in *Periods of the Moon*. Better to assign *The Catcher in the Rye* than *The Apprenticeship of Duddy Kravitz*, even though so many of our parents had grown up in Duddy's neighbourhood. That might have made the literature seem real. And when a Canadian book did come up, the selections were from another era. While Hugh Hood was publishing the exquisite stories in *Around the Mountain* and Leonard Cohen had just released *Beautiful Losers*, we were being asked to appreciate Morley Callaghan's dated moralizing, if we were asked to appreciate anything at all. I liked reading a lot, but the idea of reading in relation to nation was not even on the radar. In fact, concepts of Canadian identity and citizenship were never discussed, even though I was attending high school during Expo 67 and the Canadian Centennial, events that sparked fertile discussions of Canadian citizenship all over the country, none of which filtered down to me in my pre-university years. My central preoccupations at the time were coeducational and musical. Alice Munro may have been changing the face of Canadian fiction with *Dance of the Happy Shades*, but my tastes ran to "Whole Lotta Love" and "In-a-Gadda-Da-Vida."

My early interest in publishing had nothing to do with Canadian literature. It was focused on a dumpster that was permanently installed behind the premises of a suburban community newspaper called the *Monitor*. Every Monday they would throw their used lead type into the dumpster. At night, under cover of darkness, I would climb in to haul out the prize—thick sheets of lead covered in backwards type. I dragged them home and hid them in the basement until the next day when my parents went to work. Then, as soon as school was out, I'd run home and cut up the lead into small pieces which I then melted in my mother's prized stainless steel pots. I loved the way the lead bubbled and oozed around, the type dissolving into a grey swirl against the shiny silver. The only problem was that the pots had to be emptied while the lead was still in liquid form. I dumped it down the kitchen sink and into the sewers on the street, certainly contaminating hundreds. And there was always a little trace of lead left on those fancy pots. My mother never knew. I was troubled by lead poisoning for years.

Maybe that's what impaired my mathematical abilities. I just scraped through the high school matriculation exams in algebra. My parents were concerned about where I would go to university. McGill wisely turned me down. American colleges were way too expensive. And then Sir George Williams University (now Concordia University) saved the day. In 1969, just two weeks after Woodstock, they started a new program for students who had done badly in some high school subjects and very well in others. The program, called Explorations I, was based on the free school philosophy originated by Paul Goodman (in *Growing Up Absurd*) and developed later by John Holt, whose ideas became very popular after the publication of his *How Children Learn* in 1967. Holt believed that students should have complete freedom to choose how, when, and from whom they wanted to learn. Various programs like this were popping up all over North America at the time, but Explorations was the first example of it in Montreal. The university went all out to give the select group of students admitted to the program all the benefits of Holt's ideas. Rather than house the program in one of the impersonal, office-building-like university structures, they took over a small brownstone on Mackay Street and completely renovated it to accommodate the 100 or so unbalanced students they had admitted to the program.

Meeting with the entire group on the first day of classes, I could hardly believe my luck. Here we were in this spanking-fresh building with a cool professor telling us just how informal and self driven the program would be: there would be no scheduled classes; professors would drop in from time to time but if we didn't see them they could always be found in the big building across the street when they happened to be on campus; there was no formal grading plan because we would be grading our self-directed essays and projects on an honour system; and, from time to time, there would be some field trips. It was up to us, the professor stressed, to make it work. I still have a university publication that describes the program in the words of Fred Knelman, who called himself its "non-co-ordinator co-ordinator":

> Students want courses that have some relevance to them. They've been turned off in high school by the lecture system. They want to get away from that institutionalized atmosphere. Perhaps, most important of all, they're eagerly searching for individual identity. In fact, we have many students who are not enrolled in Explorations I coming round to the house. So what Explorations I seems to be doing is letting kids drop-in instead of dropping out.

How right he was. Within a week, the house had become a sex and drug-infested haven, populated by vagrants who had nothing to do with the program. People set up tents inside to mark off their territory. Mysterious cooking odours wafted through the halls. Jimi Hendrix and Santana blared from different rooms. The building reeked of hash and marijuana. I grew a beard and painted psychedelic orange stripes down the sides of my purple velvet bellbottoms. I refused, ever, to comb my shoulder-length hair. There were no classes. A professor did drop by, once, to give a funny lecture on penises in James Joyce's work. I could see immediately that literature would be my field of choice, but it was way too hectic at the Explorations I compound for me to concentrate on all the books I wanted to read, and besides, enough sex and drugs was enough sex and drugs.

I decided to apply for work at a bookstore and landed a day job at the big Classics paperback emporium on Ste-Catherine. I told myself that even though I was working full time, this was a moral and ethically valid part of my program at Sir George Williams because it would give me new insight into how literature worked. And in many ways, I was absolutely right, although I didn't find that out until much later. I couldn't understand how the store could possibly turn enough profit to stay open when so few of the customers actually bought books (the story of Canadian publishing in a nutshell). I began to have vague inklings of something called Canadian writing, but it was mainly limited to the names customers kept asking for: Cohen, Layton, Richler. Writers such as Atwood, Laurence, and Munro were not yet well known. As the term wore on, I began to be a little concerned about the various projects I was supposed to be completing for an odd array of vague courses over at Explorations, but then I reminded myself that by thinking about The Product, rather than The Process, I was capitulating to exactly what was wrong with the educational system. I vowed to respect The Process, and thought about my projects a lot.

Just before the term ended, we were told that it was time for a field trip to Goddard College, the infamous free-school university in Vermont where professors and students lived communally and where the students had actually constructed their own dorms. We piled onto a bus and, without the slightest security hitch, crossed the border into the rolling green hills of upstate Vermont and headed south to the quiet town of Plainfield. I had just bought my copy of *The Electric Kool-Aid Acid Test*.

Goddard started out in 1938 as the successor to the Goddard Seminary, which was run by the Universalist Church. Things had certainly changed by 1970. Goddard had become a centre of radical thought and experimental teaching that influenced the creation of independent student-teacher communities within the campus itself. It was a true hippie compound, replete with strange outbuildings decorated with tie-dyed wall hangings. Music was playing everywhere. I could smell musty vegetarian broths. Dirty jeans and skirts hung from nails outside low-slung wooden buildings scattered with books, records, and the wildest assortment of bongs I had ever seen. We attended a literature class, held in a big old farmhouse occupied by random cats and dogs. The class sat in a circle on the floor and the professor passed around a joint while one of the students handed out hash brownies. This completely convinced me that literature might be an interesting area to pursue professionally, although I had absolutely no idea, at the time, how one qualified to be a professor. Somehow, this man had made it. I could too.

Soon after we returned to Montreal, I learned that it was time to meet with a professor in order to submit my grades. I thought briefly

20

about all the thinking I had done during the term and awarded myself an "A" in every course. Most of my Explorations colleagues did the same. And then we did it again, at the end of the spring term. Much as I'm sure Sir George Williams respected our thinking and was pleased with how well we had done, the administration was not respectful and pleased enough to continue the program. Our hippie haven was shut down, and I had to get used to the crowded elevators in the Hall Building. No campus. No grass. Huge classes. I knew I wouldn't last long. In fact, I lasted two years, up to the day that I submitted a history paper to Professor Diubaldo. This time, I wasn't grading my own paper. He gave me a "D." I went running to see him during his office hours. "How could I get such a bad grade?" I asked. "It's simple," he said. "You are a not a history student. This is a literature paper. Maybe you should change your major."

What good advice. I convinced my parents to let me check out the programs in English at various other Canadian universities. As soon as I arrived at the windswept barrenness that was York University in 1972, I knew I had found a new home. Back in those days, York was still cut off from the city of Toronto proper and the university bordered on farmlands. Ingeniously, the planners of this young institution (it was founded in 1959) had hit upon the idea of putting a pub in each of the colleges comprising the university and had joined those colleges through underground tunnels, which meant that a determined undergraduate could visit every pub in a single day, even in the middle of winter, without putting on a coat or shoes. There was no need for me to look any further, and besides, a high school friend of mine was also heading for York, so we could get an apartment together.

By the end of August 1972 Rick and I had found ourselves a place near Bathurst and Wilson and, soon after, we started attending classes. I spent a lot of time in those cozy pubs, playing chess and drinking. School held little interest. I was too busy with the pubs, or setting up house, and trying to meet women. We had no furniture. We knew nothing about cooking. IKEA did not exist. I suggested that if we got ourselves a bunch of bricks and plywood we could make the furniture we needed. We found a brickyard and, over several nights, carried away hundreds of bricks, the building blocks of our newfound sense of interior design. With the furniture under control it was time to start cooking, but neither of us was particularly eager to wash dishes. I came up with the idea of the completely disposable dinner kit. The concept was simple. One pot would be used to cook all food, which would then be served in a disposable plastic bag and eaten with disposable plastic forks and knives. At the end of the meal, everything would be thrown out, leaving only one pot to wash. This environmentally responsible plan lasted exactly one night, for as soon as the baggie was filled with our first meal (hot rice and peas) it immediately melted, leaving our dinner oozing all over the table. I complained to my mother. She sent me some slightly used stainless steel pots.

They reminded me of home—Montreal—where my girlfriend and future wife was still living. Paula would make the trip down the 401 the following year, also to attend York, but for the time being she was still with her parents. I wanted to see her as much as possible, and I convinced myself that the distance separating the two cities was mainly a state of mind, especially because the highway speed limits were higher back then and, with any luck, pedal to the metal, I could make the trip in just under five hours. At one point, I was doing it almost weekly. The only thing that got in the way of my desire to sprint down that highway were the Ontario drivers, who had little sense of what the outside lane was for: reckless speeding. They would loll in that passing lane as if theirs was the only car on the road, never ever checking their rear-view mirrors. After a month of getting right up on their bumpers and flashing my brights at them while honking my horn, I realized that some kind of special action was required. They were oblivious road hogs. When I got into Montreal after one particularly frustrating trip I headed directly for an auto parts store. I described my problem in detail. The young man behind the counter made a fantastic suggestion: "Why don't you get an industrial air horn installed under the hood? We can put a toggle switch on your dash, and you'll be all set." Then he added: "Don't worry, when you hit that switch, they'll get out of the lane." Obviously this was the perfect solution, and besides, I loved the idea of having a massive air horn under my hood. I had the installation done. They had to put an air compressor in the trunk, and that took up quite a bit of space, but what did I care? I wanted those Ontario drivers out of my way.

Two days later, on the return trip, I got to try it out. Sure enough, there was a car with Ontario plates, sleeping in the left-hand lane, right in front of me. I gave him the brights. Nothing. I gave him the regular horn. Nothing. I gave him the brights and the horn together. Still no inkling that he wasn't the only vehicle on the road. Incredible. I reached down for the toggle switch. Flick! There was a momentary hesitation and an almost inaudible hum. Then a roar came out of the front of my car that sounded like a nuclear acoustic explosion. I could feel the back end lift briefly off the road. Ahead of me, the body in the driver's seat rose up as if it had been electrocuted. The car swung crazily across the road. For a moment I thought he would lose control, but no. He woke up. Finally. He got the point. He moved over. I passed him at 90 m.p.h., and shot him a dirty look. I am a student of literature, man. I am from Quebec. You are from Ontario. Move out of the way! Looking back now I can see that there was a little bit of Dr. Delicious driving down that road.

Even in those first years at York I had very little sense of anything happening in Canadian literature, even though I was surrounded by some of the most interesting and creative people in the business. John Lennox, Barbara Godard, Miriam Waddington, Irving Layton, Frank Davey, Eli Mandel, and Clara Thomas were all teaching at that time, but I never met them as an undergraduate, choosing instead to take courses on British, American, and European literature. I remember the moment I decided to enter graduate school. It was during a class on world literature given by William Gairdner, and the book we were about to study was *Madame Bovary*. Gairdner came into the class and wrote three sentences on the blackboard. The sentences resembled each other in some ways, but in other ways they were very different in terms of their vocabulary, syntax, and grammatical structure. "What unites these three sentences?" Gairdner asked. I pointed out that the first of the sentences was in fact the first sentence of the translation that we were using in class. Gairdner then made his point: the remaining two examples were the first sentences of other translations of the same work.

Could there be any more immediate and convincing demonstration of the instability of language? How could such a famous book actually not be a single entity once it had made the voyage into English? For the French, there remained but one *Madame Bovary*; yet for English readers, there were many, each with a claim to some kind of authenticity. It would also work the other way around, of course. For me, one *Ulysses*; for the French, how many? Only later would I come to understand that no book was stable, even in its original language, and that one of the most liberating aspects of literary study was the realization that in many respects, each and every text is inexhaustible, open to endless possibilities. For the time being, however, I was content in the feeling that somehow literature resisted authority. Perhaps if I continued to study it I could partake in that resistance, find some kind of liberation that would keep me free. I decided to apply to graduate school at York, got my acceptance, and found myself in the Master's program in the fall of 1974.

My first year in the program did not start out well. I enrolled in a course on the British Romantics taught by Brian Hepworth. On the first day of class I was assigned a seminar presentation for the following week, which meant I would have to talk for about 30 minutes on Wordsworth, a poet I knew nothing about. I had never read any of his poems, except a few here and there in a high school anthology. About three days before the presentation was due I began to panic. I had no idea how to proceed, absolutely no context in which to approach this monumental task. I decided to call up Professor Hepworth and confess my limitations. Surely he would give me some helpful pointers. I dialled the number:

Professor Hepworth: Hello.

Me: Hello Professor Hepworth. This is Robert Lecker. I'm in your graduate Romantics class and I'm giving the presentation next week.

Professor Hepworth: Yes?

Me: Well, the truth of the matter is that I've hit a bit of a dead end, and I'm not quite sure where to turn.

Professor Hepworth: Oh.

Me: Well, I was wondering if you could offer any advice or help.

Professor Hepworth: Yes, I can.

Me (feeling better now): Oh, thank you so much. What would you suggest?

Professor Hepworth: Do you have a towel?

Me (puzzled): Yes.

Professor Hepworth: Do you have hot running water?

Me: Yes.

Professor Hepworth: And do you have a bowl?

Me (more puzzled): Yes, I do.

Professor Hepworth: This is what I suggest. Fill the bowl with warm water.

Me: Yes?

Professor Hepworth: After you have filled the bowl with water, I suggest you dip the towel in the water, wring it out, and wrap it around your head. Then, try very, very hard to *think*. Can you do that?

Me: I think so.

Professor Hepworth: Good. Do you have any other questions?

Me: No, Professor Hepworth.

Professor Hepworth: Fine then. See you in class.

Needless to say, I immediately dropped the class. I was too embarrassed to ever show my face there again. However, I did take three courses that would shape the way I thought about literature for years to come. I still feel that what inspires us most in a good literature course is not so much the content (although it doesn't hurt to have great reading material) but the nature of the instructor, the way he or she opens up possibilities and challenges assumptions. With the exception of my Wordsworthian failure, I was incredibly lucky in this regard.

There was a seminar on the Pre-Raphaelite movement with William Whitla that brought me into a rich, evocative world of poetry, painting, music, and design. Classes were held in Whitla's cramped office, a space so piled with books and knick-knacks that it was hard to find a place for five chairs. We sat in a semicircle around Whitla's cluttered desk and talked about religion, literary values, and the making of art. I felt like I had entered some kind of secret club. Whitla was an ordained minister who had written a book on religious belief in Browning. Listening to him speak, I understood for the first time that religious experience had a literary equivalent and that if I had lost my original faith, I might yet find another. Whitla insisted that we take responsibility for our opinions, a demand that woke me up. In the second course I took with him—on Tennyson and Browning—he interrupted me in the middle of a seminar presentation and shouted "Stop! Stop it right now! I can't stand such moral relativism." I had no idea what "moral relativism" meant, but you can bet I looked it up. I began to understand that there were positions to be taken about literature, and that somehow this positioning was political. What I was missing—and how would I ever find it?—was some kind of ideological stance. Whitla had it. Where did he get it?

I had another intense experience in a class led by Hédi Bouraoui, an Algerian scholar who wrote poetry and who was interested in the politics of translation. Bouraoui's course was called "Contemporary Trends in Fiction," an eye-opening exposure to postmodernism and the theoretical problems associated with writing about contemporary literature. Bouraoui was interested in what was then still an exotic breed of critic—the French poststructuralists and critics of consciousness, who were known collectively as the French New Critics, although they bore no resemblance to the New Critics in the United States. Bouraoui introduced us to Roland Barthes and Georges Poulet, among others, and encouraged us to experiment with critical readings that employed their methods.

I had been reading literary criticism for a few years now and continued to be amazed by what a good critical article could reveal. Back at Sir George Williams, after Explorations was shut down, I took a conventional course on American literature with David Ketterer. I remember the first time I went off to the library in search of an article on *Billy Budd* and found something on hair and masculinity and Christianity in the novella. I couldn't believe that anyone could actually see these patterns in a literary work. I had seen none of them. I wanted to be able to do that kind of reading. Bouraoui's interest in the French critics sent me in search of Poulet's books, most of which were not yet translated into English. I knew that in order to really understand Poulet I would have to know more about French phenomenology, Heidegger, and especially Gaston Bachelard. But for the time being I was content to revel in the sheer liberty offered by Poulet's approach. For Poulet, an author did not exist at specific points in time, nor did his work develop over time. Rather, the author's consciousness infused all his work at every moment of its existence, so that the last word he or one of his characters uttered could stand, with equal weight, next to the first. And, no matter who they were or what role they were assigned, each and every character in some way embodied the consciousness of the author, spoke for him, provided evidence of his unwavering perception of self, time, and space.

Poulet turned the author every which way. He took the author's text, scrambled it up, cast fragments of it out in new forms, and rearranged entire narrative worlds according to his own critical whims. I loved his stylistic eccentricities, how his critical prose and imagery were always excessive, over the top:

> The true life is the life of causes. He who reaches it arrives not only at omniscience but omnipotence. By regressive abstraction he is transported to what Goethe called the Kingdom of the Mothers, the kingdom where everything *pre-exists*, and which contains all times, all places, and all forms. He has found "the motion at its origin"; he has succeeded in "placing himself within the thought of God in order to become initiate of the ideas of creation."

Or:

> All of society is "a vast field incessantly shaken by a tempest of interests." Into this whirlwind, unforgettably described by Balzac at the beginning of *La Fille aux yeux d'or*, all human beings find themselves snatched up willy-nilly; they have to

"exceed their forces," "abuse their senses," and find themselves the prey of a contagious agitation which is simultaneously a way to life and a way to death.

Reading Poulet was like entering a funhouse with crazy hallways pointing in every direction. There was no logic, no way of knowing which way to go or where one hallway would end and another begin; it was all part of the same building, and travelling through those corridors became an intoxicating, hallucinatory voyage of discovery and displacement.

Poulet disrupted sequence and broke all the rules the American New Critics had been so careful to put in place, writing out of a tradition that in fact cared little for American standards or the burdens of literary proof. I began to see that criticism was aligned with traditions that came out of philosophical and historical values that were nation-centred, self-centred, culture-centred. Every word that Poulet wrote said "I am French," in the same way that every word that Leslie Fiedler wrote said "I am American." In glimpsing this fundamental connection between criticism and nation I was also opening the door to a question that would come to preoccupy me later: how did Canadian criticism embody national value?

Although I would not be able to address that question for many years, I began to think about the relation between criticism and nation, and went off in search of writers who were pursuing similar concerns. In following this path, it was inevitable that I would stumble on other French critics, since the French were so obsessed with their own culture. That's how I ran into Roland Barthes, whose work had also been recommended by Bouraoui. Unlike Poulet, who remained relatively unknown to English-speaking critics, Barthes's structuralist theories had gained considerable recognition in North America, particularly after the translation of *Le degré zéro de l'écriture* into English in 1968 (15 years after its original publication).

The two books that really altered my path, however, were Barthes's *S/Z*, first published in 1970 (and translated in 1974) and *The Pleasure of the Text*, originally published in 1973. When I first read *S/Z* I could hardly believe what Barthes had done with Balzac's short story, "Sarrasine." I had felt an initial wave of critical liberation through Poulet, and now there was another French critic who turned reading into a multi-levelled, sensuous experience that was intense and exotic. The possibilities offered by Barthes's reading seemed endless and empowering. Now there were multiple paths to follow in any kind of interpretive act, and anything could be admitted to that act—music, painting, politics, sexuality, fashion, food—all in interaction with the critic's own life, which was itself a text, a set of codes weaving in and out of the interpretive process. As if that wasn't enough to chew on, Barthes proposed the distinction between pleasurable and blissful texts. Here was a critic who was talking about reading as if it were the same as going to a sex show:

> The pleasure of the text is not the pleasure of the corporeal striptease or of narrative suspense. In these cases, there is no tear, no edges: a gradual unveiling: the entire excitation takes refuge in the hope of seeing the sexual organ (schoolboy's dream) or in knowing the end of the story (novelistic satisfaction).

I admired Barthes's irreverent interest in the smallest detail. His commentary was so intelligent and wide-ranging, yet at the same time it was a kind of critical dandyism gone wild, a flagrant submersion in the sheer sensuousness of reading. There were no brakes on this man's thinking. There were no rules. He went wherever his reading impulses seemed to take him. ("What I enjoy in a narrative is not directly its content or even its structure, but rather the abrasions I impose upon the finer surface: I read on, I skip, I look up, I dip in again.") I wanted nothing more than to follow that lead. Looking back, I see that I was increasingly attracted to critics whose readings pursued the critical equivalence of a metaphorical dash for freedom. A seduction. A love affair. A jailbreak. I must have felt closed in, somehow, if what I wanted most was to break out, bypass the rules, admit the inadmissable into the criticism I was trying to write. I continued to follow Barthes and Poulet and finally wrote my Master's thesis on a comparison of their work. The English department's resistance to accepting this as a valid research topic was an indication of the distance between French theory and the study of English literature at the time.

During the first year of my graduate studies, while I was working on the thesis, I was also enrolled in a course on twentieth-century Canadian poetry, taught by Eli Mandel. Above all the others, this was the course that permanently changed the way I thought about literature, and it was also the experience that would dramatically affect the course of my life. I still miss Eli, who died in 1992. I don't think he was reading the French critics at the time, but the way he approached literature and teaching sure made it seem like he was following a similar path. He would come into class, rumpled and a bit late, and pause to consider the poetry he had asked us to read for that day. You could almost see the brain circuits snapping around, searching for connections, interrogating the pedagogical strategy that would be appropriate to the material. Then, out of nowhere, suddenly, he would ask a question no one could understand. Did we believe in mythopoeia? Was James Reaney a pastoral or a tragic writer or both? How did Margaret Avison understand the connection between religion and metaphor? Eli played these questions up and down, left and right. It was like he was sitting in front of a piano, and each key was a literary or philosophical concept. He would play that piano, madly and raucously and erratically and with the greatest respect, every week. He would follow a line of thought, bring in five references we had never heard of, get off the track, follow a new route, make some brilliant comparisons, get off on another tangent, pull in three new notes and then ask another question even more baffling than the first, which would excite him into telling stories about all kinds of things, until you had no idea where you were going but could not help but feel exhilarated by the ride.

I remember the day he allowed me to understand the nature of metaphor in a way that permanently changed my life. He converted me, and I had to tell others about this. I think I actually still believed what I had been taught in high school—that simile was a comparison using "like" or "as" and metaphor was a comparison without like or as. What the hell did that mean, anyhow? It was a ridiculous definition that made it certain no high school student would have the slightest inkling of how powerful and transformative a true understanding of metaphor could be. No, Eli said, metaphor had nothing do with comparison. It had to do with identity. Metaphor was about the epiphany that "A *is* B." Which could mean: *I am you.* But it went further than this, because Eli pointed out that from this perspective the biblical apocalypse was synonymous with the moment at which all human forms were identified. He quoted Blake's *Jerusalem*:

And from the thirty-two nations of the earth among the living creatures:
All human forms identified, even tree, metal, earth & stone. All
Human forms identified, living, going forth & returning wearied
Into the planetary lives of years, months, days & hours—reposing
And then awaking into his bosom in the life of Immortality.

Could I possibly understand what Eli was getting at through Blake? That true metaphor meant more than being in the world; it was about becoming the very world we inhabited. And if God or Christ was the embodiment of this becoming, then the ability to understand metaphor was synonymous with apprehending God. Metaphor was a form of being that invoked transcendence. Understanding metaphor involved the process of seeing how one thing morphed into another, and another, until, in the final transformation, metaphor became God.

All of a sudden I understood that religious experience, the drug experience, sexual ecstasy, Zen meditation, or one's possession by art were all forms of experiencing metaphor as the abandonment of the ego and the removal of time and space. Art was God. Literature could get you there. This realization had a profound impact on me, because it meant that the act of reading and interpretation could also operate on a metaphorical level. One did not have to be a poet to find identity; the critic could find it too. Perhaps the aim of criticism was not to enrich the ego but to find ways of bypassing it by opening up new kinds of identification, and, ultimately, a new identity. Now the first lines of Margaret Avison's poem, "Snow," finally made sense:

Nobody stuffs the world in at your eyes.
The optic heart must venture: a jail-break
And re-creation . . .

Although I had long ceased to be a practising Jew and felt alienated from the traditional notions of God I had grown up with, Eli allowed me to see that reading could be transformative and apocalyptic, and that I could believe in a god again, which was metaphoric identity itself. If this was true, then the study of literature could change me. It could change my very perception of the world. How often is it that you meet a teacher who really transforms your perception of yourself? How often can you say that the impact of a teacher is truly existential in its impact on your thinking, or on your life?

Eli had so many sides. We would take a break in the middle of a class and head down to one of the campus pubs that had made York so inviting to me. Eli would sit hunched over a scotch and tell stories about strange literary conundrums, various poets' eccentricities, Harold Bloom's ideas about the anxiety of influence, the complexities of prairie writing. The tales would unfold. More beer would appear. Eli had another scotch. And the class moved from written texts to oral storytelling.

He was obsessed with the role of the critic and the role of the poet. One day I met him getting out of his car at one of the university parking lots. As we walked toward the campus buildings he started naming off flowers. He had spent the last few days, he said, learning their names by the dozen. I asked him why he was doing this. "How can I call myself a poet if I don't know the names of flowers?" he responded. Eli could speak like a romantic, and obviously there was a residual part of him that wanted to believe in the connection between poetry and flowers, but more importantly he was an angst-ridden Jew, brilliant in his awareness of how the Holocaust and guilt and memory had forever compromised poetic language. He was suspicious of beauty, just as he pursued it, and it was the tension between his desire for flowers and his knowledge of Dachau that energized his aesthetic.

> I am the mouths
> of smiling old men
>
> there rises from me
> the scent of orange-blossoms
>
> I speak in the words
> of the ancient dead
> arranged
> in the raging sun
>
> in the stiffening age of days
>
> and in the temple of my house
>
> one becomes another
> I am crazed by poetry

This was my first real exposure to Canadian literature, and what Eli was doing with it was all the more amazing because most of the writers we were studying were completely new to me. It was as if a huge door had been thrown open to a world filled by writers who were all of intense interest, especially in the eyes of Mandel, who made me feel that there was an urgency to his questions, a passionate need to get to the fundamentals of this drama called Canadian poetry. Of course there was no getting to the bottom of anything under that kind of tutelage. Yet it was clear that Eli was speaking as a person who was committed to a community. He spoke about Canadian writers—both living and dead—as though they were right there with us in the classroom (or the pub). I began to get the sense that there was a converse among these writers, or that the converse could be created through critical commentary and intervention.

Although I seldom spoke to my fellow students about this at the time, I think we shared the sense that there was a common purpose in studying Canadian literature, and that in many ways, committing oneself to that kind of study was a kind of conversion experience. On one hand, we were becoming involved in the literature precisely at the time when so many books were appearing that were unlike anything seen before— from Robert Kroetsch's *The Studhorse Man* to Michael Ondaatje's *The Collected Works of Billy the Kid* to bpNichol's *The Martyrology*. Like many others, I was drawn to the experimental nature of these writers, but also to the growing debate that surrounded the evaluation of their work. While some critics (notably the "thematic critics") were promoting an understanding of Canadian literature based on models of national self-recognition, others rejected this national bias in favour of criticism that embraced a growing interest in postmodern thought, and still others tried to find a way of marrying postmodern and national values.

In *Butterfly on Rock*, D.G. Jones had suggested that finding Canadian literature was akin to coming out of the wilderness, and in fact most of the critics who were concerned with national identity presented the very recognition of Canadian literature as a means of countering absence, the wilderness, the dissolution of community and self. In contrast, those who argued against the inherent nationalism of thematic criticism positioned themselves as proponents of formal, stylistic, and structural approaches. Yet the fact remains that they claimed to be specialists in Canadian literature, despite their assertion that it was reductive to organize literatures in relation to national units. They taught Canadian poetry and fiction. They published in Canadian journals. They got money from the Canada Council. But they wanted to be sure everyone understood that, fundamentally, they did not believe that the place called Canada could be spoken about as a distinctive place with its own history, values, and cultural concerns.

One of the most militant anti-thematic critics was Frank Davey, who had been editing the critical journal *Open Letter* at York. Davey encouraged experimentation and dissidence; *Open Letter* often explored ideas about pataphysics, sound poetry, and aesthetics that seemed entirely foreign to me. I had no idea what kind of teacher Frank was in the class-room, but I was shocked, along with many of the other graduate students,

when, in 1973, *Open Letter* published a devastating article by John Bentley
Mays on the poetry of Phyllis Webb. Although I didn't know Webb's
work intimately, there was a consensus that she was a rigorous and
exacting author who had written some of the most powerful and
demanding poems that Canada had ever seen. But Mays, who was a
professor at York back then, didn't see it that way. In his view, Webb's
works were "testimony" that "as a woman and a writer" she was a "decisive,
unmitigated failure." Why? For Mays, Webb was a poet

> whose whole desire goes out, finally, to the barbarian silence
> and lithic insensibility of things; whose poetry does not 'mature,'
> but merely changes as her tactics of self-destruction vary; whose
> work is as vain, sectarian, as without acme or distinction, as
> distorted by her lusts, and as inconclusive as any in the recent
> career of literary modernism . . . if only she had given us one
> monumental poem, or had she loved or hated heroically, or
> shown evidence of courage toward one besetting sin, charity,
> let alone intelligence, would compel a reversal of verdict . . .

I couldn't understand why Mays would launch this kind of attack. Apparently it had so upset Webb that she had gone into depression and even
deeper seclusion. Mays seemed to be working through some of his own
problems in this angry critique. I wasn't surprised to learn, a year or two
later, that he had decided to leave York. But what I never really understood
was Davey's willingness to publish the essay. It was one thing to offer
criticism of a writer's work; it was quite another thing to say that a writer's
work provided evidence of personal failure. Would Davey continue to
support this kind of attack?

He was obviously willing to mount his own attacks. Davey had
delivered his pivotal critique of the thematic critics at a conference in
1974, and the air was full of rebellion. At the same time, the influence of
the thematic critics remained powerful, due in large part to the success
of Atwood's *Survival*, which had appeared in 1972. One could look away
from Canada to the models offered by critics such as Davey or Kroetsch,
or one could try to figure out, along with writer-poets such as Mandel
and Dennis Lee (in *Civil Elegies*) how Canadian writers could find an
authentic voice in the face of those who would turn away from the idea
of nation as a determining force. I realized that I was in graduate school,
studying Canadian literature, at a point of transition. I could not
understand, and never did understand, what the point was of talking

about Canadian literature if one took the Canadian out of it. Instead, it seemed to me of crucial importance to understand what made that literature different. And if literature was the reflection of a community— however divided that community might be—then it would be productive to examine that reflection. The field was completely open. The symbols of nationhood were still being born. After all, "O Canada" was only adopted as the national anthem in 1975, and it was only a decade earlier that Canada got its own flag.

The more I became aware of the tensions emerging in Canadian criticism, the more I wanted to participate in that tension. It energized the discussions we were having in Mandel's class, although he seldom took sides. Instead, he encouraged us to think about the problems posed by different theoretical models, then to bring that thinking back to a consideration of the author at hand. Still, it was clear that he was encouraging us to conceive of Canadian literature as a distinct field with its own set of problems.

It was Mandel who encouraged my own intervention in that field through a specific course assignment that would also change the direction of my life. He had complained, since the beginning of the term, about the paucity of criticism and reference material on Canadian literature, and especially on contemporary Canadian poets. He encouraged us to undertake the compilation of bibliographies of primary and secondary material on specific figures. I had virtually no idea about how bibliographies were created or about how they should be organized and edited. However, the challenge of doing a bibliography seemed to offer a welcome alternative to the term papers I had been writing for close to five years. I asked Mandel if he could suggest a figure who might benefit from such a bibliography, and he immediately answered "John Newlove."

Newlove was a highly respected poet who had grown up on the prairies and travelled the country from east to west. He was a loner whose stark, pared-down lines conveyed the sparse elementalism of the prairie landscape that had been imprinted on his consciousness. It was not happy poetry. Newlove frequently presented himself as a loser, an outcast, a marginal figure living on the fringes of a glutted material world. He became interested in Native culture and wrote some of his best poems— especially "The Pride"—about how a proud and distinct Native culture had been assimilated and wiped out. Compared to the sensuousness and polyvalent richness of so many of the poems we had read in Mandel's course, Newlove's poetry struck me as pristine in its refusal to accept the transformations wrought by metaphor:

I am too tense,
decline to dance
verbally. The flower
is not in its colour,
but in the seed.

It's one thing to read a poet's best poems—those that have been filtered out and reproduced in anthologies. It's quite another thing to head off into the rare book room of various libraries in search of the first poem, the first publication, the manuscripts stained with coffee and smelling of cigarettes, distressed by the author's notes to himself: groceries to buy, pills to take, a scribbled word that didn't work. The John Newlove I discovered in the stacks at York and the University of Toronto bore little resemblance to the poet I had encountered in Mandel's course. I found a copy of *Grave Sirs*, Newlove's first chapbook, published in a limited edition of 300 in Vancouver by Robert Reid and Takao Tanabe, meticulous typographers and book designers who had invested themselves in Newlove's art. How many of those original 300 copies still existed? Where had they gone? I began to understand that Newlove saw himself operating in the context of other artists who were pursuing strong forms of minimalism, and I began to get a sense that there was a West Coast aesthetic at work that was distinctly at odds with the more centralist aesthetic aligned with Ontario and even English Quebec.

Beyond the excitement of holding those rare early chapbooks, including *Elephants, Mothers, and Others*, and *Moving in Alone*, I saw some really eccentric material—an unbound, unboxed collection of eight poetic fragments called *Notebook Pages*, illustrated by Charles Pachter, and a strange little folder called *It #12 (Burn and Other Poems)*, published in Platteville, Wisconsin, in 1967. What was Newlove's connection to Wisconsin in 1967? It was clear that he was involved with a range of poets and artists who were definitely off the beaten track. His early periodical publications showed a similar pattern. Although his first published poem appeared in the relatively well-known *Prism*, his poetry was also printed in small journals such as *Mountain, Evidence,* and *Tzarad*. I wondered about those little magazines, the people running them, and how Newlove had entered their worlds. Somehow, his involvement in the small magazine scene made him seem even more exotic to me, and I began to realize that there were political values involved in choosing to publish with a relatively unknown magazine or press.

The research on this bibliography busied me for months, because I was not only trying to list all of Newlove's published work; I was also creating a record of the criticism (articles, sections of books, book reviews, and interviews) that had been published on him to date. When it came to this task, I could see that Mandel was right: although Newlove had been in print since 1962, it was now 1974 and only three full-length articles had appeared on his work. This says something about the kind of poetry Canadian critics were focusing on during this period—not Newlove's kind—but it also says something about the way in which research could be carried out, simply because there were so few resources allowing people to access the criticism that did exist. The main source of information was R.E. Watters's *A Checklist of Canadian Literature and Background Materials, 1628-1960*, but that stopped before Newlove had published his first poem. Although there were listings in the *Canadian Periodical Index* and the *MLA Bibliography*, these tended to focus on the better-known publications, which meant that many of the articles that appeared in newer and less-recognized journals remained sidetracked. Although I was worried about getting the bibliography completed on time, I had fun filling in the gaps and uncovering new creative and critical journals. Slowly, I began to form a picture of Newlove's evolution.

One day I found myself back in Montreal during a school break, armed with the knowledge that Newlove was then living in the city, and less than a mile from where I was staying. I decided to call him up. At this point, given all the research I had been doing, it really was like calling a myth, somebody who existed in archives and special collections, but not in the flesh. A dry, deep voice answered the phone. Could this be John Newlove? He said it was. I quickly explained my project and said I was hoping he would help me fill in some blanks. He invited me to visit him the following day. Sometime before lunch I rang the doorbell and was let in by a distinguished-looking man with a shock of white hair. He didn't seem to be too interested in talking about his own work. He asked me if I played chess. Yes, I did. We played a game. He asked me if I liked scotch. I didn't but I said yes. I got a big shot in a glass with a sploosh of water from the kitchen faucet. It was probably around 11 a.m. We played more chess. Newlove told stories. I got few answers to my questions.

He was living in the middle of dozens of boxes of books, piled up everywhere. I asked him if he was moving. "No," he said, "selling." He drew out book after book apparently slated for pickup by a used book dealer—rare books of poetry, books on Native history and culture, big art books. "Why are you getting rid of these?" I asked. "Got to pay the rent," he said matter-of-factly. Then, as he was closing up one of the boxes, a long piece of thick paper caught his eye. An early poem, written by hand, and dated. He held it out. "Take it. It's yours," he said.

I felt as if that piece of paper was vibrating in my hand. I left, clutching the poem, wondering where the peripatetic Newlove would go once his books had been sold. He seemed so calm, so desperate. I hatched a little money plan. When I got back to Toronto I took the poem down to Richard Landon at the Thomas Fisher Rare Book Library and asked if it was worth anything. Richard said it was and offered me a few hundred dollars for the poem, which I quickly accepted. When the cheque from U of T arrived I deposited the cheque and mailed one drawn on my account to Newlove with a note of thanks. Months later, it had not been cashed. I called him up again, wondering what was going on. Newlove said, "The money is yours. I destroyed the cheque." Those words told me something about the man's generosity that had escaped my most detailed research.

In the end, the bibliography was a mess, although I had no idea how much of a mess. I handed it in to Mandel and kept a copy for myself. It was getting close to the end of term—spring 1975. A few days after I submitted the paper I was walking along the hallway in the Ross Building, which housed the Department of English. The hall was lined with the little cell-like offices usually assigned to graduate students and teaching assistants—four people and four desks in 150 square feet. As usual, the doors and walls were plastered with signs and notices. Somehow, surrounded by all that paper, my eye fell on the door of room S765 and the discreet note that someone had stuck to it:

> New journal on Canadian writing
> Essays wanted
> Knock here

That sounded interesting. I didn't have an essay, but I had a bibliography. Maybe I could get it published. I knocked. The door swung open. Standing in front of me was Jack David.

CHAPTER TWO

Jack was sharing that tiny office with two other grad students who were involved in the early days of *Essays on Canadian Writing*, a critical journal on Canadian literature that he founded in 1974 after attending a meeting of English graduate students where he learned that unused funds were being channelled into end-of-term beer parties. He lobbied the graduate association, got some money, and launched the journal. One of *ECW*'s original titles was *Using up the Beer Money*. The first issue reflected Jack's interest in sound and concrete poetry. He was completing his doctoral dissertation on Earle Birney and was drawn to Birney's concrete poetry. But he seemed to be even more interested in bpNichol's artistry. Jack was collecting the eccentric books and ephemera that marked Nichol's career. He published a well-researched article introducing bp's concrete poetry as well as a bibliography of works by and about Nichol in the first issue of the magazine, which sported an image of a Canadian nickel on the cover, in recognition of the focus on his work. From a design standpoint, the issue had little to recommend it. It was so underdesigned that it looked special in its plainness. The cover price was $1.50. If you can find a copy today, you'll have to shell out about $20, which says something about the historic value that issue managed to achieve. It may not have been pretty, but it stands out as one of the first student journals willing to risk devoting so much space to experimental writing. Other articles in the issue demonstrated that the magazine was ready to embrace the irreverent, particularly when T.D. MacLulich took the unusual step of publishing an essay that defended Atwood's *Survival* at a time when virtually every other critic was howling against her thematic guide to Canadian literature.

As the editor of the journal, Jack seemed to be pretty nonjudgmental, which surprised me. I had given him my Newlove bibliography. A few days later he told me he would publish it in the next issue of the magazine. I suppose he saw the possibility of encouraging some continuity in the journal's focus on bibliography, which he had established in the first issue. He said the bibliography would soon be edited and typeset. I would be asked to come in to proof the galleys. Me? Proof? Soon I was back in the office. Jack handed me a long galley sheet in a scroll that I unfurled like a glossy postmodern Torah, putting weights on each end to keep it from curling while I proofread my work, special blue marker in hand. I felt like I was doing something important. I had no idea what to do.

I'm not sure how much editing had been done to the bibliography before it was typeset, but it quickly became apparent that the journal was far from operating according to any rigid editorial standards. The other students who were involved in editing each had an idea about where commas should go (inside or outside the punctuation marks?), whether seasons should be capitalized, whether the style guide should be MLA or Chicago or Turabian, whether the word "before" in a title should be capitalized. They were ready to argue about this. They had *positions* regarding commas and quotation marks and italics. They ranted about the insufficiencies of MLA, the horrors of American spelling, the absence of a viable Canadian style guide. Soon I began to realize that even spelling was political, that one's commitment to a certain spelling of "humour" was a statement of allegiance, a point of pride, an anti-imperial middle finger in the air.

Armed with this new concern over accuracy and consistency, I took a harder look at my Newlove bibliography, already typeset. It was full of inconsistencies! It had some American spelling! I saw yawning gaps. Contradictions in citation methods. Punctuation inside *and* outside quotes. Single *and* double quote marks. The same title given three different ways. I marked it up all over the place with that special blue pen and handed it back to Jack. What a dog's breakfast of a bibliography it was. Jack stared down at my scribbles. He raised his eyebrows. He asked me if I understood that the whole thing would have to be typeset again. Well, now I did. So it got typeset again. And probably again. This was before personal computers, of course. "Global changes" and "find and replace" did not exist. The journal was being typeset by the people who ran the leftist magazine *Alive* in Guelph. Although the first issue of *ECW* was printed by Coach House Press, the second issue was printed by the appropriately named Tim Inkster, a long-suffering master pressman who was producing beautifully printed and bound books through his company, the Porcupine's Quill, which was in Erin, not far from Toronto. Dave Godfrey's Press Porcépic was located next door.

Jack asked me if I wanted to help him paste up the second issue. A few days later we found ourselves at Tim's place, sitting over a light table, cutting the galleys to the correct text block size for the page, and then mounting them on lined paper, using a special melted wax. I snipped out blocks of text, picked up paragraphs that had fallen on the floor, tried to straighten out the unruly columns that kept squirming and wandering over the liquefied wax.

Tim was an insane perfectionist, constantly driven mad by the problems and glitches introduced into the printing process by the incompetents around him. He would emerge from under a massive Heidelberg press, fingers blackened with grease and ink, rolling his eyes about the way some setting on the machine had been screwed up by a new assistant. Again! Technical problems were constant. The day we were there must have been a particularly bad one for Tim. He walked by me as I sat, hunched over the light table, ribbons of text tumbling to the floor. I could hear him sighing and cursing gently to himself. Another loser in his shop. The funny thing about those early issues of *ECW* is Tim's hidden signature on them: while the covers may have been hideous and the editorial errors profound, those slim little journals had sewn signatures, a sign of Tim's refusal to compromise the quality of anything he touched.

Soon after my light-table initiation the bibliography appeared (together with a long essay on Newlove by Brian Henderson) in *ECW* number 2, which sported an ugly anatomical drawing of a heart on the cover. I thought it was in honour of my Newlove bibliography. Somehow, people were supposed to understand that this drawing of a heart meant the issue was mainly about New(love) because you had to have a heart to love, right? But what about the "new" in "love"? Ah well, we were graduate students. People would forgive us. In fact, the illustration was more directly related to the article entitled "James Reaney's Poetic in *The Red Heart*," by Molly Blyth. Jack told me later that it wasn't a human heart; he had taken the picture from one of his wife's medical books. Sharon was a veterinarian.

I liked hanging around that little office in the Ross Building. There was a buzz about Canadian literature there, the sense that all kinds of territory remained open, waiting to be researched and written about. The two associate editors of the journal were Ken McLean and Don MacLulich, both of whom had wide-ranging interests in Canadian poetry and fiction. They were reviewing books for *ECW* and helping Jack decide which articles should get published. As far as I could tell, everyone took the decision-making process seriously, even though their form of commenting on submissions varied widely. Don would write extended critiques. Ken worried about originality. Jack was much more to the point. He would read an essay or a review and label it "dull," "boring," "turgid," or "shallow gossip." That was it. His favourite comment, often applied to submissions from established profs, was "shit on a stick." I guessed, early on, that Jack was preoccupied with concision. He would receive long letters from people asking him various convoluted questions and he would return their letters with one word written on them: "No," "Yes," or "Maybe." I once asked him if he thought that was a detailed enough response. He looked at me as if that was an idiotic question and said, "What more would you need to know?"

My own first review appeared in the same issue as the Newlove bibliography. Around the same time, I started doing short book reviews for *Quill & Quire*. At one point they were sending me a book every two or three weeks. I learned to read and write fast. I liked the sense of digesting the broad range of material that book reviewing offered, although I wasn't so pleased the first time my precious prose got edited by the magazine. Who did they think they were to fool with my commas? After I became more experienced as an editor myself, I began to understand just how important those editorial changes could be, and I ended up resenting many of the authors who felt that their prose was so sacrosanct. Many academics, I learned, were not such great writers, and they had little sense of stylistic consistency. They told their students that grammar counted, but their sentences were full of comma splices, dangling modifiers, and run-on prose. They insisted that their students use MLA form, but they didn't use it themselves.

We had great fun reading aloud some of the ridiculous and convoluted sentences constructed by the graduate students and professors who were slowly beginning to submit their articles to the journal. The profs, in particular, really liked to hear themselves talk. A lot of them could have shaved 50 percent off their word count, but length counted in the tenure-getting game. A really intelligent short review that broke new ground by commenting on an unknown writer was worth less than a 25-page exercise in verbal diarrhea that offered little in the way of original insight, but looked hefty as a line on a *c.v.* In addition to the verbose wanderings submitted by various academics, we also began to get really crazy material from all over the place—poems about roosters from someone in Wisconsin (even though *ECW* never published poems), deranged rants about Morley Callaghan (if only I had seen those in my high school days), reviews of never-seen books by their self-published authors. A folder was created for the best of these loony submissions. We called it the "Loon File" (very Canadian, in retrospect) and added to it over the years. It got fat.

By the time *Essays on Canadian Writing* number 2 had appeared in spring 1975 I had entered the conversion phase of my involvement with Canadian literature. I vowed to read every Canadian writer I could find, to look at all the criticism, to take all the courses that were offered, to write articles and reviews, and to get involved in editing. Jack invited me on board the journal, where my name appeared on the masthead as an associate editor in the fall of 1975. Paula and I got married that same year. We rented a bungalow in a small town called Holland Landing, near Newmarket, north of Toronto. Back then, Holland Landing was not a Toronto suburb but a true rural community; there was land to spare. I sat around and read books in preparation for my comprehensive exams and spent a lot of time outside, carving soapstone figures and tending a vegetable garden. I thought I liked nature. I would drive in to the York campus almost every day to attend classes and to hang out with the others who were involved in the journal.

I was now in the second year of graduate studies and was beginning to get the sense that maybe Canadian literature would become my profession, although I still had very little sense of what professordom involved. The models I encountered seemed as different as day and night. In one course on Tennyson and Browning, Professor Whitla was talking about Victorian England, science, eros, death, and loss. During one class, he mentioned Browning's *Sordello*, a poem reputedly so difficult to interpret that it drove many of its early readers insane. This piqued my imagination. I wanted to experience that insanity. I wanted to know what it felt like to be driven crazy by reading a poem. None of my high school teachers had mentioned that possibility. I went and found myself a copy of *Sordello* and felt the first twinges of derangement:

> . . . Tush! No mad mixing with the rout
> Of haggard ribalds wandering about
> The hot torchlit wine-scented island-house
> Where Friedrich holds his wickedest carouse,
> Parading,—to the gay Palermitans,
> Soft Messinese, dusk Saracenic clans
> Nuocera holds,—those tall grave dazzling Norse,
> High-cheeked, lank-haired, toothed whiter than the morse,
> Queens of the caves of jet stalactites,

He sent his barks to fetch through icy seas,
The blind night seas without a saving star,
And here in snowy birdskin robes they are,
Sordello!—here, mollitious alcoves gilt
Superb as Byzant domes that devils built!

The poem made practically no sense. But I was determined to crack the code. I kept hacking away at it until finally the fog began to clear and I could see the magnificent structure Browning had put in place, the minute attention to detail, the twists and turns of the narrative as it spiralled through rarefied images and metaphors, the sheer power and beauty of the words sliding over my tongue. I wrote up a long interpretation of the poem, submitted it for publication, and had it accepted in a well-regarded journal. I could hardly believe the editors thought that what I had to say about *Sordello* would be worthy of print. That meant, I guessed, that I was on the professorial road, but the foray into *Sordello*'s eccentricities was only one of many roads I was following at the time.

Whitla had mentioned a nineteenth-century French writer, Joris Karl Huysmans, who had written the incredible book called *À Rebours* (1884). It was about a hyper-self-conscious dandy called Des Esseintes who is terminally bored by the predictability of bourgeois life in France and decides to live in a more creative way. A much more creative way. Like Huysmans himself, Des Esseintes embraces the "decadent" mentality. He is obsessed with the exotic and erotic and all things diseased. For example, his contemplation of history turns into an exploration of syphilis through the ages. Des Esseintes seals himself off from the world so completely that he shuns the briefest outing, convinced as he is that reality will always be disappointing. Instead, he lives surrounded by works of art "which would transport him to some unfamiliar world, point out the way to new possibilities and shake up his nervous system by means of erudite fancies, complicated nightmares and suave sinister visions." Rejecting all conventional standards of art and nature, Des Esseintes decorates his house (which is designed to feel like a ship at sea) with the weirdest art (the bizarre visions of Odilon Redon, Gustave Moreau's sensuous symbolist paintings of Salome holding Herod's head, the fantastic engravings of Jan Luyken), the most exotic perfumes, the oddest pets (a jewel-encrusted tortoise that he takes for walks on city streets), and the oddest way of feeding himself (not through his mouth, like us ordinary people, but through his rectum). In Des Esseintes's world you aren't what you eat; you are *how* you eat. Although I never adopted his feeding methods, Des Esseintes did perk my interest in tastes that went over some edge, which partially explains my continuing fondness for reeking blue cheeses, malt whiskeys so peaty that they taste like iodine, searing lamb vindaloos that can stop your breathing, a foie-gras so intense it makes you swoon.

One of the things I liked best about Des Esseintes was his experiments in synaesthesia. At one point, he decides to design an organ that will play tastes as sounds. He has a special rack constructed that holds inverted bottles of precious liquor, each of which sits over a single channel that can transport the liquor released from each bottle to a central spout. The "musician" lies on his back with the spout in his mouth, and then, by pressing different keys on each bottle above him, releases the "notes" of diverse liquors held in each bottle. As the flavours pour down the channel and mix together in his mouth, he experiences a symphony of tastes that other performers could never hear:

> Indeed, each liquor corresponded in taste, he fancied, with the sound of a particular instrument. Dry curaçao, for example, resembled the clarinet in its shrill, velvety tone; kümmel was like the oboe, whose timbre is sonorous and nasal; crème de menthe and anisette were like the flute, both sweet and poignant, whining and soft. Then to complete the orchestra come kirsch, blowing a wild trumpet blast; gin and whisky, deafening the palate with their harsh eruptions of cornets and trombones; liqueur brandy, blaring with the overwhelming crash of tubas, while the thundering of cymbals and the big drum, beaten hard, evoked the rakis of Chios and the mastics.

For some reason, although Huysmans had nothing to do with Victorian England, Whitla allowed me to write a paper exploring his increasingly eccentric experiments in art. This, combined with my exposure to *Sordello*, convinced me that the best art was really about the problem of being itself. Both Browning and Huysmans, in very different ways, had focused on the inadequacy of art to express what could only be expressed by art. They returned relentlessly to this problem, always coming back to the insufficiency of art to solve the problem they had wanted to address by creating art in the first place. This struck me as a crucial means of determining false art from true. False art was painting, or fiction, or poetry, or music, that remained unaware of the inadequacies and problems raised by its own form. True art was tortured by those inadequacies and problems, and what made it interesting was the strategies the artist developed in order to deal with them.

This was the point I think Eli Mandel was always trying to make: that the art you wanted to wrestle with was never innocent and easy; it was torn, conflicted, trying to resolve the very schisms that gave the work its power. And as a critic, to assert that you had figured out some work of literature was more than sheer pretension. It was an admission of failure, for any work of criticism that could resolve things so easily had failed to make a problem of itself and, by failing in that way, had also failed to make itself interesting to anyone except the narcissistic critic who made it. For me, this remained a powerful means of judging art and what was written about it. But it also carried big risks. I knew that I was not writing in good faith. I may have "solved" *Sordello*, but that reading showed little awareness of the problems inherent in that solving, little sense that the act of solving had disempowered the poem. I could subdue it. Yet what had the reading done to change me? How had I translated the problems I originally encountered in reading the poem into something existential, something that would end up as more than a line on my *c.v.*? I began to see that there were responsibilities attached to criticism. If you were going to be really honest, you would have to show how the reading process could throw you off track, take you away from what you were supposed to be focusing on, run you around and around until you saw all the routes you could take that you weren't taking, all the things you should know that you didn't. You could keep all those inadequacies and detours out of the reading, or you could take the risk that maybe a few other people might be interested in the problems posed by reading, and not just the reading itself. For it was the problems that made the process interesting and valid as an aesthetic pursuit.

I wasn't ready to take that plunge yet. However, it was already becoming clear that the Canadian authors who would interest me would be united not by the period they wrote in, or by a particular style or theme, but by their interest in the problem of writing itself. In Eli's course I had also completed a paper on Daphne Marlatt's *Steveston*, a gorgeous long poem published as a book about the exploitation of Japanese fishermen in the small West Coast town near Vancouver. I was startled by Marlatt's language because it was so aware of its own inadequacies. Here was an author who was writing about her doubts about writing the poem she was writing. The very problem of writing—the insufficiency of language to represent any kind of truth or essence—lies at the heart of *Steveston* and makes it a deeply moving and troubling work. What particularly interested me was its combination of poetry and photographs by Robert Minden, and the book's epigraph ("Seeking to perceive it as it stands"), which linked it to a famous American model in the same vein—James Agee and Walker Evans's *Let Us Now Praise Famous Men*.

As anyone who has encountered that work will know, it is not only about the writer and photographer's attempt to capture the lives of itinerant farm workers in the American South in the 1930s; it is even more potently about their sense that they did not have the equipment to do that capturing. By equipment I mean formal strategies: Evans could rely on previous methods of photographing poor people, but he knew that those methods tended to romanticize them, or distort them, or to turn them into some kind of commodified and acceptable art. His quest to find the appropriate photographic form is about his struggle with that form. The representation of that struggle makes the book authentic. Similarly, Agee understood that it would be easy to use language to make these people seem noble, or oppressed, or heroic, but that using language in this way ultimately served to transform them, and by doing so robbed them of the essential humanity that he had come to know and wanted to capture in words. The book is about his growing realization that those words were far from innocent, that all language is charged with value, and that in many ways it was impossible to write about these people at all. As Mandel had said, Agee saw form as a kind of murder, and himself as murderer.

I was thinking through the formal issues posed by writers and photographers like Marlatt, Minden, Agee, and Evans when I enrolled in a graduate course on Canadian fiction taught by Clara Thomas. Clara was the grande dame of Canadian criticism at the time. Maybe she is the grande dame of Canadian literature for all time. She had fought her way up through the ranks and published all kinds of material designed to introduce readers to a broad range of Canadian writing. This kind of work was crucial. There were few decent guidebooks available to help chart the basic territory and fewer still that had the kind of comprehensive overview that Clara brought to the study of Canadian literature.

As the post-structural theory machine began to claim its victims in the early 1980s, Clara was sometimes criticized for writing broad-based reference works built on the idea that a group of books and authors could be united under the rubric "Canada." Meanwhile, she was helping people get on board the CanLit ship, and she usually did it graciously. Her course was about so many of the writers who have become popular across the country—Margaret Laurence, Margaret Atwood, Alice Munro, Matt Cohen—and earlier Canadian writers such as John Richardson, William Kirby, Sara Jeannette Duncan, and Ralph Connor. She introduced a welcome historical perspective to connect these figures.

I found it fascinating to watch the trajectory of Canadian writing emerge into something called a canon. Listening to Clara speak, it became clear to me that there were certain books that had made it and others that hadn't. However, when I read what other critics were writing at the time, it became even more obvious that the idea of a Canadian literary canon (like any national literary canon) could be the site of some pretty serious debate. I began to understand that this canon really was (as the French theorist Pierre Bourdieu had shown) cultural capital. Certain writers and groups of writers became currency attached to academics, whose own reputations were made by using that currency. The more value the academics could bring to it, the richer they themselves would be, in a figurative sense, of course, since there was no real money to be made in trading canon currency. Clara was a professor, but she was also a politician; she knew exactly how the canon games were played. And even though my favourite authors were not hers, I recognized in Clara a practical and influential manager who took a no-nonsense approach to getting things done, which is why I asked her to supervise my dissertation when I entered the doctoral program at York in 1976.

In the months leading up to my admission to that program I was preoccupied with more than classes. I was getting increasingly involved in the journal, hatching plans with Jack. The first four issues were graduate student stuff, with few actual professors sending their work our way. But the journal was taking me in some interesting directions. I had run into the illustrations of Martin Vaughn-James, a British-born artist living in Canada who had published a stunning "visual novel" called *The Cage* in 1975. I was struck by Vaughn-James's willingness to break boundaries, and by the sheer mystery and freshness of his images, which had a strong narrative pull. No one would consider him a Canadian writer, of course, even though he had been living in Canada for years and had declared it his residence. His work went largely unnoticed because he wasn't the real thing.

I thought it might be interesting to meet the man. He agreed to see me at his apartment, which was filled to the brim with the curious paintings and drawings that had so attracted me. At this point in his

47

career Vaughn-James was experimenting with postmodern theories of art and exploring the relationship between text and image, trying to break down conventional categories that would treat written and visual texts as completely different forms. Vaughn-James wanted to move away from those restrictive categories. The world was all text, all language. To assign categories to art was part of the bourgeois plot to commodify creators. This is what I know today. However, I had no idea at the time that Vaughn-James was a committed Marxist. My introduction to canonical theory began when I looked around his apartment, focused on a particularly arresting work, and made the stupid mistake of saying, in my self-conscious graduate student voice, "It's a masterpiece!" Obviously I had not read enough Artaud. Vaughn-James leapt up and started screaming. "No more masterpieces! No more masterpieces!" He was really upset. His wife, who was also in the room and seemed calm, also started yelling about how Canadian critics were boors and incompetents and how deeply she hated Toronto. I muttered apologies. I said I was sorry about Canada, sorry about Toronto. In fact, I told them, I lived *north* of Toronto. And besides, I was from Montreal.

Although I had lost any credibility I may have had with Vaughn-James, I somehow managed to convince him to let us use one of his drawings on the cover of the next issue of *ECW*, number 4. My second introduction to canonical theory began with an angry phone call from Vaughn-James following the publication of the issue. "Where is my name?" he screamed. We had forgotten to credit him. He threatened to sue. Sue? From this I learned that while masterpieces may have ceased to exist and that the notion of the artist was a bourgeois construction, artists still wanted to be recognized for their work, although the idea of suing for lack of an artist's credit struck me as a particularly capitalist response to human error. Vaughn-James would have nothing to do with me after that. A few years later he left Canada and moved to Paris and later Brussels, where he continues to paint and draw.

The journal continued to evolve, but respect was hard to come by. Money started to be an issue. I remember a little cash box sitting in a desk drawer. A few dollars from subscriptions would trickle in. I suspect that Jack was funding the operation out of his own pocket, but he never complained, and he never asked anyone for money. We opened a real account at a bank on the York campus. Rather than help us out in any way, York's English department seemed to view the journal as a hindrance. Why should it do anything for a few grad students pushing boring CanLit? We asked for a bit of assistance with our photocopy costs. The answer was no. We asked if the department would back an application to the Faculty of Arts for some support. The answer was no. Where were the people who could have helped us at the time? Frank Davey was Jack's supervisor, but he didn't offer any assistance. Clara asked me to have tea with her and warned me not to publish any negative reviews of her work. Eli was not actually connected with the English department, so he wielded little influence. The chairman of the department at the time—a Brit— had as much interest in Canadian literature as a mushroom does in Shakespeare. Finally we turned to sources outside the department. The Senate Ad Hoc Committee (whatever that was) gave us a bit of cash, as did the Graduate Students' Association. The Gay Alliance decided we were a cause worthy of support, and gave us $42. By the time *ECW* number 3 came out, we had secured a small grant from the Ontario Arts Council. None of this impressed the English department, which was threatening to take away the little office space we had. Sometimes, just when it seemed like the money was about to run out, once and for all, we would get a surprise, like the first inquiry we received from a publisher about our advertising rates. Our advertising rates? That's a new one. I made up the rates on the spot, and told the publisher they were special rates, good only until the end of the month, which was in a week. Better send the cheque now. They did. We could last a few more days.

Although the journal always seemed to be in a precarious financial position, we carried on. *ECW* had broken some new ground but we had to get four issues under our belt before more than a handful of professors would send us their work. Maybe the journal looked a bit too raw. The covers still didn't have much design consistency and the typesetting and editing were pretty rough. Finally Tim Inkster convinced us to move to a more elegant design, and with *ECW* number 6 we started using the swash font that remains on the journal today. We also redesigned the interior to give it a more balanced look. In 1976 the Canada Council joined the Ontario Arts Council in providing funding for the journal. We weren't the only journal coming out of York. Bernice Lever was editing *Waves*, and Lynn McFadgen was publishing the *Canadian Theatre Review*. If York had given us a little support they would have had a nice publishing group under their wing. But, typically, they expressed no interest in the idea.

That was a crucial year in Canadian literature, due in large part to the publication of Davey's "Surviving the Paraphrase." Davey had presented the text of his essay at a conference two years earlier, around the same time as he published *From There to Here: A Guide to English-*

Canadian Literature since 1960. The book was the first concerted effort to apply postmodern theory to Canadian literature, and it implicitly questioned the conventional ideas of nation that had dominated the discussion of Canadian literature for the last century. Davey argued that writers could not be properly understood in terms of their concept of nation, any more than they could be understood in terms of a formula that explained their work as a literary expression of that concept. He attacked the thematic critics and called their work redundant, reductive, and out of touch with a post-McLuhan understanding of the world as a universe in flux, unbound by national borders and unfettered by socio-cultural paradigms that forced literary history into a sequential, determinist mould. If there was such a thing as nation, Davey wrote, it was probably in the process of breaking down. Critics had mistakenly focused their attention on linking writers via worn-out concepts of nation rather than demonstrating their distinctiveness by isolating the elements of style, structure, and form that made each of them unique.

I think Davey had several goals in mind. He was asserting some of his West Coast values against what he saw as the centrist criticism aligned with eastern Canada. He wanted to open a space for critical commentary on several writers who were experimenting with form. He wanted to empower his own journal—*Open Letter*—which had been publishing anti-thematic criticism ever since its founding in 1965. Whatever the motivation, the essay marked a turning point in the discussion of Canadian literature. All of a sudden, people became conscious of what kind of criticism they were writing. There was a war going on. The thematic critics were defending themselves. But others, sensing a seismic shift, were also renouncing their former positions and embracing the postmodern ethos, even if they didn't really like the way it felt. Commentary related to theme and nation were out. The emphasis was on form, structure, and technique.

Davey was joined by other critics who added fuel to the critical fire. A year after "Surviving the Paraphrase" came a special issue of *Studies in Canadian Literature* entitled "Minus Canadian" edited by Barry Cameron and Michael Dixon, who were running the journal at the University of New Brunswick. As their title indicated, they wanted to take the "Canadian" out of the study of Canadian literature. Cameron, in particular, wanted to promote new theoretical approaches. Over the next few years he became an outspoken defender of Theory, along with a number of so-called post-structural critics from around the country. If you were a graduate student at the time, as I was, you could see the battle lines being drawn, and you could also see the power cliques forming to defend their turf.

Some of the best postmodern critics—like Davey and Linda Hutcheon—wrote in a clear, focused style that illuminated the work in question. Others wrote in deliberately obscure prose that made the study of literature seem painful. I never objected to any kind of new experiment in theory. What I objected to was people who called themselves critics who had not yet learned to put together a clear sentence that could be understood by literate readers. Reading their work or listening to their papers at academic conferences was like being in a torture chamber.

Anyhow, the lines were drawn, and I felt that I had to take some kind of stance. Although *ECW* had never published an editorial of any kind, we found ourselves working on one in 1977, no doubt in response to the fallout from Davey's essay and the publication of "Minus Canadian." The editorial appeared in *ECW* number 7/8, the cover of which reproduced a surreal drawing by Ludwig Zeller, a Daliesque vision of exploding heads in vivisection, fragmenting clocks, and nuclear geysers rising from a sea infested with hands holding open eyelids, symbolically forcing new vision on an eye that is not permitted to blink. Some kind of explosion was at hand. The editorial itself (I wrote it) complains about critics who had abandoned their voice, who refused to see themselves as creators rather than as pure recipients of the text. I can see the ideas I had taken from Eli's class at work here, the idea that "criticism is a process of meeting, and as a process it must include uncertainty, indirection, fright." To ignore this is to write "as if we were never mystified, never in despair about *our* act." The emphasis was on the need for a more confessional kind of criticism. "An essay is a double encounter, an attempt to write about a voice about a voice." The editorial went on to argue that in the midst of the entire debate about the forms of criticism that were appropriate to the study of Canadian literature, several kinds of criticism had been marginalized, especially the bibliography as a critical tool. *Essays on Canadian Writing* was beginning to specialize in bibliographies. That specialization would turn out to be the germ that started ECW Press.

While all of these shifts in the Canadian critical landscape were taking place, there were other forces that could not be ignored, especially if you were determined to make yourself a profession in Canadian literature. Post-nationalist critics such as Davey and Cameron and Dixon were advancing their ideas at precisely the time that the Parti Québécois was taking power in Quebec. The massive exodus of Quebec anglophones from the province following the PQ election victory in 1976 permanently altered the political and literary climate in Quebec and dramatically shifted the centre of literary activity to Toronto. The influx of thousands of people and all that talent added to the vibrancy and sense of empowerment that characterized the city's development over the coming years.

A culture that feels itself empowered in this way can endorse criticism that questions assumptions about nation and the value of literary nationalism. Paradoxically, by questioning the status quo, one contributes to the myth of its value, for why bother to undermine something that is not worth undermining? The anti-thematic critics may have set out to subvert the conventional thinking that aligned the qualities of Canadian literature with ideas about the country itself, but by doing so they drew increased attention to the ideas that provoked their attack. Their subversive activity ironically empowered the idea of nation. However, it was a different story in Quebec, where an attack on the idea of Canada was more than an intellectual exercise: it had uprooted and divided families, forced people to move, and changed the entire makeup of a city and its political destiny. To attack Canadian nationalism in Quebec was to align oneself with the objectives of the PQ. In that case, questioning national values served the opposite function as it did in Ontario and the other provinces, albeit to a lesser extent. Where are the English-Canadian critics from Quebec in this period? I see D.G. Jones, writing a critical narrative about Canadian literature that is essentially a displaced meditation on how a national literature allows one to transcend the wilderness. What was the wilderness? A separated Quebec. I see Ronald Sutherland writing *The New Hero*, hoping that the founding cultures of Canada will get along. I do not see any Canadian critics from Quebec challenging the national model.

As a Montrealer living in Toronto when the PQ victory took place, I felt torn. On one hand, I was surrounded by people who were eager to put the thematic critics in their place, who wanted to abandon a naive nationalism, who were determined to apply formal and post-structural theory to the discussion of Canadian literature. On the other, I felt that I had to do something to assert the value of Canada in the face of an attack that was spreading in the province of my birth. In the year following the PQ victory I came more and more to understand my commitment to Canadian literature as a political activity that would assert my own nationalism, my own refusal to accept the separatist agenda as the norm.

Although this understanding originated in a gut reaction to the very real changes that were taking place so rapidly in Quebec, I also began to think about my response to the idea of nation in the context of a number of influential documents that wrestled with the topic. Chief among these was Dennis Lee's essay, "Cadence, Country, Silence: Writing in Colonial Space," first published in 1972. Lee was obsessed with the relation between language and nation. He wondered whether it was literally possible to speak from a space that was dominated by foreign values, and he understood that one of the problems of escaping that domination centred on the fact that one had to use a colonized language in order to escape colonization. He explored the idea that a way of speaking was (or could become) a mode of resistance. Lee's concept of cadence enables us to think of language and nation as forces that are at play in our physical bodies, in a visceral sense. Years later I found that once my students understood this concept—the idea that sound and rhythm and syntax had a physical and frequently erotic equivalent—they became much more receptive to the ways in which Lee saw his own body as a site of political enactment. However, even when they made this leap, it was still difficult for them to fully understand the depth of Lee's lament. In fact, their resistance to the essay, and even to *Civil Elegies*, was probably rooted in their embrace of technology and globalization at the expense of national self-awareness. In some ways they embodied the truth of Lee's arguments. Ironically, the issues that tormented him in the sixties exist now, more than ever, but there is little sense among the students that these issues are crucial to their own identities or daily lives. Technology has broken down national boundaries and eclipsed the pursuit of national values. And when the pursuit of those values suddenly seems important—as it did when so many young people rallied against the American and British involvement in Iraq—the discourse of nation sounds rusty, almost as if it is being tried out for the first time.

Implicit in Lee's essay was the idea that Canada had been lost but that it could be found again through the interrogation of voice. Here was a literary critic talking about the way in which language could be militant and subversive. Lee's ideas about language and the subversion of a dominant authority stood in stark contrast to the subversive ideas of the anti-thematics, who wanted to embrace a more cosmopolitan and global understanding of citizenship. Essentially, this was the difference between native and cosmopolitan values that A.J.M. Smith had identified in his 1943 anthology, *The Book of Canadian Poetry*, but it was also the difference between native and cosmopolitan values that had dominated the discussion of Canadian literature since Confederation.

Lee's theories of language were given creative expression as early as 1968, in the first version of *Civil Elegies*, a tortured poem of love and loss and the possibility of recovery, rendered as an existential voyage into language itself. The poem was revised in 1972, the same year that Atwood's *Survival* appeared. Although Atwood's book is usually taken to task for its exclusionary view of Canadian literature and for the way it generalizes about Canadian writers' response to what she saw as a dominant trope—fear of the wilderness—her critics often fail to mention that in addition to being one of the earliest books of feminist criticism, *Survival* tries to work out many of the problems confronting Lee: how to write in a culture that is dominated by America.

Atwood's idea of offering resistance by becoming a "creative non-victim" is much less sophisticated than Lee's, but it is part of a pro-national literary consciousness that emerged in the late 1960s, emanating from the House of Anansi Press, which had been founded by Lee and Dave Godfrey in 1967, the Centennial year. They tried to open up communication between writers from Quebec and English Canada by publishing a number of works in translation, and many of the English writers published by Anansi shared the strong federalist values associated with Atwood and Lee. Part of my attraction to their work had to do with the commitment to a sense of nation they supported, especially in sophisticated books such as *Civil Elegies*, Godfrey's *Death Goes Better with Coca-Cola*, and Ray Smith's *Cape Breton is the Thought Control Centre of Canada*, along with critical-philosophical books such as Frye's *The Bush Garden* and George Grant's *Technology and Empire*.

I could see that part of what I was trying to achieve through my involvement with the journal was a reconciliation with my own Quebec roots. Sure, we were not supposed to be promoting monolithic ideas of nation, but I felt that the country had been sundered. The editorial in *ECW* 7/8 announced that "we plan to devote more space to writing by and on French Canadians, not for political reasons, but because the writing is good." Today, those comments strike me as incredibly condescending, part of the very reason so many people in Quebec were ready to support a separatist government. How nice of us (me, really) to pronounce Quebec writing "good." There I was, living in Toronto, talking about Quebec literature, as if I knew a thing about it. In fact, what I had read was mainly in translation, the books that the English publishing machine had deemed suitable for consumption in English Canada. Anyhow, my good wishes about francophone writing mainly came to nought. Over the next 25 years, we would receive very few submissions in French, a testimony to how little we really understood about what was going on in French literature in Quebec.

One thing we were understanding more about was the frustrating art of bibliography. *ECW* number 6 included a bibliography of works by and about Mavis Gallant. That meant that in the three years since its founding in 1974, the journal had published bibliographies on such figures as bpNichol, John Newlove, Archibald Lampman, and Gallant, with additional bibliographies planned on Robert Kroetsch and William Wilfrid Campbell. You could see the design of the bibliographies getting more and more consistent as we explored the form. But was there any way that we could exploit this bibliographic niche? Jack and I had been working together at the journal now since 1975, and by 1977, I had become one of the editors, along with Ken McLean and Jack. When Ken went his own way in the summer of that year (to take up a teaching post at Bishop's University) there were just the two of us.

We had little money to run the journal. In many ways, the problems we encountered in running a small Canadian magazine at the time demonstrated in microcosm many of the difficulties that would eventually plague ECW Press: the search for an appropriate distributor, the struggle to improve poor sales, the relentless pursuit of federal and provincial subsidies, the politics of dealing with authors and their egos, the attempt to establish editorial consistency, the need to control editorial and production costs, the bank's repeated demands for proof of solvency, the endless headache of inadequate cash flow. At one point, hungry for cash, we sketched out a special issue devoted to "the family" and approached McDonald's in the hope of obtaining some McMoney. I imagined a string of books sporting a likeness of Ronald McDonald beside the ECW logo. No go. They did not have, it seems, a strong interest in the link between Canadian literature and the family. When our appeal to McDonald's was turned down we tried Imperial Oil. No interest there, either.

As we confronted the financial downside of publishing, the journal became more and more of a business, and I began to see that, in addition to wanting to publish a good critical magazine, I also wanted to do deals, to make this effort pay off, to put some cash in my pocket. What a dream that was, to think one could profit from CanCrit! But at least I had someone to scheme with. Jack and I were, at heart, relentless entrepreneurs. He never tired of educating himself in the ways of business. At one point he persuaded me to sign up with him for a crash course on negotiation tactics that was being given at a downtown Toronto hotel. The negotiation guru began the session with a simple question: "When you go to a department store to buy a mattress for your bed, do you pay full price?" Of course, I thought. What other price would there be to pay? "I *never* pay the full price for anything," the instructor emphasized, responding to his own question in a way that made us all understand that we had been suckers our entire lives. By the end of the day we knew all kinds of ways to get better deals and stop being suckers. Years later, when some important negotiation was at hand, Jack would remind me of some technique we had been taught that day.

For me, at least, a guiding principle in the development of our publishing program was the idea of owning Canadian literary real estate. I knew that poets and novelists had their alignments with the various publishing houses. However, no publisher in Canada had systematically established itself as the keeper of Canadian criticism. McClelland & Stewart had cornered a big part of the non-critical market with its New Canadian Library series, and there was no question that Jack McClelland was determined to bring as many authors under his control as he could. Yet, in terms of criticism, McClelland's efforts had been relatively subdued. There were some critical books in the NCL series, notably the anthologies of articles contained in *Masks of Fiction* and *Masks of Poetry*, edited by A.J.M. Smith; in addition M & S published John Moss's books, as well as a scattering of other critical studies. However, no one controlled the field, and no one really represented the interests of the professor-critics, whose circle we were gradually entering as the journal became better known.

We began to think about deals that could be done in that circle. Deals, deals, deals. We spent an uproarious few weeks imagining the creation of a service—we called it The Scholar's Butler—that would take care of academics' needs and interests. We would help them edit their work, package it, submit it for publication. The premise was that academic submissions—so crucial to the tenure-getting process—were often bypassed by editors because they were such a mess. Once the academics signed up with The Scholar's Butler they could forget about the mess they had made and leave it in the Butler's hands. Tenure would be assured. There would be a small fee for the Butler's services on an annual basis. We imagined the profs lining up for the Butler and ourselves, laughing all the way to the bank. The only problem was that our potential customers were also our potential employers. How could we tell them their work was a mess? No, we would have to find a different way to load our coffers with the profits that could be derived from Canadian literary research.

The Scholar's Butler
WORTH HIS WEIGHT

- How to get that impossible first job.

- How to hold on to that impossible first job.

- How to make your publications work
  to get you promotion and tenure.

- How to find the right publisher for your book,
  article, or review.

- How to negotiate contracts to *your* benefit.

- How to write award winning grant applications.

All correspondence treated in strictest confidence.

Send the butler your problem.
He'll treat it with kid gloves.

The Scholar's Butler, P.O. BOX 614
Downsview, Ontario M3M 3A9

You'll say the butler did it!

That's when we hatched the big plan. The big plan was to create a mega-bibliography of works by and about Canadian authors, in two volumes—one on poetry and one on fiction. Essentially, it was a spinoff of what we had been doing in the journal, but on a much larger scale. We would approach a number of specialists on different writers and ask them to prepare bibliographies modelled on our design. What could be simpler? How could we lose? Once they had agreed to contribute to our project, we could approach a publisher and use their credibility to get ourselves a nice fat publishing contract. Then, once the two-volume set was published, we could use it to get ourselves jobs, and because CanLit specialists from coast to coast would be involved in the project, chances were that some of them would be on the hiring committees responsible for picking people for those jobs, and naturally they would choose us, their editors.

Armed with this brilliant plan we decided to hunt for a publisher, and soon found ourselves sitting in the office of Peter Martin Associates, a Toronto company being managed by Carol Martin, who had published a number of reference guides related to Canadian literature, including Margery Fee and Ruth Cawker's *Canadian Fiction: An Annotated Bibliography*. Carol liked the idea. She discussed it with her colleagues and got back to us with the good news: they were ready to sign a contract. We inked the deal over a drink at the rooftop bar of the Park Plaza hotel. This was classy, even if the advance—one dollar—was somewhat meagre. Now all that remained was to contact the various researchers and to get them to produce their bibliographies in a little less than a year.

Our contract called for the creation of 45 bibliographies on fiction writers and poets. That meant dealing with 45 different researchers around the country. It meant ensuring the comprehensiveness and consistency of their bibliographies. It meant they would have to work within a predefined structure, even though that structure could never have anticipated the hundreds of questions our rules would raise. The more we tried to direct the project the more it swallowed us up. Professor A had signed up as an expert on such-and-such a writer, but it was clear that he had missed much of the secondary material. We tried to fill in the blanks. Researcher B had given us tons of information on his subject, but a quick check in the library showed that quotations and citations were incorrect; it would all have to be verified from beginning to end. Researcher C argued with us about our format and threatened to boycott the project, a threat that we feared might throw it all into jeopardy, since we were committed to delivering a specified number of bibliographies by a specific date. Professor D was not staying on schedule. His mother was ill. Professor E was having a sex change operation and could not be reached. Professor F had exhausted his photocopy budget. Could we help? It went on and on.

When the bibliographies did come in, we looked at them in horror. Entries were given incorrectly. Alphabetization was off. No one had standardized the citation format for dates of periodicals that said they were published in "Winter." Did that mean January or December? Should they go first or last in a chronological list? Should book reviews be listed? If so, how many? All corrections had to be made by hand. Everything had to be retyped. Gallons of white-out were consumed. Entries that needed to be reorganized had to be cut out with scissors and then pasted into the correct location with rubber cement. The fumes intoxicated us. The pages of each bibliography became battlefields scarred with cuts, smears of whiteout, smudged pencil markings, the detritus of erasers rubbed across entries that had been changed back and forth five times, a palimpsest of editorial compromise and angst.

As the bibliographies arrived the size of the manuscript mounted, and mounted, and mounted. Finally the contracted submission day arrived. We walked into Carol's office and dumped the fruits of our labour on her desk: about 3,000 pages of helter-skelter bibliographies in two piles, each about three feet high. Carol looked at those two piles and said she'd be getting back to us. We left, and looked forward to the publication of our book. Finally, that mess was off our hands and on someone else's desk. It would not stay there too long. A week or so later Carol called us up and gave us the bad news: there was no way she could publish that monster. It would break the bank. It could never be edited by her staff, even if someone worked on it full time for a full year. It was an impossible project that had got completely out of control. I don't know what Carol actually expected us to deliver, but it was clear that we were in trouble. All of those academics and librarians across the country who had been slaving away on their bibliographies would not be too happy to learn about this cancellation. We would never get jobs. We would be permanently blacklisted, from coast to coast. We stewed about what to do, and kept the bad news to ourselves for the time being, hoping to come up with some kind of alternative plan.

By 1977, I was getting closer to the completion of my doctoral degree, having passed my comprehensive examinations in Canadian literature, a process that involved reading hundreds of books from a prescribed reading list, then writing a lengthy exam, which was followed by an oral exam. I had Canadian literature on the brain, for sure. I wanted to get a job. Typically, one did not really qualify for a post as a professor until one had the degree "in hand," but if a prospective employer believed you had the dissertation dragon pretty well tamed, and that it would be brought to completion by a specific date, it was conceivable you might be offered a position. In truth, I had not the foggiest idea what I would write my dissertation about when I made my first job application, to UBC in the spring of 1977. To my astonishment I received a telephone call asking if I would come to Vancouver for an interview. I had made the short list! Maybe they were impressed by my "forthcoming" publications, which included a huge, two-volume bibliography of

Canadian literature, to be published by Peter Martin Associates. Or maybe it was because, incredibly, none of the profs or grad students at UBC had been conscripted for work on the project. To them, I was more or less a clean slate.

The interview was in a week. I planned it out. Other grad students at York who had been through the interview ritual helped me to imagine what to expect. Arrive in Vancouver. Be picked up at the airport by a cheery administrative assistant. Check into hotel (the Sylvia). Remember to keep receipts. Have dinner with some faculty member conscripted to entertain me for the evening. Me in fact interviewing him because my mother always told me: "You want people to like you? Ask them about themselves." Much talk about the differences between Vancouver and Montreal. (UBC Person: "I love the water, but it rains." Me: "It's cold, yes, but *so* cosmopolitan.") I would be desperate for another drink or two at dinner but would decline, of course. Wouldn't want the hiring committee to hear I was some kind of lush. Meet the committee the next day. Get grilled by six people on what I know. Give a paper to the entire department. Drinks. Another dinner with some members of the hiring committee. Pack up and go home.

That's pretty much what happened, with some minor yet disastrous variations. I hardly slept the night before I was set to fly west. Unable to sleep on planes, I was already a basket case by the time I arrived in Vancouver. It was not a smiling administrative assistant who picked me up at the airport. It was, to my horror, none other than the scary Dr. Robert Jordan, *Head* of the Department. He had the most erect posture I have ever seen. Stiff square jaw. I felt like I was being marched off to boot camp. He said little, and never smiled. I was worried. Obviously they hated me and I hadn't even met them. They were hating me *through* their Head. There was no dinner with anyone that night. I went to a bar and downed several drinks. Back in my hotel room (it *was* the Sylvia) I hauled out the paper I was going to deliver the next day, a presentation on Dave Godfrey's experimental novel, *The New Ancestors*. It was full of commentary on Godfrey's postmodern aesthetic, much of which I didn't understand. The paper struck me as wordy and pretentious. All of a sudden I started to wonder how knowledgeable my audience might be, and whether I would survive. Early the next morning Jordan picked me up and drove me up to the campus. He was still grimacing, more than ever. I was still obsessing about his title. I had never heard of a department "Head," only "Chairman." What did it mean about this department, that it had a single "Head"? I imagined dozens of shrunken professorial bodies, like clustered homunculi conjoined at Jordan's rigid neck, their heteroglossic voices rising up collectively, pouring from his pursed mouth. It was as if Jordan was some kind of master thinking apparatus, while the rest of the department served as his appendages. I knew I was getting carried away by the whole Head business, but my visions, combined with Jordan's military bearing, unnerved me.

Jordan introduced me to the hiring committee. All smiles. Today I know what those smiles hid: people rooting for their own candidates, backroom politics, all the forces in play that made it necessary to go through this interview process with several candidates, even though the committee had probably already made up its mind. They asked me what my dissertation was about. "Mediation in Canadian literature," I blurted out. "What do you mean by 'mediation'?" one committee member asked, smiling graciously. Well, I did not know what I meant. I had thought about it for a day or so prior to my arrival, and I had confused myself. But it sounded good. No, actually, it did not sound good. Someone asked me if I was using the term "mediation" to mean that I was examining liminality. "I think that's a good way of putting it," I said, never having heard the term. Liminality? Lemonality? Bill New, who knew how little I knew, was kindest. He helped me through the interview and tried to fill in the gaps and make sense of my babblings. Thank you, Bill.

After a little more torture Jordan knocked on the door. Lunch. I trundled over to the faculty club, making smalltalk with various faculty members. More conversation about "my interests." I played up my involvement with the journal for all it was worth, forgetting to think about the implications of doing that when UBC was sponsoring *Canadian Literature*, a long-established rival journal. I was taken for a quick tour of the campus. It seemed vast. I felt like I was shrinking. Then it was time for the paper. To my amazement, the room was full (later I learned that their *Head* had ordered them to be there). I delivered the paper (well done, I thought) and the audience was invited to ask questions. They took my paper all over the place, asking me to relate my findings to half a dozen authors I'd never heard of. Theory rained down upon me. I felt dizzy. Several people muttered "Foucault." Someone else barked "Derrida!" upon which several other faculty members either shook their heads, or moaned. In the nicest and politest way, prof after prof let me understand that my range of literary reference was infantile at best, and that at worst I was an uneducated self-server with a half-assed journal that he wanted to peddle to them. What a crap shoot. They packed me off to the airport. Handshakes and pleasant goodbyes.

Like a complete idiot, I wrote thank-you letters to the various profs who had interrogated me and mailed them off the day I got back from Vancouver, hoping against hope. But Jordan was too fast for me. No sooner had I posted the letters than he called to tell me they had hired someone else—Laurie Ricou—who in fact deserved the job a hundred times more than me. I was down, a horizontal man in a vertical world.

The UBC humiliation managed to distract me briefly from the crisis awaiting me back in Toronto, where Jack had been stewing about what to do with all those bibliographies. He had come up with an idea that he presented as a no-brainer: we had to start out own press. How else could we honour our commitment to all of those bibliographers? Besides, the bibliography was a great idea. We could make some money. We would establish a publishing company and take it from there. In May of 1977 Essays on Canadian Writing Ltd. was incorporated. There was no fanfare. No celebration. Jack and I were equal partners. We would finish off those bibliographies and get them out. No big deal. It only took another 17 years.

CHAPTER THREE

After we reclaimed the stacks of manuscripts that would one day become the eight-volume series called *The Annotated Bibliography of Canada's Major Authors*, we took a good look at the state of the project. It wasn't hard to see why Carol had turned it down. If it was going to have any credibility, *ABCMA* would need serious and ongoing editorial intervention. That would cost money. It would involve finding a copy editor who could make sense of the mountain of scarred paper that had become the bibliography. And we needed a place to put the mountain, which was bulging with yellow sticky notes about missing information, editorial inconsistencies, questions about titles and dates and spelling. Once we understood that all of these bibliographies would never fit into two volumes as originally planned, things began to take shape. We modified the structure so that the series would encompass eight volumes, with each volume devoted to about five writers. Half of the series would deal with poets; the other half would deal with fiction writers.

As the project developed over the next year, it became apparent that we were on the verge of running a business out of the free space provided by York. Of course, the administration had no idea about the projects we were hatching and little interest in what they must have thought of as our graduate student hobby. The first volume was set to include bibliographies of Atwood, Laurence, MacLennan, Richler, and Roy, the unifying idea being that these were well-known writers working in a realist tradition. We wanted to put some of the big names up front to draw attention to the project and to put it on the map.

The contributors to the volume were a diverse group of academics, as well as a librarian from the University of Toronto. Some of them were incredibly thorough in providing detailed, consistent information, and others really needed a helping hand. I spent hours in the library stacks looking for obscure information about these writers. The Richler bibliography was being done by Michael Darling, who knew more Canadian literary trivia than any other living soul. He was usually pretty accurate, but anyone could make a mistake, right? And Richler was a big deal. I remember the day I spent a few hours on this entry in the Richler bibliography:

"The Secret of the Kugel." *New Statesman*, 15 Sept. 1956, pp. 305-06. Rpt. "Tante Fanny's Hemmelighed." Trans. Elisabeth Rasmussen. In *Magasinet Tillaeg Til Politiken*, 31 Aug. 1957, pp. 1-2. Rpt. "The Secret of the Kugel." In *The Montrealer*, Nov. 1957, pp. 22-23. Rpt. in *Star Weekly*, 13 Sept. 1958, pp. 20-21, 54.

That was one of 366 entries listing Richler's contributions to books and magazines. I know what you're thinking. First, why would someone want to waste precious scholarly hours on a silly little entry like that? How could it matter? To whom? By asking those questions, you demonstrate that you still have the sanity I was obviously losing, because for me, that entry provoked a rich series of questions. Was Michael putting us on? I could believe that Richler had published a one-page story on kugel. I even liked kugel. But was it really true that such a slight piece would be translated into German and published in a German magazine that sounded vaguely political? I highly doubted it. That would have to be checked, of course. How could I check that? Had Darling spelled *Tillaeg* properly? What did *Tillaeg* mean? We would need a German dictionary. Maybe even verify that spelling with someone who spoke German. Anyhow, would Richler really allow his work to be published in a German magazine? He hated the Germans, right? Seemed out of character. Maybe the translation was unauthorized. Richler could sue! And what was the big deal with this story about kugel? Why was it so popular? In two years it had been reprinted three times. Was the pagination correct? Did Michael actually, physically, *touch* that German magazine? Nothing could be considered accurate unless it had been in physical contact with the researcher. I would have to check with Michael. But what if Michael *said* he had touched the magazine but hadn't *really* touched it? I imagined Richler writing us an angry letter about this German connection. Putting us to shame.

While it proved to be an invaluable way of getting to know their work, there was no end to the inconsistencies revealed by every trip to the library. Michael's little Richler entry was one of thousands and thousands. We needed help. Some money was coming to the press from the Ontario Arts Council. In July 1976 Jack accepted a teaching position at Centennial College in Scarborough and somehow he was able to convince the Association of Canadian Community Colleges to help us out a bit. We also approached the Association for Canadian and Quebec Literatures, and they gave us some assistance as well. Although we applied for funding from the Social Sciences and Humanities Research Council of Canada, their assessors took the view that we were inexperienced bibliographers who were making bad canonical choices. Who were we, they asked, to decide which authors were "major"? Wasn't it wrong, they kvetched, to assert that any Canadian author was "major" at this early point in Canada's literary development? Was it really possible, they wondered, to publish a definitive bibliography on a living writer? Eventually SSHRC did give us some money. The problem, as always, was that it was too little, too late.

In our constant search for financial assistance it was inevitable that we would find ourselves dealing with the Aid to Scholarly Publications Program, which was administered by the Canadian Federation for the Humanities. What a horror show. Publishers who wanted to obtain the benefits of this program had to submit each and every manuscript for peer evaluation, a process that could take months and sometimes as long as a year. Once the reports were received, it was up to the publisher to respond to them, and, if they were negative, to try to rebut the critique. This would add another month or two to the process. However, those ASPP grants were crucial to offsetting publication costs. It was essential to get them. But the process was skewed. The ASPP allowed the bigger presses to find one of the two readers who would be assigned to assess each manuscript submission. Since those presses could select readers who were known to be sympathetic to the manuscript, their rate of success was significantly higher than it was for the smaller presses, which were not considered trustworthy enough to find their own assessors. In the beginning, we submitted to our second-class status. Then, realizing the imbalance in the system, we asked the ASPP why we weren't con- sidered responsible enough to find our own assessors. Rather than open a can of worms, the ASPP relented.

After that, things got much better. The readers we selected were universally in favour of the manuscripts we wanted to publish, mainly because if they weren't we simply found other readers who were. This didn't make the process any faster, but at least we got the grants. Most academics whose books were funded by this program didn't understand that they could make submissions to the ASPP independently, without the backing of a press. Then, because the university presses were so hungry for these grants, a professor who already had one in hand could literally write his or her own publishing ticket. At one point, taking our cynicism about this program to its logical conclusion, we tossed around the idea of searching for those ASPP-funded manuscripts that had been obtained by individual academics without the assistance of a publisher. Why bother going through the tedious assessment process when there were lots of manuscripts out there that had already made the grade? You could develop an entire scholarly publishing program that was prefunded by the ASPP. And then you could submit the same titles to the Ontario Arts Council and the Canada Council, in the hope that they would be funded twice, or thrice.

The whole experience of applying for funding in order to support scholarly work on Canadian literature was paradigmatic. The grant-getting game never ended when it came to CanCrit. It would be played again and again as the press grew and tried to cover the mounting expenses of publishing critical books that had a limited market, at best. The story of scholarly publishing in Canada begins with the realization that the main purchasers of books of criticism and literary reference works are schools and libraries. Academics may buy these books from time to time, but usually they will try to get them for nothing by requesting them as desk or review copies. So long as library budgets remained healthy it was possible to find a limited market for series like *ABCMA*, which emerged at a time when there was no competition from online sources. Most major public and university libraries would buy the series as a core holding, even if the reviews were ambivalent.

Armed with our belief in the inevitable success of the series we pushed on, scrambling to pay for "verifiers" who would check the accuracy of entries. I was trying to work on my Ph.D. thesis, pompously entitled "Time and Form in the Canadian Novel," mobilized by the warped idea that I would create the Canadian equivalent of Georges Poulet's work in France. Knowing that I would never get a job until I had more publications under my belt, I designed the thesis so that each chapter could be published as an article. I submitted them to a variety of scholarly journals as soon as they were completed. Clara Thomas, who was supervising my work, didn't like this one bit. At one point, she called me into her office and told me to stop making these submissions. "Why?" I asked. "Because the committee doesn't like seeing too much of a dissertation published before it is defended." This made no sense to me, since everyone was telling us we would never get jobs unless we published, and the graduate program should be happy if its students were hired, right? I don't know whether Clara was actually representing the views of the committee, or whether she felt that I might write something that offended someone and therefore jeopardize my chances of receiving the ultimate degree, of being Ph-Deified, as the program director was fond of saying. I began to get twinges of what life on the other side of the academic desk was like. There was turf to be guarded. There were hierarchies to be respected. There were protocols to be followed. There were rituals to be learned. There were power plays, even wars. Literature was like property. People thought they could own it.

I learned a lot about the Canadian value of literary property in February of 1978, when, along with hundreds of other academics and teachers, I made the pilgrimage to Calgary in order to attend the most outlandish canonical event Canadian literature has ever seen: the Calgary Conference on the Canadian Novel. The moving force behind the conference was Jack McClelland. He wanted to find a way of promoting his New Canadian Library series, edited by Malcolm Ross, and he understood that academic acceptance of the series would widen its credibility. He hatched a simple plan to achieve his ends. The University of Calgary would host a conference to discuss the results of a ballot that would be circulated to teachers and reviewers in advance of the proceedings. People would vote on the best Canadian novels. Because McClelland had already obtained the rights to most of the novels on which people would be casting their ballots, the vote would inevitably solidify the status of the NCL list and make it essential reading for anyone who wanted to be involved with what was certifiably the best Canadian fiction.

Although McClelland tried to keep his involvement from the media, most of those who went to Calgary understood that it was essentially a publicity stunt designed to make the Canadian canon in fiction synonymous with the McClelland & Stewart canon. Malcolm Ross, who started the New Canadian Library with the noble intention of making Canadian literature more widely available in paperback form, was embarrassed by the apparent link being made between him and McClelland's shenanigans. And his pain was not reduced by the discussion that took place at the conference itself, which included a lot of canon questioning, canon bashing, and canon angst. Like it or hate it, there had never been a forum like this. It brought out some of the basic questions that need to be asked about any national canon: Who decides what is a "classic"? What books should be taught? Do books need to be valued for a certain period of time before they possess status? What is the relation between a national literary canon and the representation of nation? What kinds of personal and political empowerment do canonized works bestow upon those who have selected them? Who is disempowered by being left out of the canon-making process? These are crucial questions about value and how it makes us choose one book over another. I have always found it surprising to discover that if you teach literature and ask your students to articulate what specific values lie behind their literary likes and dislikes, they have a lot of trouble answering. It's not because they can't figure it out; it's because they are seldom encouraged to investigate the values behind their judgements. If this is true in terms of literature, what does it mean in terms of politics, interpersonal relationships, or the raising of children?

I returned from Calgary charged up by the fiasco. I wanted to publish the proceedings. We contacted one of the conference organizers, Charles Steele, and he agreed to edit the book, which didn't appear for another four years. It was a controversial publication. A number of the conference participants felt that it was just another means of furthering McClelland's design, and that somehow we were in cahoots with him. Regardless of those charges, which couldn't have been further from the truth, the conference changed the critical landscape in Canada. It was enormously important, if only because it forced people to think about the literary choices they were making, just as it forced them to talk about their values. Without that kind of discussion and debate, literature becomes stagnant. How many instances are there in Canadian literature of a bunch of critics getting together and really taking off the gloves? It is usually all so boringly polite.

There was a role ECW could play in the debate kicked up by Calgary. It was a role that could create an overlap for me between business and professional life. Maybe there was a way to be involved in business and to be a professor, too. By spring 1978, the tenth issue of *Essays on Canadian Writing* had appeared. It contained a brief editorial that pointed to some of our new concerns. You could see the effect of the Calgary Conference when we wrote: "In Canada, particularly, critical journals consume art; they seldom engage in the creation of an evolving critical dialogue." Then, we came out swinging, dumping on thematic criticism and raising the flag to "expressive criticism which is subjectively involved with questions of form and structure." So we jumped on the formal bandwagon, but it never really meant much. Even back then we had begun to get the sense that very few people actually read literary criticism. That feeling only became stronger over the years.

Our developing cynicism helped us laugh through the boring stuff. I remember sitting over a table with Jack, discussing the changes that needed to be made after proofreading a big fat issue of the journal, and saying that, in one sense, it didn't really matter whether we proofed the issue or not, since no one would be reading it. This got our mischievous side up. One of us suggested that we insert the following line somewhere in the middle of the issue, just to prove the point: "Screw you. We don't think you will ever read these words, but if you do, write to us and we will send you $25." No one has ever claimed the prize money.

Still, I liked the idea of prizes. How much would you have to pay someone to get interested in Canadian literature beyond the daily dose everyone got of Robertson Davies, Margaret Atwood, and Margaret Laurence? How much would it take to get people off the beaten canonical track? What kind of exercise could be designed to get the real eccentrics out in the open? You know, the people who had actually read Ralph Connor's novels about muscular Christianity, or the others who claimed to like Charles Sangster's horrid poems. And so, instead of offering a prize for finding obscenities, we created the ECW Fiction Quiz, which first appeared in *Essays on Canadian Writing* number 11. We thought up ten really obscure questions and offered a $30 prize to the scholar who returned the greatest number of correct answers. It would be followed by the ECW Poetry Quiz in the next issue. Okay, some of the questions were not that obscure: "What popular book did William Kirby consult before he wrote *The Golden Dog*?" "What is the worst proofread journal of literary criticism on Canadian literature?" "Name the author and publisher of *Maple Leaf Rag*." The only person who entered the contest was Michael Darling, the same man who had probably lied about Mordecai Richler and kugel. He got every answer right. What kind of life did he lead? Reluctantly, we sent him the prize money. Then came the ECW Poetry Quiz. Ten more questions. We offered the same prize money "to the scholar or pedant who successfully answers the most questions." Unfortunately, the only person to enter the contest was— you guessed it—Michael Darling. We got tired of sending him money and never ran those quizzes again. A better method of marketing would have to be found.

One of the problems I was facing that year was the marketing of myself. I had finished all my graduate courses and was supposed to be writing my thesis, the motherlode document I had to complete in order to get my doctoral degree. But the elusive job had still to be found and, remembering the fiasco at UBC, I wondered whether I would ever be able to make it through a job interview without sounding like an idiot. How much did a person really have to know in order to become a prof?

Besides, there were no jobs in Canadian literature being advertised that year except one, at the University of Maine in Orono. Why in the world would they want a Canadian literature professor there? I had no conception of Maine. It was the setting of Robert Lowell's "Skunk Hour." It was the home of L.L. Bean. It was a place where people went hiking or rented cottages on a beach. Well, it was a job, and I would apply. I updated my *c.v.*, wrote a covering letter stressing my editorial involvement with the journal, and sent the package off, thoroughly expecting never to hear a word about it. Ten days later, the chairman of the English department at UMO called to ask if I would come down for an interview. I would fly to Bangor, someone would meet me at the airport, take me to my hotel . . . Ah, yes, I remembered the routine.

But this was a kinder, gentler interview. The man who picked me up at the airport—Dick Sprague—seemed genuinely friendly. We drove down the interstate and then through Orono, a small New England town with a main street bordered by trees and well-kept white clapboard houses. The campus itself was almost picture perfect—stately brick buildings with ivy, manicured lawns, evergreens behind the semi-hallowed halls surrounding the campus in a ring of fragrant green. My first afternoon was spent sitting in the department lounge, drinking coffee and talking to faculty members. I felt calm.

As it turned out, the university, given its proximity to Canada, had put considerable emphasis on developing a Canadian studies program, as had other American universities close to the border. UMO had its own Canadian Studies Center, which was situated in a big house on the campus, and it had developed a network of courses related to Canada. Later in the day, I was taken to Canada House to meet Ron Tallman, the director. This was way too relaxed. Ron, with his feet on the desk, asked me if I wanted a beer. Sure. He went off to the Canada House refrigerator, and soon we were talking about Maine and university life. He gossiped and told jokes. I heard myself laugh. By the time I went off to dinner I thought it might just be nice to be here, but how could I teach in the US? I had devoted so much energy to identifying myself as anti-American. The associate director of the Canadian Studies program was Victor Konrad, a Canadian professor of geography who had been in Maine for a few years. He convinced me that it was still possible to promote Canada here; in fact, he pointed out, it was important for Americans to understand what made Canada different. If I got the job, I could use the position to do just that. I spent another day on the campus meeting with the hiring committee and the dean. I met Terry Terrel, who was editing *Paideuma*, the well-known critical journal devoted to Pound. Ah! Another editor! I presented the same paper as I did for the interview at UBC, on Dave Godfrey's *The New Ancestors*, a book no one in the room had ever heard of. In fact, most of the people in the room had heard practically nothing about Canadian writing, which, for the purposes of a job interview, served me just fine. They asked gentle questions. I left the campus feeling upbeat and relieved, although I could hardly imagine what it would be like to live in a place that was a seven-hour drive from Montreal, and worlds away from anything vaguely resembling what I had always called home.

A few days later they called to offer me the job. Of course I said yes. It was April 1978. The annual salary was $12,000. There was one stipulation: if I didn't have my degree "in hand" within a year my contract would not be renewed. And I should start thinking about the six courses I would be teaching over the next academic year: three sections of introduction to fiction (what did I know about that?), the literature of Maine (why me?), business and technical writing ("for students without a primary interest in literature"), and one course on the Canadian novel (only one?). All in all, I would be dealing with about 200 students. I felt queasy. How in the world was I going to get myself down to Maine, find a place to live, write my thesis, and learn about technical writing and the literature of Maine, not to mention fiction from Hawthorne to Borges? And then there was all the ECW stuff—the endless editing of the bibliography and the journal, not to mention new projects that seemed to keep coming our way. How could I keep my connection to the journal and the newly founded press if I was so far away?

First things first. A place to live. I had the idea that Maine would offer me the opportunity to experience rural life. Sure, I had been living in a rural community, but it was only 30 minutes from Toronto and the city was rapidly encroaching. Maine would be different. We would find a house in the country, surrounded by trees. There would be a winding country road. Some land. I would commute to the campus, then come home and tend a garden, explore the woods, write my dissertation inspired by the companionship of nature. Thoreau came to mind. Whitman. Leaves of grass and pastoral renewal.

The university put me in touch with a real estate agent. A week later, Paula and I flew down to Bangor and began the search. Bangor was the big city in this neck of the woods. We would stay away from it. Even with its 40,000 people, it would be much too urban for us. Orono was a university town. There were profs on every corner. No, we needed to be farther out, in the purity of nature. The agent brought us to an area called Hampden Highlands. I fell for the name right away. It would be like a little bit of Scotland in the middle of the northern woods. People here would sip malt whiskey. I would have friendly neighbours with family crests. The house we looked at did not seem very Scottish. It was newly constructed, on a five-acre lot that was heavily wooded. I loved the gleaming new kitchen. We sat down with the casual-looking young owners and I rolled a joint. "What do you do?" asked the owner. "I'm going to be teaching Canadian literature at Orono," I replied. There was a polite silence. (There is almost always a polite silence when you tell people you teach CanLit. Or they will say: "Margaret Atwood. Isn't she a Canadian writer?" Or they say: "*Really! That's interesting!* Who are your favourite authors?" I always give the same answer: Charles Sangster, or Henry Alline. Once, on the squash court, I asked my opponent what he did for a living. "Paper bags," he said. I didn't know how to respond. "Small, medium, *and* large?" I asked. "Absolutely," he said. Then he asked what I did. "Canadian literature," I replied. He stared at me in silence. We played our game.)

Anyhow, I told the owner of the house what I did, and turning to him, joint in hand, said, "And you?" His reply was almost jaunty: "I'm an officer with the Bangor Police Department." Hmm. I put the joint away.

Unarrested, we made an offer on the house, which was accepted the following day. Back in Ontario, we planned the move, scheduled for late May. All went well. The hundreds of invaluable bricks I had used to construct my furniture in Toronto arrived safely. We managed to settle in, and only then did I begin to realize that Hampden Highlands was not really that classy. It was definitely not Scottish. There were a lot of guys up at the corner store who looked like they belonged in *Deliverance*. They chewed tobacco, spat, and had rifle racks in their pickup trucks. When I ran into them at the local store (a mile down the road) they seemed vaguely threatening. No problem, I thought. They can do their thing, and I'll do mine.

What was a problem, however, was the looming energy crisis. The price of oil began to spike upwards soon after we arrived. By the end of the year, it would almost triple in price. People in the area saw the increases coming and decided to take action. Unlike city dwellers, everyone in Maine had access to relatively inexpensive wood. There was lots of it. But in order to heat a good-sized house with wood, you had to install a real wood furnace next to the oil furnace that would soon be defunct. My first Maine purchase was a nice big locally designed burner that cost several thousand dollars, but when I calculated how much I would save by not using oil, I was convinced I'd be laughing all the way to the bank. Not quite. A new chimney had to be built to accommodate the furnace. A master mason (who would charge an arm and a leg) had to be found. Special safety alarms were required. The new chimney would have to be cleaned regularly to remove creosote. I read up on chimney cleaning and started to worry about cancer of the scrotum, a disease linked definitively to chimneys. Instead of writing my thesis I was visiting furnace stores in search of chains, abrasive balls, and special iron coils that I would have to drag up and down 40 feet of chimney. I was advised to buy goggles, a face mask with an industrial quality air filter in it, a safety harness and belt, special boots for clambering over the roof, heavy-duty overalls. I bought it all. Now I was ready. It was time to order the wood!

If you live in a city, you may think you know something about wood. You don't. If you want to order wood in the city, you call up a guy with a pickup truck who will bring you maybe a cord, all nicely split. A full cord is a fair bit of wood. It measures 4' x 4' x 8'. That takes up space. Most city deliveries are for "face cords," which are 4' x 8' x 16", about a third as wide as a full cord. I already knew this when I got to Maine. However, I soon learned that wood in Maine is not delivered the way it is in Toronto. I looked up "Wood" in the local yellow pages and called one of the many numbers listed. The furnace manufacturer had estimated I might need ten cords to heat the house for the full winter, but I didn't want to take any chances. "Can you deliver 20 cords?" I asked the wood man. "No problem," he said. I told him to dump it in the back yard, imagining that I would hire some neighbourhood boys to stack it up. That's not what happened. When I got home the next afternoon, I saw trees—big thick trees—sticking up at all angles. It was a mountain of trees, an avalanche of trees, almost as high as the house. In a panic, I called the wood man back. "I asked for 20 cords of wood! What is this?!" The calm voice on the phone said dryly: "That *is* 20 cords."

My back yard was ruined. It had been occupied by a horizontal forest piled to the sky. Absurdly, some lines from Gwendolyn MacEwen's "Dark Pines under Water" flashed through my mind:

Explorer, you tell yourself this is not what you came for
Although it is good here, and green:
You had meant to move with a kind of largeness,
You had planned a heavy grace, an anguished dream.

MacEwen was right. I was sinking in an "elementary world." What to do? There was only one solution, I realized, already regretting my decision to become a professor-landowner. I would have to get myself a chainsaw and start cutting. The next day, over at the chainsaw store, I learned again that it would not be quite that simple. Some of those chainsaws were huge. They were lethal. I saw myself slipping, just once, instantly slicing off a hand or leg. I was going into battle and I came away fully armed: steel-toed boots, knee guards, chainmail armoured gloves, goggles, earplugs, sharpening blades, mysterious tools, storage cases for the weapon, and containers filled with gasoline that I imagined exploding in a fireball ignited by a stray chainsaw spark.

It took me three months to cut up that wood. Every day I revved up the chainsaw and thought about "Time and Form in the Contemporary Canadian Novel" as I sprayed myself with bug repellant, cursing and tripping over mounds of sliced up logs that I could hardly lift. Why could I not lift those logs? Because they had not yet been split. I bought an iron splitting wedge, a sledgehammer, and an axe. I split wood for about three hours. I ached. At the rate I was going, it would take me months. There was only one solution. I had to rent a hydraulic splitter. That got the job done in five days. Finally I was able to find some local boys to stack it up, although it would still have to be carted down to the basement after it dried. I decided to worry about that later. My new job called.

As September approached I started to make frequent trips to the campus. It was about a 30-minute drive. I had a Norton anthology that I was supposed to use for my Introduction to Fiction course. I blasted through the stories it collected, wondering what in the world I could ever say about William Faulkner, or Virginia Woolf, or John Barth, or James Joyce. At least I had taken a course on Melville. Naturally, Norton's editors assumed that Canada did not exist. There was not a single Canadian story in that book, more evidence of the fact that Americans generally believe that if Canada exists at all, it is simply another American state, and an impoverished one at that. Every time I opened that anthology I thought about their ignorance of Canada and got pissed off. How many times in the future would I be enraged by American authors who submitted their work to the press with a self-addressed envelope that bore American postage, as if it would work in Canada, as if Canada was just an extension of the US? Not to mention the fact that as soon as I set foot in Maine I immediately became "Bob," as if the name Robert was some kind of nickname. "Bob." What a dumb name. I hated it. I hated this country that wanted to make me a Bob, without my consent. But I had no choice. I was Bob (except in the classroom, where I had magically become "Dr. Lecker"). And Bob would use Norton or nothing. I spent hours cramming at the library. Truth be told, I loved the American stuff. Well, I loved a lot of it. But when it came to the literature of Maine—and that course was looming up—I got truly sidetracked trying to make sense of it all. The big author seemed to be Sarah Orne Jewett. But there were also all kinds of strong poets who had come out of Maine. I discovered Marsden Hartley, Wilber Snow, Louise Bogan, and Richard Eberhart. No one had put together a comprehensive anthology of Maine literature. I knew that the only way I was really going to learn this stuff was to put myself in a position where learning it would be inescapable. I headed over to the University of Maine Press and pitched them on an anthology of Maine literature. They signed me up. I learned my stuff.

Maybe it was my experience in the deep woods of Maine that came to affect the progress of the bibliography series, which was still being edited. The English department at York continued to threaten ECW's meagre office space in the Ross Building, and finally, that summer, they gave us the boot. Jack was hauling around boxes of the journal in the trunk of his big used American car, which sagged under the weight of publication. A new home would have to be found for the journal and the press. Hédi Bouraoui had at this point become the master of Stong College at York. Although his new title made him sound like the star of an S & M film, he was in fact the man running the college. He was interested in publishing his poetry. We were interested in an office. A deal was struck with the Master. We got a room that was about 100 square feet. No windows. Bouraoui allowed us a special storage space for the excess books—the walkway around the building's furnace, in a hot little room at the top of a narrow stairwell. Certain that the books would be set on fire by the furnace, we took out insurance on those unsaleable scholarly volumes. If only the building had been engulfed in flames we might have escaped years of debt.

Jack had met a woman named Ellen Quigley, a brilliant and dogged student and editor who wanted to get involved in publishing. We set her on the bibliography. She ripped it to shreds, undoing our painstakingly glued entries, highlighting the gross inconsistencies that marred the work even after months of corrections and debate. Finally, it was getting to the point where it could be typed up in a final form, ready for the typesetters (who would have to type it all over again, of course). I volunteered to find a typist and a typewriter in Maine. I went out and bought an IBM Selectric and hired a typist who lived deep in the Maine woods, not too far from the campus. She assured me that she had electricity. Day after day she would type away at those entries. We would correct things, change, edit. The typist would retype. The manuscript moved back and forth from Maine to Toronto. The typist would retype. Raising the cash to pay for this operation was no problem. I simply went to the bank and got an advance on my ECW Visa card. The bill would come later. Why worry?

My office at UMO was nothing special, but it was my first office. I was a professor. I was terrified. Some of the other profs lived in Orono while others had real farms with animals in barns. I wondered about my colleagues. When I expressed uncertainty about unresponsive students to one of the older profs, he told me his secret: bring a stopwatch to class, ask a question, press the button, and see how long it takes before someone answers. "My record is 22 minutes," he said. "You mean 22 minutes of total silence?" I asked, thinking that would be tough. "Easiest way to teach," he said. "Works every time."

Next door to my office was a prof who I think fancied himself a Mormon prophet. He was continually talking about his visions, the proper place of women, how they were designed to serve men and bear their children. Once, I was invited down a dark country road to visit his farmhouse for dinner. Some female faculty members were there. Things got out of hand. At one point, one of the women grabbed a knife, pushed our host onto the table, and threatened to give him a vasectomy.

Next to his office there was a strange man who was always typing. He couldn't feed the typewriter fast enough. I was reluctant to bother him. He seemed so intense. As Tom Waits asks in one of his songs, "What's he building in there?" One day I got up the nerve to knock on the door. "Hi," I said. "My name is Robert Lecker and I'm the new guy on the block." "Hi," he replied, "my name is Stephen King." Could it be? Yes, it was. We struck up a conversation, and soon I was telling him about my course on Maine literature, which was rapidly going down the tubes. He was a Maine author, right? He could help out! I asked if he would be willing to come to a class to discuss two of his short stories, which the students would of course read in advance. He seemed a bit reluctant, but finally he said yes. The day arrived. I intro-duced him triumphantly to the students, who seemed unaware that the author of *Carrie* had an office just down the hall. We talked about his stories, and then I turned to him and asked if he could say a few words. Steve got this very strange look on his face and started shaking his head. "I can't," he said. "They're too scary to talk about." Was he putting me on? I never found out, but he always maintained that while he could talk about the act of writing, he found it impossible to talk about the deep terror inspired by his fiction. There was Sarah Orne Jewett and *The Country of the Pointed Firs*, and there was Stephen King and *Carrie*.

While I was struggling to learn more about Maine literature, I was also desperate to keep up with the Canadian literary scene. I felt cut off from the community at York and out of the loop when it came to the larger community of academics working in the field. Through the Canadian Studies Center I managed to connect with a growing network of profs in the US who were developing courses in Canadian literature. As I learned, it was much harder to teach Canadian literature to American students, because so much that one took for granted when living in Canada did not apply here. The students I encountered were pitifully ignorant about Canada. Perhaps this was a reflection on the kind of students who came to UMO (it consistently achieved one of the lowest rankings of state universities in the country), but I think it was a broader indication of just how little interest Americans in general had in Canada. That lack of interest filtered down into the elementary and high school education systems. My students knew something about France and something about Africa, but if you asked them what the capital of Canada was they would stare back blankly. I remember reading an interview with an American army general who was asked about the US military policy regarding Canada. "Canada is a pimple," he responded. "We don't operate on pimples." My classroom operation seemed more demanding than that. How was I supposed to teach students about Margaret Laurence's imaginary Manawaka when they had never heard of Manitoba? What did the symbolic northward voyage of the female protagonist in *Surfacing* mean when the geography of Quebec had never registered on their mental map? I think they actually believed the stereotype that Canada was a country of snowshoes, igloos, and frozen tundra. Once, to counter this, I rented a van and took a dozen students on a two-day trip to Montreal. I drove them around the entire city, showed them the bistros, the nightlife, the universities, the house where Leonard Cohen grew up, the Museum of Fine Arts. When we returned, I asked what had impressed them most about their visit. What struck them as particularly Canadian? There was a long silence. Then one of the male students said, "I really liked the cars."

My colleagues teaching Canadian literature at other American universities understood these limitations and ran with them. I learned to bring in maps, to start from square one, to give little lectures in history, to show pictures of places and people. The more I did so the more lonely I felt, talking about my country as if it was on the other side of the world, or as if it were some incredibly foreign and exotic culture. The only way I could ground myself was to pursue that culture with a vengeance. Studying Canadian literature, teaching Canadian literature, writing about Canadian literature, editing Canadian literature, publishing books about Canadian literature: all of those activities were a means of reminding myself who I was, what I stood for, where I had come from, why I was here. The longer I stayed in Maine the more militant I became. Maybe it was because my first teaching job was so grounded in the need to identify Canada that I was never really able to think about its literature in post-national terms. At one level, which I knew to be politically incorrect, I resented those critics who spoke about Canada as an artificial construction, as some kind of monolithic dream that was just that—a dream. They had the luxury to say that, the luxury to take it for granted. They were living there; it was invisible to them. But to me, half a day's drive from Montreal, it was all too real. Crossing the border on occasional visits back home, I never lost the sense that I was finally safe, in a better place, home. Sometimes, my response to that border became maudlin: I would spot a maple tree on the Canadian side, its leaves turning orange and red in the autumn, and I would start to feel choked up.

The contrast between my life publishing CanLit and my life teaching CanLit became starker and starker. In publishing, I felt like I was entering an esoteric realm of detail that few people could really share. As a teacher, I knew I was covering the basics, even as I longed to connect with more advanced research. As the first term rolled on, the first volume of *ABCMA* was coming to completion and would soon be ready for typesetting. By this point Jack and I had become obsessed with bibliographical formats. We studied the *MLA Handbook* as if it were some kind of oracular code open only to the truly initiated. Sometimes the handbook was vague. We argued about how to interpret its nuances, the truth behind what the MLA gods had really meant. A few times we became convinced we had found an inconsistency. We fantasized about writing MLA a letter, demanding an explanation.

Some of their pronouncements just did not make sense. If, for example, you were going to give a title in quotation marks and include punctuation (as in, "Clark Blaise wrote a story called 'Eyes,' which he published in 1969"), why should that comma go before the quotation mark? The comma is not part of the title, but including it inside the quote marks makes it seem like it is. That's not fair to Blaise. It distorts his story. MLA said the comma had to be there, but we disagreed. We decided to change the policy. After all, we were publishers. And we were Canadian publishers. We did *Canadian* literature. We didn't have to take our marching orders from the Modern Language Association of *America*. Unfortunately, we made our decision after the first full version of the bibliography had been typed in the Maine woods. All of those commas that were inside quote marks—thousands of them—would have to be changed. We had it all retyped. Then we sent it to the typesetter, who typed it all again. The proofs came back. Wait a minute. Those commas looked weird! Maybe they made more sense inside the quotation marks after all. Maybe MLA was right. Our name was on the line here. We decided to change it all back to the way it was before. So the bibliography got typeset all over again, from beginning to end, with the commas inside the quote marks. It cost thousands of dollars to change it, and change it, and change it again. But principles were principles, right?

If we were smart, we might have stopped at that point and recognized a near-fatal error. Instead of capitalizing this project from day one, we allowed ourselves to get into increasing debt in order to support the publication of these outlandish projects, which were wonderful research tools, but which cost way too much to produce, given our limited resources. The quest for perfection in publishing is a deadly habit. As the debt piled up over the years with more and more reference series and critical books coming out, it became a constant race to find money, and usually that meant borrowing money, a practice that would inevitably land us in trouble. Jack was fond of pointing out that if only the history of ECW had been backwards, everything would have worked out fine: we should have started by publishing trade books that some people would actually buy, and that would have given us the capital needed to produce the critical books and the library reference series, which were so costly and yet limited in their potential market.

The bibliography was set for publication in 1979. We had just put out an issue of the magazine with a focus on Michael Ondaatje. By the time it appeared, in 1978, we had legally incorporated the press and had designed a company logo that would be used on ECW Press books and the journal. It looked like this:

People often asked about this curious colophon. I found the original illustration in Cirlot's *A Dictionary of Symbols*, a book I had been using in connection with my various undergraduate courses. It seemed mysterious and alchemical, perfect for ECW, a reflection of our profound and abiding interest in alchemy. Within a year of settling on the logo, we managed to turn those alchemical symbols into a convoluted expression of our publishing philosophy:

> Our logo is the alchemist's athanor. At the top left are the symbols for water and digestion. At the top right are the symbols for fire, glass, earth, and the crucible. The retorts show the transformation and purification of materials over a fire. Since alchemy is not simply for the transmutation of materials into gold, but also for curing ailments, ECW has chosen the athanor, the place of digestion, not simply to indicate a marvellous transformation of dross into valuable matter, but to suggest a curative transformation of already existent material. The heat in an athanor is maintained by a tower which provides a self-feeding supply of charcoal. Similarly, the constant production of manuscripts with few publishing outlets provides the energy and demand for the press. Publishing and writing are also not unrelated to alchemy. One alchemist's manuscript reads, a "disciple shall hold in his hand paper, ink, and pen, and another a naked sword." In refining manuscripts, we use only the finest material and believe that the contents of the books match their production quality.

I'm not sure which one of us was holding the writing materials and which one was holding the sword, but the outlandish nature of this description was in fact an ironic expression of our growing doubts about the mystical dimensions of publishing. Back in the real world we were learning that it wasn't some marvellous transformation of dross material that sold magazines or books. More often than not, it was the canonical status of the subject in question. The Michael Ondaatje issue drew a lot of attention and, untypically, it sold in stores. What could account for this? Part of it was Ondaatje's growing popularity, although he had by no means come near to achieving the canonical status he enjoys today. However, what became apparent was that people would invest in authors, even if they would not invest in ideas. A new strategy began to take shape: *Essays on Canadian Writing* would begin to publish more issues focusing on specific writers. At the same time, the press could branch out into publishing books on Canadian authors as well.

It is difficult to appreciate today just how little in-depth author commentary there was at the end of the 1970s. Once we understood this, it only remained to put in place the plan of covering the field by commissioning studies of as many Canadian authors as possible. To me, this was the heart of the ECW plan. Eventually, financial considerations would force us to question the model, to modify it, and then to abandon it in pursuit of books that could attract wider audiences, or bigger government grants. I believe the barriers faced by Canadian publishers today—and three decades ago—make it virtually impossible to run a viable company devoted to the kind of vision we initially embraced. To understand this, one need only answer two simple questions: 1) how many copies, on average, will be sold of a book of Canadian literary criticism? and 2) how many copies, on average, will be sold of a similar kind of book in the US? Because the market in Canada is so small, a sale of 500 copies of a scholarly book would not be unusual. Some might sell 250, while a successful one might do 1,500. Even though the population of the US is roughly ten times that of Canada, this does not translate into ten times sales. However, if you have a much bigger market, chances are that a good sale for a scholarly book in the US might be 700 copies, with a really successful book selling a few thousand. Of course, there are always exceptions to the rule. Atwood's *Surfacing* sold thousands of copies, and there are other eminently successful critical works. But generally speaking, you cannot make money selling 500 copies of a book, especially a scholarly book, which demands rigorous editing of text, notes, references, and so on. However, you might be able to make money selling 1,500 copies, if you were very careful. That's why it is still possible for scholarly studies of American literature to appear by the dozen each year, while the output of critical studies of Canadian literature has virtually dried up.

The government grants that are needed to offset the inevitable loss have been cut back or eliminated, while the disappearance of independent bookstores has further eroded sales potential: chain bookstores have little interest in stocking titles that will be bought by a handful of people across the country. And remember: most of the academics who might buy these books will first try to get them for free as desk copies or review copies. Very few of them will be willing to put down hard cash, even though the cherished idea of building on others' research is dependent upon successful dissemination. However, no publisher can disseminate without a return. The refusal of academics to buy academic titles eventually impacts their own chances of getting published, for as publishers become increasingly sceptical about the market potential of these titles, they cut back on them, making it more and more difficult to share ideas. A perfect example of this is the shift at UBC Press when Peter Milroy became director in the mid-1980s. Peter looked around, checked out the sales figures, and said the press would no longer be publishing CanLitCrit. Other publishers simply kept raising the stakes, demanding higher and higher government subsidies to offset the cost of publishing books that would never be sold.

Those are the realities. However, they were the realities we learned down the road. In the meantime, there were still lots of opportunities to lose a pile of cash. A year earlier, in *ECW* number 6, we had published an interview with Margaret Atwood, conducted by J. R. (Tim) Struthers (we called him "The Parenthetical Man"). Why he signed his name that way remained a mystery to us, but one thing was clear: Tim was determined to carve out a niche for himself in Canadian criticism. He was particularly interested in the Canadian short story and was one of the few Canadian academics who had focused on the novels and short stories of Hugh Hood. I agreed with Tim that Hood was one of Canada's most neglected writers, a neglect that stemmed, I thought, from the fact that he was a practising Catholic who believed that moral and religious insight could be gained through fiction. That kind of view did not sit well in the postmodern era that had been unfolding for close to a decade. But Hood soldiered on and continued to write some of the most provocative and finished fiction Canada has seen. One chapter of my thesis was devoted to *The Swing in the Garden,* the first book in Hood's twelve-novel epic called The New Age, which aimed to be for Canada what Proust's *Remembrance of Things Past* was for France. Inspired by Catholic theology and his incredibly eclectic reading in world literature, Hood produced deceptively simple novels and stories (about baseball, or flying a kite, or a trip to the corner store) that were moral allegories, rich in metaphor and symbol.

Tim proposed a special issue on Hood, and we agreed. He vowed to assemble a cast of critics who would give us a stellar collection of essays. Eventually, after endless and inexplicable delays, we gave Tim a final deadline and he delivered a wonderful collection that remains unsurpassed to this day. Always thinking about our ballooning debts, we came up with a plan to sell the hell out of those essays. First, instead of just publishing the essays in an issue of the magazine, we would print extra copies, slap a different cover on the volume, and also sell it as a book. Then, when the book was published, we would hold a conference on Hood and ask the contributors to present short versions of their essays. That, we thought, would draw in a crowd, who would eagerly buy the book, which we would offer at a special conference discount.

The beauty of this plan was that we could have our cake and eat it too. The issue of the magazine would be funded by the Social Sciences and Humanities Research Council of Canada and the Ontario Arts Council, who supported the journal through grants, while the book would receive additional funding from the Canada Council and (again) the Ontario Arts Council, since they funded the press through more grants. The magazine subscribers would pay for the special issue, while the book would be sold to non-subscribers, with a different cover and no discernible link to the magazine. The collection of essays on Hugh's work was the first title published by ECW Press, in 1979. We asked Hugh if he had any photos we could use on a poster we were designing to promote the conference, and he provided us with a shot of himself in a pair of tight swim trunks, a good indication of his self-confidence. Although the conference was not that well attended and very few people bought the book (surprise, surprise) the double-dipping strategy worked. It became a strategy we used for years, with special issues on such figures as Alice Munro, Timothy Findley, Leonard Cohen, and other prominent writers also being sold as books. In any case, Hugh seemed grateful for the attention his work had received. We struck up a friendship that would introduce us to other authors and book projects not too far down the road.

While we were anticipating the release of that first ECW Press title I was trying to cope with my teaching responsibilities and the joys of home ownership in Maine. The first few months of teaching awakened me to many of the odd circumstances that conspire to make professordom such a weird pursuit. Most of my students were from Maine. Many of them had grown up in the country and had gone to rural schools. Others came from coastal areas. Their fathers were fishermen, some working lobster farms near Bar Harbor. Strange things happened in my fiction class. One day, a student came in and put up his hand. I was encouraged, since he had never said a word about any of the stories we had studied. As soon as I recognized him he stood up and proudly announced that "I got my first buck." This did not compute. Was he talking about the money he had made at his first job? I asked him to repeat. He did. "I got my first buck, Sir." Still made no sense. Then one of the women in the class made it clear as a bell: "He shot a deer, Dr. Lecker. Killed it. Gonna eat it for his supper."

Now I understood. The ritual of fall hunting season had begun and, sure enough, over the next few days I began to hear gunshots around our house. Everyone seemed to be wearing fluorescent orange vests and walking with a pronounced stoop, as if they were ducking the next shot. Up at the corner store the *Deliverance* guys sat around drinking beer and telling stories of the hunt, their high-powered rifles slung casually over their laps, while outside, dead deer with glassy eyes adorned the hoods and roofs of rusted pickups, their tied-down bodies leaking brownish blood. I walked carefully during those weeks, certain that a stray bullet would pick me off. It suddenly dawned on me that I'd been jogging happily down the road listening to Pat Benatar's "Hit Me with Your Best Shot!":

Hit me with your best shot!
Why don't you hit me with your best shot!
Hit me with your best shot!
Fire away!

A very stupid thing to do in hunting season. In fact, it was Jim, our neighbour, who got hit. One day I ran into another neighbour who did mechanical work on my car. "Where's Jim gone to?" I asked him, since I hadn't seen him in a few days, and that was unusual. "Shot," he said. "Shot for a deer. Gone for good, Jim is." That gave me a whole different feeling about Hampden Highlands. I would stay close to home, wear bright clothes, finish my thesis, turn off Pat Benatar, and hope for the best.

As a young and inexperienced prof, I was entitled to make certain mistakes. For example, I would walk into a class and ask "How many of your fathers fish lobster?" Many hands went up. Smiling, I would say,

"Anyone who brings me a bunch of lobsters gets an 'A' in this course, no questions asked." My big mistake was not in making this offer, but in forgetting that I had made it. Understandably, I wanted something to perk up my day. The students didn't seem too interested in all those wonderful short stories. In the Maine literature course I had reached the low point of covering heartfelt poems about trees and woods. Even worse was that technical writing course for business students I had been forced to teach. There were multiple sections of this course, each with about 30 students. I have blocked from memory the exact number of times I taught the course, but I remember it all too well. How to compose a letter of application. How to design a good resume. How to effectively describe the detergent you are selling. Soon after the term began, the course director told me that an important phase in the course was about to begin. It was time to teach the students how to write assembly instructions, just in case they became engineers or town planners and needed to tell others how to put together helicopters or municipal sewage systems. "Do you know our method?" he asked. No, I didn't. "It's called LARCS." Teaching students how to write assembly instructions would be a lark. He told me he would see me at class the next day, and show me how the pedagogy worked. LARCS. It sounded like fun.

The following morning I saw him coming down the hall towards the classroom with a little blue wagon in tow. The wagon was stacked with boxes of wooden Tinker Toys, the kind you fit together to make windmills, merry-go-rounds, and cute little cars. LARCS, I found out, stood for Linearly Arranged Cellulose Stringers, a humorous attempt to make the Tinker Toys sound like sophisticated building materials. But of course, as it said on the boxes, these LARCS were made for children, ages 4-6. How would this work? The director showed me how. The class was divided into ten groups, with three students in a group. Their job was to build something with the Tinker Toys—the more elaborate the better—and then to write out the assembly instructions that would allow someone else to re-create the object. The students had great fun doing this. Tinker Toys littered the classroom floor for days as they tried out their designs. They shrieked and laughed. It was a kindergarten riot. I didn't have as much fun. After they had packed up all the little wheels and sticks and cogs and buttons they had used for their projects, the whole mess was handed over to me. Who else would be able to determine whether the instructions worked? I would have to assemble all of the projects and give each a team grade. So for hours and hours I sat in a room at home, Tinker Toy pieces spread out around me, trying to replicate the far-flung imaginative creations of the students, who obviously knew I would be doing this and had tried to create the most outlandish designs possible in order to torment me. A helicopter with three parallel rotors and emergency landing mechanism. A solar-powered train riding on 32 wheels per car (with special double axles). A merry-go-round that generated enough electricity to power a wheat-grinding mill, attached by a rotating tunnel that lit up inside (batteries not included).

I needed a break. Now that my wood had been cut and stacked, I took solace in the idea of planning a large garden that would sit in front of the house. Even though it was autumn, it was difficult to find any kind of retreat in the great outdoors, since the Maine woods were filled with killer insects that swooped down on you from every direction. Undaunted, I cleared the space for my garden and pondered the next step. Fertilization, obviously. This was a large garden. Mere bags of fertilizer would not do. Using the trusty Yellow Pages again (I never learn) I called up a company listed under "Fertilizer" ("see also Manure"). Could they send up a load for my garden? No problem, I was told—the load would be delivered that very afternoon. I felt a surge of pleasure at the idea of getting the garden all ready now for planting in the spring. That evening, returning from the campus after another day devoted to LARCS, I pulled into the driveway and saw that my nice level garden had been turned into a mountain. And there was no way around it: this was a mountain of crap. I had failed again to understand that in Maine, when they said "a load," they really meant it. An entire dumptruck of manure had been deposited on my garden. There was no alternative but to begin spreading it out. But there was far too much of it to spread through the garden. I got out the red wheelbarrow, and started carting it off to the surrounding woods. So much seemed to depend on this.

As a glorious fall unfolded, the trees turned their brilliant colours and I dug into my various routines: cram for fiction course, read Maine poets, try to understand postmodernism, assemble Tinker Toys, write dissertation, edit journal and bibliography, clean chimney, feed furnace, avoid hunters, haul manure into woods. One day, as I lifted the handles on the wheelbarrow, one of a zillion deerflies that had been buzzing around my head made an all-out attack on my nose. That was it. I realized that the only way I could finish clearing the garden in the midst of this deerfly pestilence was to find a way of dealing with their relentless onslaught.

Remembering some philosophy course from my undergraduate

years, I hit upon the idea that if I did not hear those deerflies, they would not exist. Specific actions to achieve this kind of deafness called for a change in my habit of dress. I strapped a Walkman to my belt and plugged it into some heavy-duty industrial earphones, the kind used by those airport guys who work close to the roar of jets all day long. I put a long white towel over my head and draped it to my waist, securing it over the headphones with a multicoloured headband. I wore large, dark sunglasses and black cotton gloves. To keep the bugs from biting I found a long, robe-like, white vinyl raincoat that I cinched at the waist with a braided purple rope. Knee-high black rubber boots completed the protective disguise. I looked like a bewildered Arab sheik who had made some very bad fashion errors. Outside, it was hot. Very hot. I hit the button on the Walkman. That wonderful song by Foreigner blared into my brain:

Ooh, ooh, ooh, cold as, cold as ice
You're as cold as ice
You're as cold as ice, cold as ice, I know
You're as cold as ice, yes I know

It worked. I could be cold as ice. Somewhere out there, around me, the deerflies buzzed and stung, but they were at the far end of a tunnel, and I was in my own world, a Jewish Canadian Assistant Professor Literature Sheik tending my transcendental Maine garden, thinking cold, thinking Foreigner, thinking bliss.

All went well until one day, while I was hauling away manure to the sounds of "Hotel California," I saw an unknown car turn into the driveway. I was in my complete anti-deerfly outfit. Who could be turning into the driveway at this time of day? The car stopped. The door opened. Out came three of my students! I recognized them immediately as the sons and daughters of the Bar Harbor lobster fisherman, the students who had so quickly raised their hands and been offered an "A" in exchange for lobster home delivery. They came right up to me and asked if Dr. Lecker was around. Was it possible for them not to recognize me? I knew I had to make an instant decision. Either I would have to raise or lower my voice a pitch, disguising it and claiming I had no idea who Dr. Lecker was, or I would have to 'fess up to being a part-time sheik in rubber boots, hauling around a pile of crap. I peeled off the headband and tore off the towel. One of the students gasped. The others took several steps backward, as if they were standing in front of a zombie. I calmed them down. Explained the outfit. They looked at me, and I knew that life at the university would never be the same again. Within an hour every student in English would know what I really did in my spare time. I began to calculate how this might affect tenure decisions, and whether any student would ever hang out with me again. They left me with a huge bag of lobsters. I was not content.

As winter approached I started to panic about all the things that assistant professors usually panic about. I wouldn't have enough publications to get tenure. The faculty members evaluating my dossier would be unfamiliar with Canadian scholarly journals and would therefore think them marginal at best. My teaching evaluations would be bad and some of the students might complain about my alternative lifestyle. Worst of all, I might not complete my dissertation by the spring, and I would be fired. They might be calling me Dr. Lecker today, but I knew it was all a sham. In fact, I was not yet a doctor, and might never be one. No other university would even think of hiring me if I messed up my diss. Every night I wrestled with the works of those authors I was discussing in that godforsaken thesis: Hugh Hood, Dave Godfrey, Matt Cohen, Jack Hodgins, Robert Kroetsch.

They were all so different, yet what their works had in common was a deep preoccupation with the relationship between identity and time. Hugh was a Catholic novelist who believed that apprehending Canada was one means of finding grace. I became preoccupied by the way in which his Montreal stories depicted the landscape I knew in terms of Christian motifs. Godfrey was experimenting in the techniques of the French *nouveau roman*, particularly the work of writers such as Alain Robbe-Grillet and Marguerite Duras, in whose novels story and theme are secondary to structure and the attributes of the physical world take precedence over human feelings. Godfrey was interested in the way these writers used filmic techniques in their fiction, cutting and splicing and juxtaposing to make readers aware of the constructedness of the text. Cohen was a more traditional novelist, but he was definitely obsessed with personal and social history, returning again and again to the myths of identity formed through various confrontations with memory and time. Hodgins was a magic realist determined to break the bounds of linear narrative in a quest for identity that was self-made, rather than inherited. Kroetsch was deeply involved in postmodern aesthetics and had become the leading spokesman for the postmodern sensibility in Canadian writing and criticism. His enigmatic way of speaking about Canadian texts made them seem rare and exciting, a breath of fresh air after the conservatism that marked so much Canadian criticism in the seventies. Fortunately, not that much criticism had been written on these authors, so there was a remote chance that I might finish the thesis on time. The only problem was that life—and new publishing opportunities—kept getting in the way. And there was also the issue of my home life. Paula was not happy in those Maine woods. Nature was good, but it was not Toronto or Montreal. It seemed hard to keep things on track. Then things got more complicated. Paula was pregnant.

CHAPTER FOUR

By the end of my first year in Maine I was a father. It was a girl! I was overjoyed. This was exactly what I had hoped for. If it had been a boy, I would have been condemned to a life of soccer, football, hockey, or some other horrid team sport that involved endless chauffeuring and cheering from the bleachers at some mosquito-infested field or chilly ice rink that reeked of sweat-soaked hockey gear. I said to my father-in-law: "It's a girl!" Without missing a beat he said, "Great. Now you have something to worry about for the rest of your life." The truth is that I was worrying even before Emily was born. Who would her playmates be on this lonely country road? Even Bangor was a 20-minute drive away. And how would I get that damn dissertation done? There were diapers that needed attention and some kind of termite had started chewing through the floors. Somehow, I pushed on and managed to finish the thesis just in enough time to hold on to my job. I was still married. Lobster arrived regularly. A new academic year began. The well-fertilized garden started to grow, and grow.

Emily arrived in August, just around the same time as our collection of critical essays on Hugh Hood, the first baby of ECW Press. Hugh and John Metcalf were both publishing with Oberon Press in Ottawa, a company owned by Michael Macklem and renowned for its inactivity when it came to promoting its authors. They were dissatisfied with Oberon's performance and didn't have much faith in its future. After some lengthy discussions with us, Hood decided to make the break and left Oberon for ECW in May 1979. The next month Metcalf did the same. They would be joined a year later by Leon Rooke, who also wanted out of Oberon. By 1980 we were publishing the fiction of three of Canada's most accomplished writers.

As soon as John and Hugh came on board we started investing heavily in their books. We worked out an arrangement with Oberon to buy the rights to their previous titles and talked to other publishers in the hope of controlling all the rights to their earlier works. We reprinted

The Swing in the Garden (the first novel in The New Age series) and acquired the rights to some of Hugh's other previously published books, including the groundbreaking short story collection, *Flying a Red Kite*, as well as an earlier novel, *A Game of Touch*.

Hugh was an obsessively organized writer. He wrote every day and read voraciously. His schedule called for the production of a short story collection one year, to be followed by a novel in The New Age series the next, back and forth until the series would be finished, just in time for the millennium. Only his death stopped Hugh from completing that last volume, although he made a very good start on it. We published *None Genuine without This Signature*, a strong story collection. Much as we loved Hugh's fiction, we should have chosen a different path to follow in the early days of a small Canadian publishing company. This might seem puzzling to most people unfamiliar with the publishing industry in Canada. How could a Canadian publisher be making a mistake by aligning itself with an established Canadian writer who was an excellent businessman to boot? How could we go wrong republishing some of the finest fiction ever produced in Canada? Surely people would see in us the same quality they saw in Hood's work, and our stature would rise through the association. Not to mention sales. This is not how things work. First, it is rare for novels in Canada to sell thousands of copies— very rare. Yet in order to make any money, that is what must be sold. A well-established company with significant inventory can take a chance on a new writer, or on a writer who is excellent but does not sell in the thousands, because they can support their operations through the sale of backlist titles; often, those backlist items provide the major source of revenue for publishing operations. But a young company does not have a backlist, so it must hope to make its profits on pure sales of frontlist titles. However, since we were reprinting a number of Hugh's works, we faced a double disadvantage. First, the market had already been exposed to the books. If we could get grants to support their republication that would have helped, but the grants available from the Canada Council to support that kind of reprinting are not nearly as hefty as those assigned to first-time authors and original editions. We had to rely mainly on sales, which were never high enough to justify our investment; however, we believed in Hugh and felt that if only we kept publishing his work, people would eventually see the light, and we would profit from having seen it long before them. If lesson one in publishing is not to engage in projects that you can't fund, lesson number two is not to get involved with poetry and fiction with the idea of making serious money.

Although the debt was growing, we kept developing ideas. What kept glimmering, I think, was that whole untouched field of Canadian literature, and in particular Canadian literary criticism. Day after day I was struck by how few reliable resources existed. ECW would fill the gap, take over the terrain, execute project after project, become the leader in the field. This wasn't an active kind of territoriality; it was simply a plan of action born from the realization that no one had systematically made the field accessible through criticism and research. The more CanCrit projects came our way, the more we were inclined to sign them up. At the same time, we continued to pursue good creative writing. All the company money had to be borrowed by us, personally. I got my first loan for $5,000 in 1979. It seemed like a huge amount at the time.

John Metcalf was living in Delta, Ontario. I had a vague sense of his place in the literary firmament, mainly through my knowledge of his stints with the Montreal Story Tellers. I couldn't understand why his fiction was not on any of the Canadian literature courses I had taken at York, or why no one had really given it the critical attention it deserved. However, as I became more familiar with the canon and the players, I began to get a better sense of John's crimes against the CanLit establishment. First, he was born in England, and spoke with a British accent. Many of the authors he liked to read and respected were also British-born. Shame on him. He was not Canadian enough, despite his citizenship. Worse, he seemed to be pursuing modernist values in fiction at a time when Canadian critics were eagerly embracing postmodernism. Metcalf was a painstaking craftsman, forging every sentence again and again until the sense and rhythm were poetically just right. He didn't work quickly, but what he produced was beautifully wrought, exquisitely timed, and full of humour and pathos. Despite the growing interest in style and form, most critics were not really capable of commenting on literary style at the level of lyrical prose. They could talk about meta-fiction, self-reflexivity, parodies of conventional literary forms, historiography, and the fragmentation of consciousness, but they seldom were able to put their finger on what made a sentence beautiful to read, or what made a paragraph click.

Some people were offended at the idea of our paying such high-class attention to Metcalf's work. His most serious offense, of course, was to criticize the government grants and subsidies designed to assist Canadian publishers and writers. This made people nervous. What if there were no grants?! Metcalf argued that literary value would eventually be recognized, and that to support writing through grants was not only to introduce artificial value but also to perpetuate the mediocrity he saw in a good deal of Canadian writing. I still think that one of the funniest scenes in Canadian fiction occurs in *General Ludd*, where Metcalf describes a visit to Canada by two prominent Russian writers, who are astounded to learn about the subsidies available to Canadian writers and publishers. Metcalf's descriptions of these subsidies may sound like fantasy, but in fact they are completely true. The Canada Council did have a program to buy unsold books by the truckload in a bid to assist publishers faced with an audience that was reluctant to read, and the Ontario government did give a discount on books to people who had invested in provincial lottery tickets. Gambling contributed to Canadian literacy, while truckloads of unsold books were shipped off, in Metcalf's words, "as compulsory gifts to underdeveloped countries, hospitals, institutions for the blind, prisons, and lunatic asylums." In fact, it was later discovered that many of these books had found their final resting place in the Pickering dump.

Metcalf had great fun lampooning the system. Obviously he was a traitor to the cause. But how many people really took the time to see that his curmudgeonly stance was born out of a real interest and investment in what Canadian writing could achieve? He had standards. He championed many authors, established and new. He didn't try to hog the stage. He sought out talent. When young writers caught his attention, he promoted them for all they were worth, and when he became the editor at the Porcupine's Quill, he brought into print many excellent first-time authors whose work might otherwise never have seen the light of day.

ECW published some of John's most trenchant criticism (I think especially of *Kicking against the Pricks*) and encouraged him to edit some controversial essay collections. Although John's stuff was gutsy and funny and shrewd, few people bothered to respond. He had poked at so many sacred cows that he was put off limits—a sign, I think, of an unhealthy trend in Canadian criticism—the tendency to marginalize or ignore those who question the status quo; or, more precisely, those who question it from outside the professional club called professordom. My own involvement with that club made me realize how easy it was for professors to sit back and let the newspaper reviewers do the dirty work. We were professionals. We were above the fray. We had a more developed sense of quality. We had our own terminology. We didn't want to step on too many toes. After all, you never knew who might be evaluating your next grant application. We knew the canon and were secure in it. Challenges to the canon could be amusing at times, to be sure, but you couldn't rock the boat too much, because then you would be pushing figures like Margaret Laurence and Roberston Davies into the water, and if that happened, who knows who would be left in the boat? Mind you, I wouldn't have minded the decanonization of writers like Laurence and Davies, whose work, I had to admit to myself, I found boring. I wanted to hear some profs stand up and say that, but they all remained far too polite. In fact, it turns out that rampant politeness ultimately made the whole CanCrit industry much more boring than it might have been if only people felt more comfortable taking off their bourgeois gloves, an argument made persuasively in Stephen Henighan's *When Words Deny the World*. Not too long ago I was visited by a graduate student who was interested in finding out more about the state of Canadian criticism. I asked her which Canadian critics she enjoyed reading. She seemed genuinely stunned by the question, by the implicit assumption that criticism might actually be enjoyable to read. I challenged her to find me even two Canadian academic critics, under 40, who were writing against the status quo, younger critics willing to make a bit of a stink about something that rubbed them the wrong way. I am still waiting for her to give me a single name.

I shouldn't really complain. As a young critic teaching Canadian literature in the early 1980s, I wasn't doing much to stir the pot. I think my chief concern was to create some kind of consolidation in the study of Canadian literature, not exactly a task that lends itself to undermining existing models. On the contrary, ECW was building up the canon, entrenching writers, and providing the critical tools that ultimately increased their currency. At one level, this made me cynical. It was so easy to manipulate the canon. On another level, though, I wanted to create a canon as a sign of national value. I remembered the words of Edward Hartley Dewart when he wrote, in one of the first anthologies of Canadian poetry, way back in 1864, that "a national literature is an essential element in the formation of a national character."

If my mission was political, it would be achieved by consolidating the relation between literature and nation through a publishing program that glorified that connection. No doubt I was spurred on by the events leading up to the Quebec referendum in 1980, a shatteringly anxious period for all Canadians and a particularly trying time for anglophones in Quebec, many of my relatives among them. I thought of the feelings I had about returning home every time I crossed the border into Canada and realized that if the referendum succeeded I could never call a separate

Quebec my home. And if that was true, where *was* my home? I felt the potential loss of that home every day in the months leading up to the referendum, a loss that I'm sure would be difficult for someone living in English Canada to imagine. Quebec might leave, but Canada would still be their home, and they would remain within it. But the place where I grew up would have become another country, a country based on the repudiation of the nation that had provided a spiritual and professional centre for my adult life. There was little I could do to get politically involved, given my location, but I did participate in a radio program on the topic for the Maine Public Broadcasting Network in April 1980, a month before the referendum. When the results were finally announced I felt a huge wave of relief. The Canada I had known would never be the same, but it had survived a massive test. Little did I realize that the whole tortured referendum process would be repeated 15 years later, and that it would involve me in political currents that were infinitely remote from my life in Maine. I remember wondering at the time, trivially, how the Quebec vote would affect ECW's various projects. Could there be an *Annotated Bibliography of Canada's Major Authors* that covered writers such as Hugh MacLennan, Irving Layton, Anne Hébert, and F.R. Scott if those writers lived in a country that was no longer Canada? With the outcome of the referendum uncertain, we had continued to follow our initial plan. The second volume of the bibliography was in process, along with several novels, critical books, and special issues of the journal.

Things had changed dramatically in the production of the bibliography, due to the fact that I now had access to a computer terminal connected via modem to the university's mainframe. In order to get online I had to reach the campus by 7 a.m., at which time I would dial a special number and pray that it would not be busy. If I was lucky and the call went through I had to push the phone headset into a specially designed plastic modem and hope that everything connected. This was before personal computers and word processing programs as we know them today. We used Waterloo Script, an early word processing program developed in Canada at the University of Waterloo. Now we could make global changes and see the results on the screen before printing things out. I threw out my bottles of rubber cement and put the Selectric in a cupboard. But things were still cumbersome. It was impossible to print out a single page. All printing was done in a central building on the campus in huge print batches. If we wanted to check a few edited pages of the bibliography to see how our changes looked, we had to run the entire document, sometimes printing out and trashing 300 pages in order to see three. And converting the Waterloo Script files to typeset pages was no easy matter, since very little progress had been made in achieving compatibility.

The higher-ups in the English department at Maine didn't know much about my various projects, but they knew how to make good use of an ambitious assistant professor. Early in the semester of my second year I was summoned to the chair's office, where I was told that some special funding had been made available to bring in distinguished speakers, and wouldn't it be nice if we brought down a Canadian writer. Of course, it was stressed, the event would have to be a real success, since future years of funding depended upon the success of this first venture. It went without saying that the speaker would be appearing in the largest lecture hall on campus. Maybe 400 seats. It also went without saying that I had no choice but to accept the challenge. Hmm. How would I fill 400 seats? The visiting speaker would have to be someone special. I got in touch with Margaret Laurence, who graciously accepted my invitation. But then family and health concerns forced her to cancel. I thought of Margaret Atwood. If anyone could bring in an audience, it would be Atwood. I wrote to her. As it turned out, she was scheduled to be part of a creative writing course at the University of New Hampshire. If I agreed to pick her up there she would come back to Maine with me and read from her work.

I was worried. I had never met Atwood. The only contact I had had with her was in connection with a review I had asked her to write of a new book of criticism by Robin Mathews. She had turned me down, and I had written back to ask if it was because she didn't like doing reviews. "No," she responded, "I do not in the least mind being asked to write reviews. But Robin Mathews? Come on now! He can't count!" Ouch. I hoped she thought I could count. I was nervous about saying something dumb, but I was even more nervous about filling the hall. I decided to blitz the state with posters advertising her visit, with a special campaign directed at high schools in the area. I followed up with personal phone calls to teachers around the state, stressing how fortunate their students would be to see this first-rate writer. Initial feedback was good, but there were a lot of seats to fill. I worked feverishly up to the day I was supposed to pick up Atwood. I drove down to the University of New Hampshire and found her in a little cottage on the campus that they used for these writing classes, sitting on a sofa surrounded by students who were commenting on each others' poems. It was one of those feel-good creative writing seminars in which participants tell each other oh-so-delicately that they really can't stand each other's work. How many polite ways are there to say "Your writing *really* sucks"? Those seminars know all the ways. Atwood wasn't saying much. The instructor, a perky young woman·who was no doubt an assistant professor like me, encouraged her to make some comments. "We're all so happy to have you here with us," she said, "and we've been so looking forward to your thoughts." Atwood looked around at the expectant circle of faces. "You really want my thoughts?" she asked. "Of course," said the prof, looking pleased. Atwood paused. Then she said: "None of you know how to use punctuation properly. You need to learn how to use punctuation before you can write. Why are you going to university? None of this material is very good." The prof looked shocked. Then I could see that she had started to cry. She ran out of the cottage, followed by her supportive and injured students. I was left in the room with Atwood. "Are you ready to go?" she asked. We got into the car and headed back to Maine. Given what I'd just seen, I realized that anything could happen. I decided this would be a good time to confess. When we stopped for an ice cream at a Howard Johnson's I summoned up my courage and told her I was worried that the big lecture room would not be full. "Don't worry," she said. "It will be full." That didn't relieve me much, but I crossed my fingers and hoped for the best.

As it turned out, Atwood was right. For a while. There were dozens of school buses outside the lecture hall. My high school campaign had worked! Inside, every seat was taken by happy-looking young students whispering and chewing gum. I even saw some of my own students and a handful of faculty members. Things would be fine. They were not fine. The chair of the department stood up and commented on the new lecture series and invited me to welcome our very special guest. I read my prepared introduction to Atwood and thanked her for being with us. The room burst into applause as she approached the podium. What a relief. Then she uttered the sentence that turned everything around: "I'm going to read some torture poems," Atwood said. She started reading some of the gruesome poems from *True Stories*, which would be published later that year. I looked around. The high school teachers were shifting anxiously in their seats. Atwood continued to read—rape, murder, atrocities, torture. She read in her flat, level voice, almost without expression. The juxtaposition of the voice and the subject matter made it all the more chilling. I became aware of a general movement around me. The high school students were being marched out of the hall! I saw lines of them forming near the exits as Atwood read on. Most of the room cleared out. I was aghast. After the scattered applause I stumbled to the front of the lecture hall, looked up into the vacated seats, and thanked Atwood for her wonderful and provocative reading. She remained serene.

A few days after Atwood left I received a call from a reporter working for *Chatelaine* magazine in Toronto. They had selected Atwood as their Woman of the Year, and the reporter had been following her recent visit to the United States. Apparently she had been speaking to various people at the University of New Hampshire, who were a little put off by Atwood's attitude toward the students' writing. The reporter asked me why Atwood's audiences often seemed frustrated by her readings, by what she called "that monochromatic telephone recording of a voice informing them of political atrocities overseas and emotional brutality at home." I wanted to be positive. "I have no idea why they are frustrated," I said. "I found Atwood to be very pleasant and we got along quite well." Before the reporter ended the call I asked her if she would mind sending me a copy of the special Atwood issue when it was published. She was happy to oblige. About a month later the issue arrived. The cover was filled by a photo of a heavily made-up Atwood, looking quite unnatural as a superwriter glamour queen. Inside was the long article on Atwood, whose reputation the reporter characterized as "cold, humourless, bitchy." Then the reporter turned her attention to my comments:

> On the other hand, a reputation like this gets shattered in the most delightful ways. Robert Lecker, an assistant professor at the University of Maine, Orono, invited Margaret Atwood down for a reading last spring, not knowing what to expect, although the word strident figured prominently in her advance billing. "I think he thought some monster would crawl off the plane," says Atwood. Instead, Lecker found a "funny, warm person completely in control of her work—I fell in love with her."

Whoaa! I never said that! I said she was funny and nice, but "love" was stretching it a bit. I rushed to call Atwood. "I didn't say I fell in love with you!" I squeaked, wondering what fate would now befall me, since I had certainly offended the most important writer in the country. Atwood was still calm. "Journalists will do that," she said, reassuringly. "Don't worry about it."

Despite her graciousness, it took me weeks to recover from the whole ordeal. I wanted to disappear. I wanted to hide out at home and never set foot on the campus. However, there was a problem at home. There was a smell. A bad smell, coming from one of the walls. What do you do when you have a bad smell in a wall? You talk to the neighbours and they suggest that you have a carpenter take a look at that wall. Two days later Ron shows up and sniffs the wall. "You have a dead rat in there," he says. We strike up a conversation about the rat. "What do you do?" he asks. I give the standard answer (I've now learned to keep it brief): "Teach Lit." He looks around the house. "You sure could use some new clapboard on that wall." What's he getting at? "How would you like to trade skills? No money. I write science fiction. You comment on my science fiction, and I'll fix your house." For months after that Ron gave me his stories and I would try to help him make them work a little better.

Seemed to me like I was getting the best part of this deal. The rat was gone, my siding had been replaced, and Ron was now working on the roof. However, he claimed to be happy with the arrangement. No one, he told me, had ever read his writing. He was shy and reserved. For him, somehow, it was a means of connecting with the world. I thought of how our exchange gave me a new sense of what my own training was worth. At that point, it was worth a rat in the wall, new clapboard siding, and twenty shingles on a roof. But at least the value was concrete. It wasn't the same as getting a pay cheque from the university every two weeks. I read something, I commented, and a man showed up and hammered on my house. That made it seem so real. I never stopped getting a thrill from earning concrete rewards for my esoteric skills. Later, when the ECW list got bigger, I would love selling books to people at street fairs and conferences. Even if I sold it for half price, there was still the sense that someone was willing to put real cash in my hand for this literary artefact that I had helped to produce. It was a completely different feeling than receiving money from a distributor for the total number of books sold in a given month, 120 days after that month ended (if you were lucky), minus returns, provided that the distributor was still solvent and willing to pay. Most people imagine that the revenue from books sold in stores flows directly to the publisher. But in fact there is almost always a crucial intermediary—the distributor—who is responsible for getting the books to the stores and then collecting from the stores on a regular basis. Only after that collection is made does the publisher see its revenue, which is reduced by the commission paid to the distributor for supplying the stores.

Although actual dollars were paid for books and skills from time to time, more often than not we were searching for cash. Our signatures were on various forms at the bank. I had taken out two loans totalling

$20,000. It was getting a little scary. Things had been pledged in security. Things like our modest houses, not to mention personal guarantees. The Internal Revenue Service apparently recognized my plight. Soon after they assessed my first tax return as a professor at UMO they sent me a cheque for $2,500 because my income was below some national poverty line and I was therefore entitled to emergency aid. I wish they had helped ECW, where the challenge was always to make the next payment, to stay just one step ahead of the bank raising some kind of flag. The cash flow depended largely on the library market. No individual would be interested in owning a bibliography, and few others seemed passionate about owning some of the publications that marked the early 1980s: a collection of essays on prairie poetry; a book of verse by our landlord, the master of Stong; a comparative study of the relation between English- and French-Canadian literature; a book about little magazines in Canada. To supplement our income we turned to packaging books for a number of publishers, editing anthologies of poetry and fiction for companies like Nelson Canada; Holt, Rinehart and Winston; and Harper & Row.

All of this exposure to Canadian criticism and its very limited audience made us understand that if we were ever going to pay off our loan we would have to develop large-scale projects for the library market using a formula that could be repeated again and again. That's when we hit upon the idea of a critical series. Two factors contributed to our concept of such a series. In my first year at Maine I had contacted Twayne Publishers in Boston in the hope of writing a book on Robert Kroetsch for their Twayne's World Authors Series. At that time Twayne was one of the dominant players in the field of literary criticism, mainly because they had learned to tailor-make series for the library market in the US, and they had subcontracted the acquisition process to a general editor who was responsible for finding authors and vetting their manuscripts. Twayne responded to my request by informing me that the acquisitions editor for TWAS was about to retire, so things were on hold. Modestly, I wrote back and suggested myself for the job. A few months later, I found myself acquiring titles for Twayne and striking up a relationship with its publisher, who was naturally interested in developing series for the library market. If Twayne could succeed in the US by producing books on hundreds of American writers (along with a handful of Canadian ones), why couldn't we do the same exclusively in Canada? The benefits of developing a series were also highlighted by a second factor, which was our experience with the journal. We had learned that once a library had subscribed to something, it very seldom let it go. This situation would change in coming years as library budgets shrank, but in the early 1980s and throughout most of that decade the library market remained strong and positively committed to the concept of subscription, whether to a magazine or a consistently well-executed series of books.

Operating with the subscription concept in mind, we conceived several new series that would draw us further and further into debt. The biggest sink-hole was a massive project called *Canadian Writers and Their Works*, which was originally titled *The Critical History of Canadian Literature* (*CHCL*), or chuckle, which it definitely was not. The idea was to produce 20 volumes of critical essays, with half devoted to fiction writers and the other half to poets. Each volume would contain five essays on five writers, structured according to a format that called for a biography, a discussion of the writer's milieu, a summary of criticism, a chronological survey and discussion of the author's work, and a bibliography of primary and secondary sources. This meant that we would have to commission 100 essays of about 15,000 words apiece on a very diverse group of writers, and we would have to ensure that each and every essay conformed to the series' design. In other words, we were talking about coordinating and editing 1.5 million words.

You'd think we would have learned about the nightmares this would involve from our experience with the bibliography series, which, even at this point, had only seen the publication of three volumes; five more were still in the works. We hadn't learned. We wrote letters to academics and critics all over the country, asking them to participate in the project. Many said no. We wrote to others. Finally, 100 said yes. We set strict deadlines. Almost no one delivered their essay on time. This was not in the least bit odd. In academic publishing, everyone will always be late. And the essays that did come in posed problems we had seen before: despite our clear instructions, the essays were not editorially consistent in any way. Some were not even up to date. Others had incorrect or missing information. Everything would have to be verified. Some kind of mystical copy editor would have to be found to make sense of the mess. It wouldn't be us; we had already sniffed way too much glue.

The series was supposed to be finished within a few years. It never occurred to us that it would have been impossible to fund the publication of all those titles in such a short period of time; nor did we have any idea of the enormous costs involved in editing those books, making them consistent, verifying their contents, getting them typeset and printed. We had to put together a three-person editorial team to handle the volume and keep things on track. They met regularly to ensure that consistent stylistic and citation standards were applied across the board. To add to our costs and frustration, we decided that we could issue each of the essays in each volume as a discrete monograph. That way we could do a double hit on the libraries: they would buy the bound volumes for their reference sections and the monographs for the stacks, where they would sit with other books on the author in question. In fact, this plan worked quite well over time. Gradually the libraries came to recognize the series and to invest in standing orders for new volumes as they appeared. That certainly increased cash flow. But the problem was that we were way overextended. Authors wanted to be paid. Editors wanted to be paid. We got in touch with Don Evans, an accomplished cartoonist and illustrator who worked under the pen name Isaac Bickerstaff, and commissioned him to provide illustrations of every one of the 100 writers in the series so that we would achieve a consistent look. Don wanted to be paid. We had no money. Our houses were on the line. We weren't even paying rent or light or heat or expensive lawyers and accountants, yet it was impossible to make ends meet. By 1981 we owed $50,000. We tried to take advantage of every grant under the sun. This is when we began to learn that many books just don't qualify for some of those grants—books like collections of critical essays, or multi-volume library reference works. Well, screw the grant-givers. We believed in the projects. We would push on with new ones. We drew up a proposal for a series of annual anthologies called *The Best of Canada*, which would collect first-class material published on Canadian life and culture every year. No takers. We developed plans for a series of travel guides devoted to Canadian cities. Too expensive. We worked with Evans to design a book called *Bald Is Beautiful* and found an agent who tried to flog it to US publishers, without success.

Sometimes I found it hard to believe that I was invested in these books and series and still teaching Canadian literature in Maine. Something about that was not quite right, no matter how I cut it. Almost every day, something happened to remind me how far I was from home. It might have been the continuing difficulty of acquainting my students with Canada or the constant sight of the American flag or the oddness of the stationery I had printed up: *Essays on Canadian Writing*, Department of English, University of Maine at Orono. On other days, it might be some baffling student-related exchange, as in the following conversation I had one day with the coach of the UMO baseball team, who didn't know that I don't care about baseball and didn't even know the team's name and, most important, that I was from Canada and didn't know the code:

> *Coach*: Is this Dr. Decker?
> *Me*: No, this is Professor Lecker.
> *Coach*: I'm looking for Decker.
> *Me*: Then I think you want Art History.
> *Coach*: No, I want English.
> *Me*: OK, I am English.
> *Coach*: Are you the one teaching that LARCS course?
> *Me*: Yes, I am. It's a course on technical and business writing. LARCS is a project.
> *Coach*: Good, good, well we have a student in common!
> *Me*: We do?
> *Coach*: Yeah, Jason Fledge. He's in your class, right?
> *Me*: Yup.
> *Coach*: Well, you see, he isn't doing too well in your course.
> *Me*: That's right.
> *Coach*: He's on the team.
> *Me*: That's good.
> *Coach*: I was hoping we could come to some kind of arrangement.
> *Me*: What kind of arrangement?
> *Coach*: He has to pass the course to stay on the team.
> *Me*: Well, then, he should start working harder on his assignments.
> *Coach*: Yeah, yeah, but like if he doesn't pass he'll be off the team.
> *Me*: I hope he passes, then.
> *Coach*: Yeah. Right. Well, how can I put this? He has to pass.
> *Me*: If he passes, he passes.
> *Coach*: I don't think you get it. He has to pass to stay on the team.
> *Me*: I hope he passes.
> *Coach*: I'll be calling you back.

The coach did not call back. Jason passed. In fact, his work improved dramatically during the last few weeks of class. His essays were models of their kind. It was almost as if I was dealing with a completely new person. But quality is quality, right?

Another student in Jason's class had just the opposite profile: from day one, he was a star achiever. No one could write instructions like Derek. His resumes were perfect. His job application letters were unsurpassed. Even his LARCS instructions were impeccable. He told me he was headed for law school, and I had no doubt he would vault to the top of his class there too. Toward the middle of the term each student had to submit a proposal for a lengthy project they would hand in two weeks before the end of class. The project was supposed to relate, some-how, to their major. Derek handed in a nice proposal. He wanted to do his project on the restructuring of electoral districts in Bangor. That's a bit weird, I thought, but the guy is going into law and maybe that's the kind of thing potential lawyers are into. I gave him the green light. Ten days later he handed in the finest project of them all, a beautifully complete document with graphs and statistics and detailed information.

As I was reading this, a little bell went off in my head. I would hear this bell many times in the future, but this was the first time I had heard it at Maine. The bell said: This is plagiarized. But if it was in fact plagiar-ized, how would I prove it? What did I know about the electoral districts in Bangor? I fretted about this for a few days, poked around in the library, got nowhere. Finally, I headed over to the law library and threw myself upon the mercy of the reference librarian. She looked down at Derek's paper, flipped through it, and said, "Come with me." We walked through the stacks. She stopped in front of a shelf and picked out a slim volume. "Here is your student's essay." I could hardly believe my eyes. He had copied it lock, stock, and barrel. All of the diagrams too. His student ID number was entered neatly in the back of the book. Derek, Derek, Derek.

When the time came to hand back the students' papers, I held onto his. It didn't take him long to show up at my door. "Have a seat," I said. "Is there anything you want to tell me about your paper?" His eyes were going twitchy, but he kept his cool. "No, what would I want to tell you?" I looked him in the eye and asked: "Is it possible that this work is not yours?" "No, it's mine," he said. This was pissing me off. "Look," I said. "I'm going to give you one last chance to tell the truth. If you tell the truth, you will only fail this paper. But if you don't tell the truth you are going to fail the course." "I'm telling the truth," he replied, at which point I brought out the book itself and asked him if he had ever seen it. He denied ever seeing it. "That's funny," I said, "because your ID number is in the back of the book."

He continued to deny. That put me over the edge. I flunked him in the course. Two weeks later he wrote me a letter. In it, he said that my unjust actions had caused the law school to refuse him admission and that if I did not revise the grade and pass him in the course he would kill himself. He gave me a deadline: 48 hours. I panicked. Here I was, in my second year as a prof, and already I had received a suicide threat in connection with a grade. That wasn't supposed to happen until you were a full professor. This was scary. What to do? I ran up to the chair's office, described the situation from beginning to end, and showed her the threatening note. "What should I do?" I think I wailed. "It's very simple," she said, as if the answer was so obvious it hardly needed to be uttered. "Let him kill himself." This I could not accept. I would be responsible for someone's death! I ran around to the offices of other professors, asking them all what I should do. Every single one said the same thing: "Let him kill himself." I had a lot to learn about the prof business, that's for sure. What did they know that I didn't? What they knew was that someone with an ego like Derek's would never have the balls to off himself. I saw him crossing the campus a month later, no doubt formulating plans for his altered career. From this I learned that when you are a prof, crazies can show up anytime. Stand your ground.

I was still standing. As the end of my second year of teaching approached, I tried to take stock of my situation. Living in the US, I still felt out of the CanLit loop, even though I was attending conferences, publishing in various journals, and dealing with all kinds of academics through the press, the journal, and the Twayne series, which continued to expand. I plugged into the network of academics who were teaching Canadian literature in the US, mainly through my involvement with the Association for Canadian Studies in the United States, one of the few scholarly organizations that seemed to want its members to have a good time. I loved going to their bi-annual conferences. There was a little bit of ego there, but nothing like the Canadian conferences where people showed up to stake out their turf or to take ungenerous shots at others who were threatening it. I used to go to the annual Canadian conference of English professors held at the Learned Societies meetings, but I gradually tired of hearing people beat their theoretical drums and of listening to graduate students present papers that demonstrated very little command of the extant research on the authors or ideas they were talking about. It was all so narcissistic and territorial. Worse, there was little sense that this dissemination of research was achieving the desired ends. The idea behind conferences was similar to the idea behind scholarly publication: a scholar built on other people's work in relation to a problem or an issue or an author, and through this communal effort the research moved forward. What often happened, however, was that scholars became reluctant to get involved in the existing research, or, if they did, they would cite others' work in order to make the politically correct gesture, or, more frequently, to set up someone else's argument

in order to have an object to attack. There was nothing wrong with disagreement, of course. I'm all for that. What started to bother me, however,
was this sense that there was no genuine CanCrit community out there.
It was clear that there was a vibrant community of feminist scholars
who were truly sharing ideas and who saw their inquiries working in
communal terms. The poets and fiction writers found communities that
provided dialogue and support. But the critics tended to remain aloof.
Again and again I got the sense that there was little generosity of spirit
there, little sense of welcoming others to the professorial club.

I got a taste of that unwelcoming stance when the reviews of the
first volumes of *ABCMA* started to appear. The reviewers tended to be
cranky. They didn't like the word "Major" in our series title. Who were
we to decide who was major and who was not? They found items that
had missed our net. They complained that some of the entries were not
up to date. Did anyone stand up and point out that no one had done
this before? Did anyone say that now it was possible to get a sense of the
trends in Atwood criticism, or to find out what was in the manuscript
holdings in various rare book rooms? Did anyone wonder how we had
managed to research and organize these thousands of entries, or how
we had dug up information about international book reviews? As the
series moved on, and more volumes got published, I learned to expect
this kind of response. More often than not, it was a non-response.
Bibliography and works of literary criticism just went into the void. You
put out an issue of the journal, mailed it out to hundreds of subscribers,
and there was a resounding silence. You published an article on some
topic of apparent interest to others, and no one said a word. I think
most academics just get used to this silence. They know that very few
people will read their work but they carry on anyhow, either because
the research is self-fulfilling in some way, or because they want the salary
increase that is tied to the quality and scope of their publications, or
because they believe that one day someone will actually communicate
with them about their ideas. I didn't reach this level of cynicism until
later. Even in those early days as a prof, however, I had the uneasy sense
that in many ways this would be a lonely profession, one that was made
less lonely by the classroom teaching so seldom considered a vital element
when it came to merit increases or raises in salary.

Although teaching could offer a sense of community, it wasn't easy
to feel comfortable in the classroom. In order to relax in front of students
you have to feel in control of the material. You have to know exactly
where you are going, and if you get sidetracked, you have to know how

to let that happen without worrying that you have screwed up the lesson plan. This is particularly important in lecture situations, when anything can happen to mess up the plan. I discovered this the hard way when I gave my first lecture at York, back when I was a teaching assistant in a course that enrolled about 300 students. I knew I had 45 minutes to give my lecture, and I became obsessed with the idea that I would either run overtime and not finish, or that I would run undertime and be left with nothing to say. So I planned the timing of the lecture obsessively, plotting the exact moment that every topic I wanted to cover would be delivered. At 9:10 I would be talking about point A; at 9:15 I would be dealing with point B; at 9:25 I would hit upon concept C, until my perfectly timed lecture came to its perfectly planned ending: 9:55 on the nose. Everything in my lecture notes was flagged and colour-coded according to the clock.

At the beginning of the lecture things went well, although I was shaking in my boots. I talked. The students took notes. I hit all my topics at the minute specified in my plan. The lecture rolled on. Hey, this wasn't so bad. Then, the thing happened that was not supposed to happen. I had never imagined this. A student at the back of the lecture hall raised her hand. A question! There was no time in my lecture plan for that. I decided to ignore the hand. Today, with the students being so polite and accommodating (most of them) the hand would eventually have gone down, melted away. But this was the seventies. It was a militant hand, attached to a militant arm, which was no doubt attached to a militant person wearing high leather boots. I continued to ignore it. The hand and arm that were waving in the air did not like this. The person in charge of the hand and arm rose from her seat. I was still on time. Maybe she would sit down. She did not sit down. No. She climbed up on her seat and waved her hand, calling out "Hellooo, hellooo!" Her whole body seemed to be waving at me. Everyone was looking. I had to recognize her:

Me (briskly): Yes? You have a question?
Her: Yes, Sir, I have a question. I've had it for a while.
Me (checking the clock. Maybe I could just talk faster): Go ahead.
Her: About ten minutes ago you used a word I did not understand.
Me (OK, a quick definition and I'm back on track): What's the word?
Her (gleefully): Existentialism.
Me: I used that word?
Her: Yes. You did. I would like to know what it means.

It was all downhill after that. Sometimes you just have to abandon everything and go with the flow. This became a teaching rule that I applied more and more diligently as time wore on. I learned not to be afraid to tell some stories, to spread a little gossip, to bring in elements from my own life. When it came to teaching Canadian literature I tried to relax enough to bring in other forms of Canadian art. And because I wanted to entertain the students as much as I wanted to entertain myself, I got more and more interested in Canadian music, Canadian painting, Canadian history, legend, lore. Sometimes, I got even further off track simply in order to get back on it. Once, when the class seemed bored, I launched into an impromptu lecture on the scale of malt whiskeys, explaining the ladder of taste that rose from the warmth and fragrance of Oban to the peat and smoke of Lagavulin and upward to the heavenly extremes of the iodine-scented Laphroaig. My central conceit was the possibility of transcendence via malt. This took about ten minutes. The students seemed vaguely interested. They perked up. I said: "Any questions?" One woman raised her hand: "My father says it is OK to put a drop of distilled water in Lagavulin. What do you think?" That kind of question was music to my ears. I would try to craft my answer in such a way that we could segue back to the syllabus. The detour seemed to have worked.

I was teaching a pretty standard canon, falling back on some of the titles I had studied as a graduate student, many of which were already making me tired. Mrs. Bentley in *As for Me and My House*. Unreliable narrator. Got it. *The Diviners*. Memorybank movies. Laurence trying to be postmodern. Looking way too forced. Robertson Davies and Carl Jung. Did anyone besides Davies believe that Jung's theories had a place in daily life? Susanna Moodie's *Roughing It in the Bush*? A sure way to turn off a group of students was to force them to read it and then give them a test. W.O. Mitchell? The contrived innocence of *Who Has Seen the Wind* made me wince. Frederick Philip Grove? As Mordecai Richler observed, the best thing that could be said about Grove was that he was a very good speller. It was a confusing time. The list of the 100 greatest Canadian novels produced by the ballot at the Calgary Conference left me shaking my head. Gabrielle Roy's *The Tin Flute*? In 1981? Ernest Buckler's *The Mountain and the Valley*? If its hero, David, had one more phenomenological epiphany I would definitely lose my breakfast. I could see from looking down the list that the books that interested me most were those that were implicitly about their own formal assumptions, self-conscious books that problematized their own existence, tortured books that wondered about the status of language. I was drawn to writers such as Michael Ondaatje, Robert Kroetsch, Phyllis Webb, Gwendolyn MacEwen, A.M. Klein, Leonard Cohen, Clark Blaise—the heavily obsessed writers who nearly went crazy trying to overcome some central paradox or problem.

Ondaatje had taken all kinds of risks with his *Collected Works of Billy the Kid*, which was as much about writing as it was about Billy. I loved the way the book's blurry photos made me want to see more clearly, and then the way that wanting forced me to question my need for that kind of clarity. I felt the same admiration for *Coming through Slaughter*, and Ondaatje's exploration of the relation between art and madness. I went to the library and found Bellocq's Storyville photos and was amazed by their innocence and violence. I knew there were no recordings of Buddy Bolden's blues, but I went searching for the early New Orleans music that must have sounded like his and started to get lost in that idiom. Ondaatje's books moved between sanity and insanity, between the dream of formal perfection and the recognition that such perfection was a dream, a sham, an ideal that would inevitably destroy you.

Ondaatje lived on the line between extremes. That was the line I was looking for in art and literature, the place in the abstract painting where the line breaks down, the ambiguous space where you could go either way and be energized by the tension. The blur forced you to fill in the blanks. It made you a participant in the story, rather than a passive observer. I could see that Ondaatje was inviting me to fill in blanks all over the place, that he was always implicitly telling me that the story was about my reading of it. Jack and I decided that we could probably sell a critical book that focused on some of the incredible scenes in Billy and other books that interested us at the time. We made a valiant attempt to co-author an analysis of the scene in the poem where Billy is raped by the sun (my favourite scene) and discovered that it was virtually impossible for us to merge our critical voices. Jack's was succinct, concrete, and visual. He liked short, direct sentences. My sentences ran longer and my words were more multisyllabic. Whenever he edited my prose he was always getting rid of "ands" and commas, proof that, as a writer at least, I could never really call it a day and let a sentence end.

I could see that much of what interested me about Ondaatje could be found in the works of those other writers who were claiming my attention. Kroetsch had just published *The Sad Phoenician*, which followed *Field Notes*, an incredible testimony to the flux of human experience, a series of poems that allowed me to see that poetry was intimately linked to place. I loved the way Kroetsch was ready to celebrate uncertainty, how he could make meaning out of seed catalogues or farm ledgers, how he described the Canadian long poem as a pre-orgasmic, desire-ridden voyage into the delights of textual foreplay and delay. In terms of fiction, I was being drawn into the obsessive world of Clark Blaise, who kept coming back to the stories of his childhood in the American south and later Pittsburgh. The stories were funny, tragic, gothic, sexualized. Blaise was never able to escape his role as writer and observer. His ultimate subject matter was him translated in a hundred ways by the symbolic landscapes that marked his short stories and the novel *Lunar Attractions*, a lusciously dark and obsessive tale of sexuality, depravity, and loss.

Although I was able to discuss these writers' works in my classes at Maine, it was clear that teaching Canadian literature was not going to be a full-time activity so long as I remained there. Other "service" courses needed to be taught. I was frustrated by my inability to make Canadian literature the central focus of my teaching, and frustrated more by my growing sense of the distance that separated me from the ECW activities in Toronto. Jack was dealing with most of the administrative issues. He was schlepping around books and mailing off packages every day. We didn't have a distributor at this time, so he essentially played the role of the distributor—packing orders, issuing invoices, sending stuff out. I wanted to get closer to that activity. Besides, family life in Maine was encountering problems. Paula felt lonely and dislocated with a house in the woods and a two-year-old child on her hands. We wanted to be in a city. A Canadian city. As my fourth year at UMO began, I decided that it would be my last year there. Either I would find an academic post in Canada, or we would move to Toronto and I would find some kind of work and co-manage the journal and the press.

Soon after the fall term started I learned that McGill had an opening for a post in Canadian literature. Hoping against all hope, I sent in my application. Then I got the call. Shortlisted! Early in 1982 I drove up to Montreal and got interviewed for the job. It was mostly a blur. I remember having drinks at the faculty club, meeting with faculty and students, and presenting a paper on Margaret Atwood. I remember being introduced to Louis Dudek, who was retiring, and him asking, "Well, are you ready to step into my boots?" What a ridiculous idea. Here was one of Canada's most accomplished poets and teachers asking me if I was prepared to replace him. But I said "I guess so," wondering what this all meant. I remember a dinner with the hiring committee at an Italian restaurant. Too much wine. Surely I said something inane. The next morning I headed back to Maine, knowing that whatever happened, I could not remain in the United States. About a week later the chairman at McGill called me up and offered me the job. I would be heading back to the city of my birth. Post-referendum Montreal, still part of Canada, a quick plane ride from Toronto. I could hardly imagine how many things the move would change.

By the time June rolled around we had bought a house in Montreal and put the one in Maine up for sale. We would have to carry two mortgages for a month or two until the place in Maine was sold. No big deal, since it was sure to sell quickly. But not too many people seemed to be interested in making an offer. I discussed the asking price with our real-estate agent who suggested a slight reduction. I put the price down a bit. Now it was close to the price we had originally paid, despite all our improvements. Still no offers, and the summer was marching on. Our move to Montreal was scheduled for July. When the moving date was just around the corner and no buyers had shown up, I knew I had to take action. I hired a trusted student, Debbie, to place an advertisement in the local paper in the hope of finding someone to rent the place, on the understanding that it was for sale and that the tenant could be asked to vacate with a few months' notice. I could handle two mortgages for a month or two, but not beyond that. It was imperative that we rent the place. If it remained uninhabited it would surely be claimed by animals or squatters. Besides, winter was not far off.

Soon after we settled in Montreal, Debbie called from Bangor with some heartening news. She had found a good tenant whose references had checked out well. He put down a deposit and signed a lease. It wasn't a perfect solution, but at least it would pay the Maine mortgage until the place was sold, and someone would be there minding the furnace, so the pipes wouldn't freeze. The first term at McGill got underway in September. I was worried about the Maine house all the time. However, the tenant had paid in August. He paid in September. His cheque was just a little late in October. Still no action on the house. I realized, with a little frisson, that I'd heard nothing from our real-estate agent in two months. As if she had read my mind telepathically, a few days later she called me up. After the small talk, the conversation rapidly boosted my nervousness. "Mr. Lecker, we're having a little trouble showing your property." Why? I thought. What's wrong with my property? Too far in the woods? No.

"Well, Mr. Lecker, we have a bit of a problem with the pictures on the walls."

"What pictures do you mean?"

"The pornographic posters."

"Pornographic posters?"

"Yes, there are porno posters in all the rooms. And big spikes nailing them to the walls."

"I can't believe that. I'll call the tenant and tell him to get them down right away."

"That would be good, Mr. Lecker. And there is one other thing . . ."

"Yes?"

"The marijuana plants in the basement. We cannot show the house with those plants down there."

"Jesus Christ! OK. I'll get him to remove the plants. How many plants?"

"Enough."

The next day I called the tenant:

"What is this business with the porno pictures on the wall?"

"It's no big deal. Just a few sexy pictures."

"Well, they have to come down."

"No problem."

"And what about those plants in the basement?"

"Just a few friendly houseplants."

"Get rid of them, OK?"

The weeks went on. The rent cheques stopped coming. It was getting colder outside. I didn't know what to do. I called up Debbie. I called her on the wrong day:

"Debbie, we have to get this guy out of there."

"Yeah."

"Whaddya mean 'Yeah'?" Like, we have to do this now."

"It's too late."

"Too late?"

"The house got busted this morning by the state troopers."

"Busted!? For what?"

"Grass. Cocaine. You name it. Picture is on the front page of today's paper."

She mailed me the picture. A trooper stood in front of the house, grinning, a large marijuana plant suspended from his outstretched hand. "Drug Bust in Hampden Highlands," the headline read.

Sometimes you just have to bite the bullet. My house had become a pornographic drug den. There had been wild parties. The place was trashed. Even after I replaced all the carpets and had the walls plastered and repainted, no one would come near the place for months. It was a drug-bust house. Kiss of death. A year later we finally sold the place to a new arrival from California, a man who didn't know, or didn't care, about its tainted past.

CHAPTER FIVE

There was a wonderful irony in getting hired at McGill, the university that had found me inadmissable as a student twelve years earlier. I was back in my home town, back to familiar streets, family, the places I knew as a kid. Despite Quebec's dire objections, the Canadian constitution had been repatriated just a few months before my return, Trudeau seemed to have a handle on things, and the whole separatist agenda was on hold, however temporarily. I felt like I had run a long race and made it to the finish line.

But a new race had begun. The Department of English at McGill was coming out of a hiring freeze that had lasted many years. Along with another person hired in the same year, I was the youngest prof in a department that had deep historical roots. It was housed in the Arts Building, the first structure erected on the McGill campus in 1839. There were a good ten years between me and the next-youngest professor, while several others were within five or ten years of retirement. They had their ways and they had their traditions. They would trade barbs and jokes in staff meetings made raucous by eccentric personalities who wanted to be centre stage. It was not easy to fit in. Although the department was staffed by some of the most respected names in Canadian literature at the time—Louis Dudek, Hugh MacLennan, Alec Lucas—I got the sense that Canadian literature was still seen as a lesser literature, something a young opportunist might take up as a hobby, rather than as a serious body of work with its own complex aesthetic problems that went back more than 200 years. Many of the professors were American, hired at a time when little emphasis was placed on recruiting Canadian graduates. Much of the departmental business took place over drinks at the Faculty Club, a prestigious old mansion with a ballroom, a ladies' lounge featuring floral upholstery, a hushed reading room with padded leather wing chairs, and one of the classiest billiard rooms I've ever seen. If I'd learned to keep my mouth shut a little more in those early days, I might have avoided some of the nasty consequences that came from speaking my mind about various issues that had already been decided by the power brokers running the department. But at least the departmental politics did not extend into my classes, where I was given a completely free hand to do what I had always wanted to do: teach multiple courses in Canadian literature, on every period, and on any figure that interested me.

At the University of Maine my office had been a small cinderblock cell in a new building made of concrete slabs. I had a slit of a window that looked out on the dilapidated temporary building that had become the dilapidated permanent building used by the History department. McGill gave me a fine office on the main floor of the Arts Building with a window that looked out over the campus and into the heart of downtown Montreal. Students would stand and smoke in front of my window, wafting me a scented combination of tobacco, marijuana, and patchouli oil.

In fact, in 1982, they were smoking everywhere, even in the classrooms. They would light up and argue about poems and ideas. They would get emotional about Canadian literature. It must have meant something if they were so passionate about it, gesticulating at each other in frustration, defending their ideals. I was in heaven. There was a devotion to Canada here that I had not seen since my days at York. We would argue about the value of Bliss Carman, E.J. Pratt, Archibald Lampman. A student wondered how Lampman's poetry might sound if we could resurrect him and hear him reading it aloud. That made me think about the recording of dead poets' voices. I brought in the brief, garbled recording of Tennyson reading his own poetry that Edison had captured on a wax cylinder, 40 seconds of hypnotizing rhythm that had survived a warehouse fire. We played sound poetry by The Four Horsemen and bpNichol, listened to some of the music that inspired Ondaatje in *Coming through Slaughter*, debated the merits of Kroetsch's belief that Canadian long poems were displaced forms of sexual desire. In one class devoted to textual erotics, a female student (who later became a distinguished doctor) got up on a table and did a partial strip-tease. None of my students at Maine had done that. But McGill had somehow unleashed the primal impulses attached to the ardent study of literature. And more. In one of the comments scribbled on the student evaluation forms that were completed at the end of each course, someone had written "Nice ass!" Yes, I was home.

I was teaching all kinds of Canadian material—a course on contemporary women's fiction that included the mysterious *Passing Ceremony* by Helen Weinzweig and Elizabeth Smart's *By Grand Central*

Station I Sat Down and Wept, with its despair-driven lyricism. I was drawn to the tortured stories of self-doubt that made up Clark Blaise's *A North American Education* and the self-immolating fantasies of Hubert Aquin (which prompted a resentful call from the French department asking why I was teaching Aquin in translation). I was standing, twice a week, in front of almost 300 students enrolled in the compulsory lecture course on Canadian literature. I was terrified. I remembered my experience back at York, the day my lecture was interrupted by that unruly student with her impertinent question about existentialism. This time I would take command of the room, relax, be open to questions. The only problem was that the students refused to arrive on time. What was wrong with them? The lecture was at 9 a.m. I had been awake for hours. But most of them looked like they had just gone to bed. (By the end of the year, I understood that they *had* just gone to bed.) This was a difficult lecture. I was talking about the crisis of language that had developed after the Second World War. I was trying to convey the predicament faced by so many writers who had come to understand that poetry could not be counted on to convey ideas about truth, beauty, or essence, simply because those ideas had all been shown to be relative, transient, and perpetually in flux. The door kept opening and closing, banging each time someone entered the hall. Each bang of the door cut into my concentration, my desperate bid to appear relaxed. The door opened and banged. A student walked in late. OK, five minutes late. No big deal. It banged again. A few more students. Ten minutes late. I was getting pissed. It banged again. Fifteen minutes late. I said to the student: "This class starts at 9. Please come on time." The door banged again. Twenty minutes late. A scruffy looking guy tried to slink into the back row. "Get out!" I shouted in a fit of rage. He kept his cool. "Fuck you!" he yelled back, and stormed out of the lecture hall. So much for the crisis of language.

It wasn't always this way. The greatest luxury of all was not in a course on Canadian literature but in one devoted to Tennyson and Browning. On the first day of class I walked into the small classroom that had been assigned to the course and found two students sitting there. I waited for other students to arrive, but no one else showed up. Figuring this would mean the cancellation of the course, I told the students I wasn't sure whether the class would continue. Later in the day I found the program director and asked what the replacement course would be. "Replacement course?" he answered. "You've got two students. Consider yourself lucky." This wouldn't happen today, but back then it seemed incredible to me that a university could make that choice, choose to devote a prof to such a small course. As the years rolled on, I saw the university making other choices, and, in my case, they were almost always choices that earned my loyalty and respect.

My own interests in Canadian writing were pulled in two contradictory directions. On one hand, I was drawn to authors who were fundamentally modernists, often working in the modernist short story tradition. I latched on to the idea of doing a book that would bring together some close readings of stories by Hugh Hood, Clark Blaise, and John Metcalf, perhaps in some kind of subconscious identification with them as writers who either inhabited or had once inhabited Montreal. But, more importantly, I was drawn to the concision of their prose, its lyrical quality, and the subtlety of the metaphors that inspired their deceptively easy-to-read stories.

How different could three writers be? Hood's fiction was inspired by his deep and abiding Catholicism, but you'd never know it from his subject matter, which ranged from baseball to music to war to the Toronto Public Works Department. After I understood that the image of the swing on the opening page of *The Swing in the Garden* was really a backyard version of the crucifix, I could never read Hood's stories the same way again. I still think one of his strongest books is *Around the Mountain*, a collection of interrelated stories about life in different Montreal locales. Hood put a completely different, spiritual spin on what it meant to climb the mountain in the centre of the city. I decided to focus on the story called "Looking Down from Above" and to allow myself to digress on it, to see the interpretive process as one that could illuminate me as well as the text.

From that kind of reading I learned that every act of interpretation is simultaneously an act of self-interpretation. In a way, you formed yourself through every reading you did by choosing a voice, an idiom, a pace, an identity appropriate to the text in question. Literary interpretation was a collaborative affair. There was no text without a reader. So why not capitalize on the reader's role, cranking up the level of critical self-awareness to the point that the reader's own values were inescapably part and parcel of the story? As I spent more time in the classroom, I began to understand that most students and readers have no idea why they like the books they like, mainly because they've never been encouraged to let their own values into the liking or disliking process. It's easy for someone to say "I really liked that book by Leonard Cohen," but if you ask them to list the values that account for that judgement they don't know where to go.

Many of my students seemed to be unconscious of the values embodied in their own writing. They spent years completing essay after essay for a variety of classes. Yet if you asked them to comment on their own prose—on its grammatical, syntactical, rhetorical, and punctuational qualities—they drew a blank; essentially, they didn't know what they were saying. Once you could get them to focus on the rhythm and structures of their sentences, on the repetitive patterns they could break, they began to write in a different fashion that freed them to think in different ways. The most repressed writing came from students who had attended private schools, usually in Ontario. What was going on in those expensive schools? Their graduates would hand me essays that were as evenly paced as the ticking of a metronome, and just as boring. I would say, "You were at a private school before coming here, right?" They looked shocked. Had I looked up their file? No, it was all in the writing. Four or more years of learning to write nice, sanitized, orderly sentences had robbed them of the passion that comes if you feel free to bend the rules a bit, get out of the syntactical rut. Grammatical conditioning is social conditioning. A culture is the grammar it learns to use. If your own syntax and grammar are repressed, how can you be expected to respond to the intricacies of form and style? How, in that kind of environment, can literature ever make you feel free? The only way is to break the pattern by forcing students to confront the limitations of their own prose. Once they got beyond the regular, monotonous sentences they had been taught to write, all kinds of stuff started to happen. Their critical voices came alive. They started to have fun. Once they began to enjoy language, instead of seeing it as a chore, they became much more open to the way others dealt with language. You can't be a literary student or a critic if your own grammar is enslaved.

In my own writing, the experience of forcing myself to slow down the reading of Hood's fiction by allowing it to become deliberately self-conscious prompted a form of self-examination that ended up with practical applications in the classroom and with a different take on how writing worked. It was one thing to stand in front of a class and to ask everyone about theme, or conflict, or symbols. Most students could respond to that, however dull the exercise might be. It was another thing to say, "Tell me about how Alice Munro and Margaret Atwood use punctuation," or to ask, "Which of these authors is most preoccupied with multi-syllabic sentences, and why?" What are the politics of punctuation? The point was driven home one day when I invited Russell

Smith to visit my class on contemporary Canadian fiction writers. The students peppered him with the typical questions and then one said: "If you were one of us asking *you* a question, what would it be?" Smith didn't hesitate a moment in delivering his response: "The question I would ask," he said, is "Why did you use that particular comma in that particular place?"

The point Smith made—that readers usually don't see style as content—was a concern that characterized all of John Metcalf's stories, which had to be read, first, as musical expressions, crafted lyrics shaped into prose. You could read Metcalf simply on the level of timing. You could write an essay on the way he engineered delay. The hesitation in the way a sentence unfolded marked the hesitation of a character. The staccato pitch of another revealed self-confidence. One of the reasons Metcalf's fiction is not more widely appreciated, I think, is because content has trumped style. Another reason is that even though some of the best living short story writers are Canadian, including Metcalf, book buyers tend to resist the short story form. Although there are obviously a number of writers who have escaped this resistance, the most prominent being Alice Munro, the fact remains that it is very difficult to sell short fiction, which calls for a different reading sensibility, one attuned more to concision and nuance than to the broad canvas offered by a fully developed novel.

Blaise was another author whose reputation would have unfolded in a very different way if he had not chosen to start his career by writing short stories. Was there ever a more alienated or self-conscious writer in Canada than Clark Blaise? He had grown up in the swamplands of Florida and moved again and again as his salesman father pursued job after job, each situation more desperate than the last. Clark spent a lonely childhood entertaining himself while coping with the parade of eccentric personalities connected to his father's business dreams and personal lusts. He became an autodidact, reading everything he could get his hands on, amassing an encyclopaedic collection of facts and trivia about everything from baseball teams to astronomy to fashion. He was the perpetual outsider, a literary nomad, a loner isolated by his hunger for knowledge. I loved the strangeness of his characters and the bizarre situations they found themselves in. I loved the grotesque images of violence, usually attached to the natural world, and the urbane images that populated Blaise's Montreal stories. If Blaise had stayed in Canada, he would undoubtedly have become one of the country's better-known writers. However, true to his peripatetic origins, he never stayed in one place very long.

While I was working on Hood, Metcalf, and Blaise, I was also follow-ing my interest in a writer whose understanding of literature was dia-metrically opposed to their modernist leanings. Robert Kroetsch zipped to prominence after the publication of *The Studhorse Man* in 1969. Although Kroetsch had been writing novels and poetry for almost a decade before that novel appeared, it was the story of Hazard Lepage's search for the perfect mare for his stallion Poseidon that caught on with academics across the country. The novel embodied the postmodern values that had come to prominence in American fiction and critical thinking during the late 1960s. Kroetsch, who was teaching at the State University of New York at Binghamton, was also working on the postmodern journal *Boundary 2*, a position that gave him access to ideas that he was able to incorporate into his fiction.

By the time I showed up at McGill in 1982, Kroetsch was already being called Mr. Canadian Postmodern. He moved back to Canada and started to rediscover his prairie roots, turning childhood experiences into the material for an extended series of meditations on everything from the recovery of vernacular diction to the erotics of the long poem to the fear of women in prairie fiction. However, what really set Kroetsch apart was his ability to command the stage in so many genres. His poetry was built on elaborate metaphors derived from commonplace local sources—a seed catalogue, a farm ledger, the story behind the paper-weight on his desk. Each one of his novels seemed to tackle a different theoretical problem, but Kroetsch brought humour to the theory; he was always willing to take risks and to play. As his criticism developed he became increasingly preoccupied with Canada, and he managed to theorize the country in a voice that was approachable, not intimidating. Kroetsch's writing fulfilled the criterion I began to apply to a variety of Canadian works: it was literature about the problems inherent in its own form. I wrote a couple of articles on Kroetsch's poetry and fiction and got up the nerve to send them to him. His response was predictable: "You need to take more risks," he said. I planned to write more about Kroetsch. I thought about the nature of taking critical risks.

One area that did not require more risk-taking was ECW. By 1982 we had published around 25 titles. Over the next five years we would publish another 40. Considering that most of the money behind these books came from loans or government grants, we were not in an enviable financial position. Although enough public, high school, and university libraries had picked up on the bibliography series to provide us with modest cash flow, there were a lot of other projects underway that were swallowing up cash. We were publishing new works by Hood, Metcalf, and Rooke as well as reissuing some of their out-of-print books, even though the market for those older titles was extremely slim. Why do it? I think we were driven by the belief that if these authors had come over to ECW it was our duty to support their careers. We finally published *Taking Stock*, the proceedings of the by-now infamous Calgary Conference on the Canadian Novel, a book that had limited appeal, judging from sales. (Fortunately, the publication was supported by a grant from the University of Calgary.) And we were still ramping up for 20 volumes of the *Canadian Writers and Their Works* series, even though we had no idea how that project would be funded. Were we poor businessmen? I guess so, since a more experienced publisher would have done up a profit and loss sheet for each title and, in our case, probably would have concluded that most of the books should never have seen print. Undaunted, we plunged ahead, buoyed by the belief that the next book would be a winner, that some special grant in aid of publication would come in. We were getting lots of proposals, and many people seemed to want to work for us.

What would it really take to make a winner? What was a "winner" book in Canada, after all? I am always struck by the earnings figures announced by profitable businesses when they have a good year. Loblaws, or Research in Motion. Profits can double. Costs can be reduced by 20 or 30 percent. An entire corporate mentality can be applied to cutting out wasteful or non-productive parts of the business. A plan can be put in place, certain financial objectives can be achieved, and there's hell to pay if those objectives are unmet. None of this business mentality had much to do with the way we were running ECW at that time. It probably didn't have much to do with the way most small presses were running their businesses back then, and even now. Sure, we had a sense that we were filling a market niche—reference books and criticism on Canadian literature—but if we had really looked hard at the figures I think we would have seen that it would have been virtually impossible to make real money by following our early plan. The market was just not big enough to generate enough sales to cover costs and leave a reasonable profit margin. Nevertheless, the big business model was obviously inviting. Desperate for revenue, we toyed with the idea of selling shares in the *Canadian Writers and Their Works* series to Canadian academics, and we even went so far as to draw up a little prospectus. The figures were impressive: we figured the costs would be $400,000 and sales would be $804,000, leaving a profit of $404,000, which would be divided equally

To Whom it may Concern:

      I understand that you sometimes use freelance writers.
While I realize that every other person thinks he or she
can write, I know I can.

      I have never writen to a publisher befor. I supposed
I would try. What could I lose?

      Here is a sample of my writing. If you would like to
see more, you have my address and phone number.

> I am the one that stalks in the night.
> Iam the one that lies everywere.
> I am the one that lies *VES* in the shadwos.
> I am the one that feasts on your fear.
> IAM THE ONE, I AM THE ONE.
> I am the one that steals your sole.
> I am the one that makes the hatrede you feel.
> I am the ultimet siner the ultimet evil.
> I AM THE ONE THAT YOU WILL FOLLOW.
> I am the one, I am the one.
> I AM THE FALLEN ANGLE.

I apperciate your time. I know you must be verry busy.

                              Turly me,

From the Loon File

among the investors. Simple as that. The precision of these figures struck us as convincing. After all, if we told people the project would earn $400,000 they would never believe us. The number was just too round. But $404,000? Now there was a number that was totally credible. There were no takers.

The reference books were hugely expensive to edit and produce. They were big books that required heavy-duty library binding. The editorial and production process was complicated. We would convene meetings so that the three copy editors working on the series—Ken Lewis, Scott Mitchell, and Ellen Quigley—could discuss editorial issues and standardize their rules. The accuracy of citations had to be checked and rechecked. I still find it amazing that we hired all kinds of people to go into libraries to check on this data, a process we also followed with the journal, as if someone actually cared whether the correct page range of an essay was 96-104 or 96-105. Was it really worth it to submit hundreds of interlibrary loan requests so that we could check the initial in a name or the way an author had spelled a single word? We thought people cared. Yes, it would have mattered if the people who used these books found huge errors and gaps, but for the most part they were sound. Did it really make sense to spend all that extra money to hunt up missing page numbers? It took almost 20 years for us to abandon this verification process when it came to the journal; in other words, it took that long for us to realize how little people really cared about the accuracy of quotations and the number of a page.

We had big ideas about how to capitalize on our reference series. I think we were inspired by the concept of spinoff publishing that had been developed by a number of American publishers, especially G.K. Hall, Twayne Publishers, and Gale Research. They would produce one book full of essays, and then cannibalize them, packaging them with other essays from other books to form whole new titles. Our spinoff concept involved the idea of printing the individual essays and bibliographies that comprised *ABCMA* and *CWTW* as separate monographs. It seemed like a good idea, our thought being that those who could not afford the full book would zero in on the specific, cheaper titles hived off from the mother book. And we could do this by increasing the print run of the main book, then just pulling out the relevant sections for each monograph, slapping a paper cover on them, and giving them a separate ISBN, thereby effectively getting, say, five small books for a little more than the cost of printing the original full volume.

That's what we got, but we seriously misjudged the market for these monographs. We might sell 100 or 200 of some of them, but others, devoted to more obscure writers (Hugh Garner? Ernest Thompson Seton?) would sell just a few, mainly to the university libraries that bought almost everything. There is just no way you can make money doing that. In order to make money selling books you have to sell thousands, not hundreds, and certainly not a few dozen. It might be possible to break even selling 500 copies, but in order to really make money you had to sell 5,000 or 10,000 copies of a title, and, of course, that was not real money in the true business sense. It would mean a very modest profit. However, because no publisher could sell that many copies of every title, the poorer sellers would inevitably erode those profits.

It wasn't only a question of focusing the product line and choosing titles that would have a broad market. The bottom line was that in Canada, the trade market was, by definition, small. And if the trade market was small, how much smaller was the academic/library market? Way too small. For years we continued to pursue these projects that ate away at capital, making it more and more difficult to find cash for new projects that might have pulled us out of the hole. We always imagined the scenario of getting a call from the bank, informing us that our loan had been called, that it would be necessary to repay it all within 48 hours, or something disastrous like that. We had no contingency plan for this. I suppose we would have had to take additional mortgages on our houses, sell our cars, beg, borrow, or steal. Who knew what it would mean? We told ourselves that if we shut down the operation, totally eliminating costs, that eventually the inventory would sell off enough to pay down the debt that kept rising. I doubt this would actually have worked. Our sales projections were not always particularly accurate, and besides, book sales would certainly slow down over time. We were too deep in debt to count on sales. I spent a lot of sleepless nights thinking about bailiffs coming to the door, imagining my car being towed away, furniture being auctioned off, the house itself repossessed by the bank.

Eventually, financial circumstances would force us to make a number of decisions that we probably should have made much earlier, but we weren't seasoned businessmen ready to make those hard choices. It took years for the real cynicism to set in. At this point, despite the company's spiralling debt, we were pursuing an unrealistic ideal—the dream of making money selling Canadian fiction and criticism. Although it was crazy to think we might have been able to create a profitable business following this path, it's probably true that we were no better or worse than many other small Canadian literary publishers that emerged in the same period. Most of them were run by people following dreams, be it the publication of Canadian literary criticism, or experimental poetry, or unconventional short fiction. Most were plagued by the same problems we faced: undercapitalization, poor cash flow, limited market, inability to promote the books as effectively as possible, competition from big-name publishers, lack of bookstore shelf space.

In this kind of climate, it became essential to obtain government grants. Any grants. We tried to leave no stone unturned. We pored over lists of foundations that might support some of our projects. We considered every government agency and thought of how we could spin things to get some funding. In 1983, with the encouragement of John Metcalf, who had a friend at the Department of External Affairs, we submitted an application for $104,000 to offset the costs of distributing *Canadian Writers and Their Works*. We wanted External to buy one copy of the first volume in the series for every major library in the US and overseas. That was 5,500 libraries. This little plan would fit well with External's mandate of promoting Canadian culture internationally. At the same time, it would encourage the libraries to invest in the remaining 19 volumes in the series. Clever, clever, clever. The best part of the application was for funding of what we called "utilization workshops," which would involve External flying "the series editors" (me and Jack) to Canadian studies conferences around the world so that we could "offer three-day utilization workshops on a number of topics related to the study of Canadian literature and the effective use of *CWTW* as a reference tool in Canadian studies." Nice. Workshops in Switzerland. Workshops in France. Workshops in Tuscany. We only wanted $18,000 for those workshops. No big deal. To this day, I can't understand why they turned us down. Well, sometimes we did actually get the grants. The journal was funded by grants from the Ontario Arts Council and the Social Sciences and Humanities Research Council of Canada. The press was getting money from the Ontario Arts Council, the Canada Council, and (sometimes) from the notoriously hard-to-please Aid to Scholarly Publications Program. It didn't really matter whether the publication in question was the journal or a book. The challenge was always to get the grant that would offset the inevitable loss that would result from publishing a title that would never sell enough copies on its own to cover the costs, let alone make a profit.

The business of grant getting is a complicated affair that transformed the Canadian publishing industry. Most commentators on the industry recognize the importance of agencies such as the provincial arts councils, the Canada Council, the Book Publishing Industry Development Program (referred to by insiders as "Bippy-Dip"), and the Social Sciences and Humanities Research Council. However, what hardly ever shows up on the radar is any recognition of how the granting criteria applied by these various programs determine the kinds of books that get published and those that languish in the slush pile. And what seldom gets mentioned is the extent to which publishers inevitably came to conceive of their books in terms provided by the agencies. Sometimes, as was certainly the case with ECW, this could lead to a single publication being described as if it had multiple personalities, with each personality constructed in order to satisfy one agency or another. For example, the Ontario Arts Council won't fund journals that are academic or scholarly in orientation. They want to promote readability and accessibility. As a result, the journal called *Essays on Canadian Writing* that is pitched to them is a broad-based magazine devoted to Canadian writers and writing, a magazine that could appeal to a wide variety of readers. But SSHRC wants to fund journals that are scholarly and that promote advanced research. The journal that gets pitched to them is highly academic, specialized, and filled with cutting-edge research by noted specialists in the field. The Ontario Arts Council seems to like magazines that publish the work of new and upcoming writers. So, for them, *ECW* is a journal devoted to promoting younger critics from around the country (we don't call them academics) who are changing the literary landscape. However, SSHRC wants to give its money to established journals publishing the research of senior scholars. For them, *ECW* is a specialized, academic publication serving the needs of graduate students and professors. We make a special point of calling the audience "professionals."

In these grant dealings, it is crucial to read all of the guidelines carefully. One year we learned that after 12 months of evaluation and negotiation, we had been awarded a grant from the ASPP for a biography of Margaret Atwood. This was terrific news, since advance sales for the book looked strong, and we planned to print a few thousand more copies than originally planned. In order to obtain the ASPP grant, we were required to submit an estimate of our print run. Pleased by the advance orders, I reported that we were going to print about 5,000 copies. No sooner had the ASPP received this estimate than it immediately cancelled the grant. Why? Because our estimates indicated that the book would be too successful, and therefore it did not merit assistance. Clearly, ASPP was a program designed for titles guaranteed to lose money. It was a negative funding program that wanted nothing to do with success. There was an important lesson here: never tell the ASPP you expect a book to do well. Instead, tell them you are only printing a few hundred copies and that it will surely be a loser. Then, sit back and wait for the grant to roll in.

Over the years, as we got better at grant getting, we understood more about how the eligibility requirements established by various funding agencies could affect the entire publishing program. When the Canada Council introduced its block grant program for Canadian publishers in 1972, it also introduced a list of categories that were ineligible for funding. At first, the list of ineligible categories was relatively small. But gradually it expanded, which meant that publishers who wanted to take advantage of the program had to pay increasing attention to pro-ducing the kinds of books the Canada Council wanted to support. They didn't want to support travel guides or self-help books, so those were out. They didn't want to provide funding for any kind of guide at all. They liked poetry, and fiction, and especially books by younger writers, which meant that if you really wanted to capitalize upon the grant, you would turn away from several unsupported genres towards poetry by young writers, or fiction by a first-time author.

The irony was that although these were exactly the kinds of books that usually sold in very limited numbers to a small audience, the funding formula made it more inviting to publish 500 copies of an obscure poetry book than 3,000 copies of a travel guide. If the portion of the block grant allocated to that poetry book amounted to, say $3,000, and if you knew that after receiving that grant you might break even, why would you take the risk of publishing a book that would not be funded, knowing you could easily lose $3,000, and potentially much more, especially since the guide book would have to be promoted, and promotion can be costly? In an ideal world, you would take the chance because you believed that the travel guide would succeed and bring you more profit than the obscure poetry book. However, if you were up against the wall and were worried about losing money at every turn, you might choose the more conservative route of publishing mainly books for which funding was assured.

In the end, this kind of strategy could seriously compromise a publishing program and create a book market filled with experimental poetry and fiction that few people wanted to buy, rather than a market truly driven by the tastes of the broader reading public. This explains why you can look at the catalogues of so many Canadian publishers and ask, "How in the world can they sell enough copies of *that* book to make any money?" The answer is that they hardly need to sell any copies at all. They could print a minimum run of 500 copies, sell 50 to the author and his or her friends, warehouse the remaining 450 copies, and collect a handsome grant, all the while promoting themselves as a cutting-edge press. This is why Fiddlehead Poetry Books was able to publish 44 slim and uneven poetry chapbooks in 1973, the year after the block grant Program started, whereas in previous years they had published fewer than ten titles per year. The same kind of activity was taking place all over the country in the years following the introduction of that program. Canada was awash in bad poetry chapbooks and lame first novels published by small and aspiring presses, while the canonized writers sought out the big publishers like McClelland & Stewart, and even they got grants for publishing books by Margaret Atwood and Alice Munro, books that would certainly have earned their keep.

Although the publishing program that we were developing at ECW in the 1980s was driven by a naive idealism combined with literary nationalism, the fate of each book instilled in us more and more cynicism. It was very difficult to get funding for the projects that seemed to need them most—*ABCMA* and *CWTW*—because the agencies would not support bibliographies, or because they were reluctant to give their blessing to a series, worried, perhaps, that it would commit them to the long haul. The temptation was always to sign up the book that would get support from somewhere—from the author; from the author's university; from a "grant-in-aid-of-publication" which was really a way of supporting a vanity publication without calling it that; from the Aid to Scholarly Publications Program; from some kind of guaranteed sale to a company or individual; from a professor agreeing to a large-scale course adoption that would guarantee sales.

As our cynicism increased, we began to hatch plans based on the recognition that if we were to remain in academic publishing we would have to get the support of the profs, since they held the key to sales. One project that emerged from this understanding was the two-volume anthology called *Canadian Poetry*. Ed Carson was editor-in-chief at General Publishing at the time, and his relationship with Jack went back many years. He was responsible for the New Press imprint at General, which was a line of paperback books designed to mass market Canadian literature. We pitched him an anthology concept built on idealism and cynicism, one that would sell like hotcakes in the cheap and accessible New Press format. Although we would be named as editors of the volume, the actual contents would be chosen by dozens of professors around the country, each of whom was a specialist in a particular author. Because Professor X would be responsible for choosing the poems by a particular author to be included in the volume, he had a vested interest in seeing it succeed. To make the anthology more useful in the classroom, we asked each of the professors to write mini-essays on the author in question, which meant that the professors got to choose the poems they liked and write about the poets in short essays that could then be inflicted upon their students. But what we really needed was a big-name draw that would give the anthology the credibility that our names lacked.

We screwed up our courage and approached George Woodcock, asking him if he would be willing to write introductions to each volume. Woodcock was the editor of *Canadian Literature*, the most prominent journal of criticism back then, and he was also the author and editor of all kinds of books and articles devoted to Canadian writing. He was perhaps the best-known name in Canadian criticism in the early 1980s. We offered him a small sum to complete the introduction to each volume. For whatever reason (Woodcock was by training a journalist and he didn't let his personal beliefs get in the way of his ability to write for a living), he accepted our invitation. This put him in an awkward position because, given the fact that the anthology's contents were dependent upon the selection of a wide group of people, George found himself forced to make sense of many selections he would never have endorsed had he been the volume's editor. He had to lend credibility to an anthology that, at a number of points, I don't think he really found credible. He complained a bit but remained professional throughout the project, sending us two introductions that I thought did a remarkable job of synthesizing the contents and providing a coherent overview. Having established this kind of relationship with George, we thought about how he might lend credibility and consistency to some of our other projects, and we hit upon the idea of asking him to introduce all of the 20 volumes in the *Canadian Writers and Their Works* series, a task which again called for him to synthesize the commentary on the five writers we covered in each volume. Although George objected to some of our combinations, he completed the task from beginning to end, an incredible overview that only someone with his breadth of knowledge could have produced. Both the anthology and *CWTW* turned out to be successful ventures in the end. Woodcock's name on the cover undoubtedly had much to do with that success.

What did I learn from this? That once something had achieved canonical status (in this case, Woodcock himself) people would invest in it. Needless to say, that rather basic insight could easily compromise the originality of a publishing program, because if you really followed up on the idea that what sells is the canon, there would be little reason to pursue all of the non-canonical subjects that were certain not to sell. But the more you bypassed those non-canonical subjects, the more canonical your own program became. You could do weird things like publish an obscure book of criticism if it was backed by a grant. However, it was a different story if you decided to publish fiction by non-canonical writers, and that is exactly what ECW had done.

By 1982 we had published several works of fiction by Hood, Metcalf, and Rooke, in addition to buying the remaining stock of a number of their previously published books, so that we could authentically claim to be these authors' publisher. Not content to lose money on the regular editions of their books, we decided to put out deluxe, numbered editions of their new works, deluded by the belief that a dozen fans might buy the special editions at $50 a pop, helping to cover the printing costs. So we produced a deluxe edition of *General Ludd*, bound in exquisite leather, and another of *None Genuine without This Signature*, with a spine covered in calfskin. This strategy also backfired. Very few people were willing to shell out that kind of money for a book. Meanwhile, the stock we had acquired of those writers' previously published work had to be ware-housed somewhere; the furnace room at Stong College was getting awfully full, and how long would it be until the fire department drew attention to the inescapable hazard of parking all those books around a furnace?

Were we really going to sell enough books by these authors to cover the costs of acquiring them? Sadly, the answer was no. Although we believed in their writing, it gradually became clear that it would be very tough for their books to break even. With the bills from the critical books and reference works arriving at a furious pace, it was obvious that something had to be done to stop the bleeding. I remember the day Jack called with a typically blunt message: we had to get out of the fiction business as soon as possible. This was a really tough decision. I think we had built up the authors' faith in the press, and to admit failure in this way was the last thing I wanted to do. We had already made plans to send Metcalf, Hood, and Rooke on a cross-Canada reading tour we called the ECW Roadshow, which would be the last attempt we made to promote our fiction writers for many years. The cost of that trip alone almost took us down. Jack was right: there was no sense pursuing a program that was sucking us dry. Probably, if we were smart, we would have also cut out or cut back on many of our other projects. However, it was difficult to extricate ourselves from some of those long-range commitments, especially because we were dealing with multi-volume series that were partially complete. Many of the libraries had purchased standing orders for the series, so it looked like there would be some future cash if we kept investing in those works, even though the big reference projects, as much as the fiction, were eating up the cash.

With the reference books and spinoffs and general inventory increasing every day, it became clear that the little office at Stong would no longer serve our purposes. Jack started to look around for a rental space that would serve our needs and give him a bit more room in his own basement, which had been turned into another ECW office. In 1983 he found a building on Coxwell Avenue that had been a dry-cleaning store. He hired some of our editors to spruce up the place and had storage shelves installed in the basement for our growing stock. The walls and trim were painted in what had become the ECW colours—burgundy and cream—and we moved the whole operation there. Although the roof leaked every time it rained, it was wonderful to have our own space. Still, there were lots of problems, one being that we were handling our own distribution, which meant that we soon had to hire staff to pick books, do the invoicing, pack orders, and prepare them for shipping. Jack managed to tackle all of this. He would load books into his big used American car every day and haul them down to the post office. How long could he keep doing that? He was teaching full-time at Centennial College and running the head office of a growing company. He was dealing with the bank and the people hassling us for payment. His location in Toronto meant that many of the day-to-day needs of the business were handled by him, a fact that eventually led to resentment and tension between the Montreal and Toronto offices—but not yet. The most immediate challenge was to figure out how to make some money making books.

That challenge inevitably altered the way I looked at literature. Once, back when I was an undergraduate, and later as a graduate student, literature was literature. I never thought about the material side of publishing that literature, never stopped to consider what kind of risks a publisher had to take, or how books might look one way or another, depending on the publisher's approach to controlling costs. I never thought about what the author was getting paid for his or her writing, or what the book designer would charge, or how much the typesetting charges would be per page. The notion of overhead simply didn't exist.

The legal and financial negotiations that took place in order to bring a book to print eluded me. Now, however, I began to see that every book was incredibly conflicted, contaminated by all of the various factors that accounted for its production. The editor felt that the author's language was derogatory and patriarchal. She tangled with the author, which got his back up and prompted him to complain to the publisher. The designer wanted the book to look one way; the author didn't like the design. The novel had already been typeset with an entire paragraph left out. Would anyone notice? What should we do? The book had been ruled ineligible for a grant, but it had won the grant after a lengthy appeal that called for the publisher to describe it as something other than what it was. The book was published and then we received an angry note from a reader who said his own work had been quoted without permission. What were we going to do about it? He was going to call his lawyers. The book was published and the original print run sold out. Terrific. We reprinted the books, hoping to capitalize on the apparent momentum, but then the demand dried up and bookstores started to return copies, forcing us to pay for an additional print run that would never be sold. We received a wonderful collection of short stories and turned it down because only a few hundred copies would move. We received a tired collection of criticism and responded positively because we could break even if the book got a grant.

Once the publishing cynicism was in your head, it became difficult to see the literary landscape as a force that existed outside material concerns. What became pretty clear to me by the mid-1980s was that the business of Canadian literary criticism was controlled by a few players who made their publishing decisions in response to many of the same factors that influenced ECW's decisions. Would the book get a grant? Would the libraries buy it? Could it be packaged as a series that would make it an obligatory purchase?

Some of the least useful books in Canadian scholarship were produced because there was a positive response to one of these questions. Many of the critical books produced by university presses were accepted for publication on condition they receive a grant in aid of publication from the Aid to Scholarly Publications Program, which meant that the university presses generally shared the assumption that when it came to Canadian literary criticism practically no work could stand on its own or draw a readership sufficient to rationalize its publication. Other critical books or series were produced because the author or editor had received a large grant to support a large-scale research project, with part of the grant being allocated to the publication of the research. A good example of this kind of project was the series of books that emerged from the Centre for Editing Early Canadian Texts at Carleton University, which was founded on the basis of a huge SSHRC grant awarded to Mary Jane Edwards in the early 1980s. What was the purpose of this grant? Ostensibly, it was to fund research that would allow Edwards to produce definitive, scholarly editions of some of the earliest Canadian texts, books that interested fewer than ten people in the entire country. Practically, the grant allowed Edwards to create a self-contained publishing enclave at Carleton. Every year they would churn out a volume or two. They had no reason to worry about finding a publisher, since part of their grant was dedicated to covering the publication costs. SSHRC understood that no publisher would touch those books without some serious funding. Once she had this funding in place Edwards approached a number of publishers, including ECW. We designed a mock volume for her and described a detailed publishing plan. However, what became apparent was that Edwards wanted to keep that grant money right at home. After going through the motions with various publishers she settled on—surprise!—Carleton University Press. In the end, those hefty volumes were far too expensive to use in courses and besides, having to pay such close attention to the words of Frances Brooke's *The History of Emily Montague* or Thomas McCulloch's *The Mephibosheth Stepsure Letters* could threaten your mental health.

Well, there are those who get grants and spend public money on these kinds of projects, and then there are those who are much dumber, the ones who spend their own money on endlessly complicated series that very few people will use. For ECW, the killer project along these lines—The Best Way To Lose Money Project—was certainly the *Canadian Literature Index*, affectionately known as *CLI*. The concept for this series originated in 1983. As we became more familiar with the library reference material on Canadian literature, we realized that there was no Canadian equivalent of the *MLA Bibliography*. What was needed, we thought, was a comprehensive index to primary and secondary materials that would cover periodicals and newspapers. The plan was to collect the data in cumulative, annually published volumes, but also to release quarterly updates. We knew that this was a massive undertaking, but we had no idea how huge it would become. Bolstered by the belief that we were engaging in a project that was completely original and comprehensive (it was) we hired two full-time researchers, Janet Fraser and Richard Hanson, to gather the data. Later, we successfully obtained a SSHRC research grant that allowed us to hire a third researcher, Allan Weiss, for three years. They worked out of Fraser and Hanson's Toronto home, which quickly filled up with the hundreds of periodicals and newspapers we needed for indexing purposes. The house was awash in paper. Mountains of material would arrive every day. This was not an automated process: all the material had to be read, cited, cross-referenced, and then cross-indexed.

Things did not always go smoothly. The editor of the series—Fraser—differed with us about the methods and principles to be employed in collecting and citing the data. Each annual reference-sized volume ran to more than 500 pages and included thousands of citations, all of which were annotated and cross-referenced by author, title, subject, and keyword. The editors viewed 12,800 periodicals and 780 newspapers per year in search of citations related to Canadian literature in that year, and then classed those citations under 5,000 different subject headings. The average number of citations per newspaper reading was only one, which meant that each of those 780 newspapers, read every day, produced an average of a single citation each per day. The challenge of collecting this massive range of material would have been daunting to a well-capitalized university press; for ECW, it was lunacy.

We announced that the 1985 index would be published in 1987, and that a subscription to three quarterly updates as well as the cumulative volume would go for $275. The project moved forward, and a lot was banking on it. We were paying the editor, paying for research, contributing to the editor's office costs, and generally putting a lot of money into a program that was already stressed to the limit, with so many resources already directed to the bibliography and *Canadian Writers and Their Works* series. Somehow, incredibly, we managed to publish the *CLI* indexes for four years before we were forced to cancel the series due to insufficient sales, 2,000 pages later. Even at the relatively high subscription price there were just not enough libraries willing to invest in the series to make it work, and we had no real way of reaching American libraries. The debt grew.

Although we had entered into a distribution agreement with G.K. Hall in the US, we had no effective sales team to represent us to university libraries. We had to rely mainly on promotional mailings, which cost a lot of money and delivered few subscriptions. It was simply impossible to find the money to do it all. Every day we would talk about schemes to raise more cash. One plan involved building up a distribution business in Canada for foreign reference book publishers. By 1987 we had approached and signed on with Twayne Publishers, Ohio University Press, University of Nebraska Press, Magill Books International, and Salem Press. This distribution arrangement proved to be a lot more trouble than it was worth. It increased the demands on the Coxwell Street office, which was now filled with books from a variety of publishers, each of whom wanted accounting, payments, inventory figures, and so on. Of course the distribution did produce some cash flow, but, as usual, not nearly enough to offset the costs we were incurring to produce all those books and series. How could a publisher ever make any money?

In this business, just breaking even on a title could seem like success. One of our publications that continued to break even was the journal itself, mainly due to the funding it received from the federal and provincial governments. When that money was added to subscription revenues and the payments we received for various rights sales, it was possible to cover the costs. As Jack put it, the journal was "a wash." Yet surely there was a way to make it even more profitable. We thought about several possibilities. McDonald's had already turned us down; so had Imperial Oil. Obviously they weren't supporters of CanCrit, and their response was so discouraging that we immediately rejected the idea of turning to Wendy's or Burger King. Besides, those were American operations, and what would our readership say if they saw that the fine criticism we published was ultimately aligned with Whoppers and Big Gulp Slurpies? Tim Horton's was not (yet) in the picture.

There had to be a better way. We hit upon the idea of making the journal the publication of a charitable organization, so that we could then receive money from companies and individuals, who could write off their donation as a tax deductible contribution. We came up with the name Canadian Literary Research Foundation and had some spiffy stationery designed with a subtle beaver on it, just to prove how Canadian we were. With issue number 31, a little more than a decade after the journal's founding, we began to credit the journal as a publication of CLRF and started working through the various bureaucratic and governmental hurdles that would allow the foundation to issue tax deductible receipts. Unfortunately, we were never able to satisfy all the various requirements and were forced to abandon the idea after trying to milk it for eight years. By 1993 the journal had returned to being a publication of ECW Press. We had spent money on lawyers, money on accountants, money on stationery. But in the end, the charitable organization concept didn't bring us a dime.

Another cash-raising plan was built on the perception that in many ways the Canadian publishing industry was a kind of huge vanity press, with the money to support books coming from the government rather than from individuals. Regardless of the source, the effect was the same: the money to support the publication came from a source exterior to the press and the supporter understood that sales alone would never cover costs. Maybe we could set up a vanity publishing arm of ECW that would do in Canada what a number of subsidy publishers had done in the United States. We tossed around different names for the subsidized publishing venture. The first was Slazenger & Wesley. (Jack's mind was obviously elsewhere during this exercise. He was thinking about his tennis game that day, while I, much more grounded, was thinking about John Metcalf, whose middle name is Wesley.) In the end, however, we settled on Emerson House. Why a Canadian vanity publisher would want to call itself Emerson eludes me, especially because neither of us was particularly fond of Ralph Waldo. Besides, we were as nationalist as ever. And we had already proved, definitively, that if you build a better mousetrap, the world would not necessarily beat a path to your door. Driven by whatever conception we had of our subsidized publishing division we designed an elegant logo and a brochure for prospective authors. There were very few takers. The only publications of any significance to emerge from Emerson House before we folded it was a book called *Notes to My Children*, by William E. Caswell and an anthology of poetry put together by a Montreal high school class. I think we missed the key to vanity publishing in this little detour from our central publishing program. Vanity was fine, but people did not want others to know they had paid. The solution was reasonably simple: convince the authors to buy 500 or 1,000 copies of their title and then publish the book under your regular imprint. That way, you could be assured of a sale (to the author) and of collecting your regular grant, which you could never do if the book was released by an outright vanity house. Although it was against the Canada Council's rules to fund books that had already received support from the author, there was nothing in the rules that prevented us from publishing a book that we knew would sell, well, to someone ... Many years later, we understood that some books that were ineligible for government grants could still be profitable if a person or a company committed to buying sufficient quantities, or if there was a back-door injection of funds. Clearly, several Canadian publishers have profited from the same understanding.

The whole business of publishing left me with a deeply divided feeling about books. In one sense, the book was always an antagonist, threatening to take your money, invade your life, cause conflicts with a variety of people, leave you feeling like you had wasted endless hours on an artefact that almost no one used or saw. In another sense, the book was an object of pride, the concrete product of a stream of decisions, negotiations, and creative teamwork that produced something unique, bearing the name of the company that I helped create. In yet another sense, the book was still somehow connected to the world of literature that involved my professional life at McGill. For a professor, books inhabited a special domain. They stood lined up on my office shelves, symbols of what I had decided to do with my life. They were the raison d'être of the profession, the reason we taught and wrote. Ideally, those books united us in some kind of community; they were the focal points around which our research would cohere. They were the currency we used in the classroom, and, knowing this, we devoted inordinate energy to getting the reading list right. A class was only as good as its teacher, but the teacher also knew that the class was only as good as the books it covered. Put a tedious book on the course and the students would be unhappy. Put a challenging and original book on the list and they would rise to the challenge, eager to experience new ideas and techniques.

In order to keep my ideals about books intact—the ideals that had led me to become a prof in the first place—I tried to separate the publishing experience from the teaching experience. The books I taught existed in some kind of pristine vacuum, untouched by money, calls from the bank, editorial squabbles, rent to pay—all the factors I knew were attached to every book, whether it was produced by a big house like McClelland & Stewart or a little one like ECW. The books I published were made of real paper that cost a certain amount. I remembered the arguments over a specific cover, or the typesetter's frustrated insistence that my decisions about hyphenation were misguided, ill-informed, and wrong. He wanted Garamond, to give the book the authority it deserved. I wanted Sabon, to highlight the elegance of its ideas. We settled on Baskerville as a compromise. But, in truth, I never liked Baskerville. The book hurt my eyes every time I opened it. What really killed me was those series. I had a vision of all 20 volumes of *Canadian Writers and Their Works* lined up on the shelf, each one perfectly aligned with the next, the gold horizontal stamping on the spine forming a continuous, unbroken line that would speak to the authority and unity we had achieved. We printed 18 volumes out of 20 and got them just about perfect. Then, something happened to the last two volumes. Somehow they were shorter than the other books. Stubbier. The golden line was broken, perhaps the printer's subtle reminder to us that no publishing project was without its flaws, and that if you believed in the perfect line, it was better to get out before the inevitable problems began to unfold.

Even after I got away from the multiple book personalities I had begun to recognize as part of my life, I still had to sort out the divided feelings that confronted me about the field I had chosen to pursue: Canadian literature, and, more particularly, Canadian criticism. I wasn't a writer. I was supposed to be a critic. I was also publishing literary criticism. The publishing experience created a cynicism about criticism that made it difficult to validate as a professional pursuit. So much criticism on Canadian literature was being published at the time. Some of it really made me wonder where things were headed. One of the most revealing books of CanCrit to emerge during this period was *Future Indicative*, a collection of the papers presented at a conference on literary theory and Canadian literature at the University of Ottawa in 1986. It was attended by many of the CanCrit heavy-hitters. The conference itself provided ample evidence of just how insular Canadian criticism had become. Any non-professor attending the conference out of sincere interest in Canadian literature would have been baffled by all the jargon, the buzzwords, the pompous appeals to the literary elite who had gathered to celebrate the way they talked, or, as John Moss so aptly put it in his introduction to the published proceedings, these were the "esoteric" and "baffling" words of professionals who were "deconstructing the box" so enthusiastically that what they said remained "the arcane pleasure of a few genuine and brilliant eccentrics."

Well, I was not so impressed. Imagine that you are an intelligent undergraduate, or just a plain old interested reader, who has shown up at this conference to find out what the big guys are thinking about CanLit. You've read a few Canadian authors. Loved the direct colloquialism of Al Purdy. Sunk your teeth into some of Phyllis Webb's *Naked Poems*. Even appreciated the sorrowful lament about time and mortality that makes Bliss Carman's "Low Tide on Grand Pré" so poignant. Now, in front of you, Barry Cameron is introducing his paper on Canadian literature and Jacques Lacan:

> My paper is dialogic in a second, more Bakhtinian sense, too, for it dilates rhetorically between two modes of discourse and the subject positions inscribed in those discourses: phallic assertion and hysteric interrogation, master or analyst and hysteric. I want to deny (disavow), however, the specular image

of any authority I might be presupposed to have over Lacan's texts by my dialectical use of an assertive mode—for one thing, the master's mode is usually imperative, not assertive—in an effort to release myself from one of the effects of phallocentrism that dictates that one should cover one's inadequacy, one's lack, in order to have the privilege of speaking as expert, especially at academic conferences that try to situate subjects. I can only hope, too, that my "denial" is not an example of Freud's *verleugnung*: the refusal of a disturbing element of unconscious life, a refusal whose particular characteristics mark it as a desperate defence against—and therefore a confirmation of— that very fact. It is not insignificant that Freud first used the word to describe the man's response to the "traumatic perception" of the woman's "castration," the mark of her radical otherness, her difference. Am I, like Lacan, caught in the paradox of my own utterance?

Cameron then adds:

> I speak from neither the position of master (identified with phallic supremacy and control) nor the position of analyst ("the subject who is presumed to know"), but rather from the position of the hysteric or slave—a position of vulnerability constructed on my recognition and acceptance of my inevitable "castration" in language. (In my first draft of this paper, when I typed castration I left out one *t.*) Indeed, as Jane Gallop has argued, Lacan's primary ethical goal and therapeutic purpose are that one must . . .

You get the idea. Now, I like Barry Cameron, and he has made some significant contributions to Canadian criticism. In this case, like many of the other conference participants, he went over the theoretical edge, finally speaking in a way that would leave an intelligent undergraduate, and many others, shaking their heads. I came away from the conference deeply disillusioned. If this was the current state of affairs, if this is how professors were supposed to speak, what would happen to all those people who didn't know that as readers they were really hysterics and slaves? And how could I ever pitch ECW's critical books to the dwindling audience of professors who sincerely believed that they were hysterics and slaves? ECW was ramping up to bring out a string of scholarly studies, reference books, and a whole new series devoted to individual Canadian novels. There was the journal, pumping out article after article, year after year. There were a host of other journals and publishing companies developing a variety of critical books in the field. CanCrit was expanding, encouraging profs to submit grant applications, generating conferences at which research would be "disseminated," supporting research projects that would allow graduate students to be hired, computers to be bought, overseas trips to be funded. For what?

The publishing aspect of my life made me realize how few people were really willing to invest in all this critical material. Ideally, that material would advance our conception of the field. We would share ideas and by doing so come to a better understanding of ourselves as a community devoted to the national literature that accounted for our professional lives. But that isn't what usually happened. As it turned out, Canadian criticism seemed to be a relatively isolated affair. An academic would produce a manuscript and hope to get it funded. A university or trade press would publish it. There would be a smattering of reviews, most of which would appear a year or two after the book was published. This delay in reviewing got so bad that some journals, like *Canadian Literature*, were even publishing reviews of books that had long gone out of print. In this kind of system, the idea of dissemination was a joke. Even at academic conference, there was little opportunity for a real exchange of ideas, mainly because most of the papers were quite specialized and members of the audience would not have delved into the topic in sufficient depth to create a meaningful exchange. There would be a few polite questions and then it would be on to the next speaker. What was gained through this kind of activity? In fact, as was the case in most industries (which CanCrit had become), the players were really getting together to shoot the breeze, assess the power structures, and position themselves in strategic alliances that would allow them to advance their own careers by publishing more books and articles that practically no one would read.

Even though my scepticism about publishing criticism was increasing with each new publishing venture, I remained profoundly interested in a number of Canadian writers, and I continued to produce criticism, working against my sense that it would fall on deaf ears, trying to convince myself that if it was really good enough there would be some kind of market out there. I had been focusing on Robert Kroetsch's poetry and fiction for a number of years and continued to be impressed by his range of reference, by the way he could take the most insignificant events and invest them with meaning, radically undermining the status quo. In some ways, reading his creative works was like working through an intricate critical problem. Kroetsch set traps for himself. He put up barriers and then asked his writing to destroy them. He was a postmodernist but not a pretentious one. He could speak about Derrida in the same breath as he spoke about prairie beer parlours. He even had enough self-confidence to allow Shirley Neuman to conduct a full, book-length interview with him, a crazy tangle of ideas sparking with energy. Every day I would descend to my basement and tap away at my book on Kroetsch. At Christmas, when Paula, Emily, and I visited my parents in Florida, I rented a typewriter and laboured away indoors, determined to finish that study.

No wonder my marriage was stressed. Well, in truth, it was more than stressed. It was falling apart. By 1986 the book on Kroetsch was released and I was getting divorced. I was involved in a new relationship with Mary, a graduate student I had met in a class at McGill. Less than a year later, we were living together. The divorce settlement put even more strain on my already strained finances and made it impossible for me to borrow any more money. Nevertheless, I had been lucky enough to secure one of those grants that profs coveted, a time-release stipend that would allow me to stop teaching for a year while I worked on another book I was planning—a full-length study of Clark Blaise. My interest in Blaise had been piqued a few years back when I wrote an overview of his short stories, but now I wanted to sink my teeth into Blaise's obsessions. After a transition period in a dark and cramped apartment, I rented a larger place in Outremont, just down the street from Jacques Parizeau and poet Nicole Brossard. Gwynne Dyer lived upstairs. Mary moved in a few months later. Emily was with us every other night. It was a new life with new demands. And there was a book to write.

I spent day after day thinking about Blaise's weird childhood, the eccentric turns his life had taken, the significance of his marriage to the well-known novelist Bharati Mukherjee, his strange stories of swamps, salesmanship, and sex. Blaise had just published *Resident Alien*, a book that made me even more curious about his life. How much of *Resident Alien* was fantasized? How much was real? One day I was reading a Blaise story and the phone rang. It was Clark. I had met him a few times through John Metcalf and we had corresponded over the commentary I wrote on his stories in *On the Line*, but I had never spent any extended time with him. He was teaching a creative writing course in New York. He explained that he would be commuting to Montreal weekly to give a course at Concordia as well. He wondered whether we could put him up for two nights a week. How often does this happen? Was this a signal from the sky? The author I was writing about had just called me up to ask if he could come and live with me. I explained the situation to Clark, reminding him that the biographical fallacy would make it impossible for me to relate anything he told me about his life to his work. Without missing a beat, he told me that I could be his Boswell, spying on his private life, enriching myself through his story. Still, it was difficult to think of Blaise as Doctor Johnson.

Clark showed up in the fall. Mary and I could hardly believe that this man whose fiction had meant so much to us was actually sleeping in the room at the end of the hall. Clark had an incredible set of literary connections. One day he came in wearing a pair of grey flannel pants and announced that they were Bernard Malamud's. Malamud had died recently, and his widow had offered Clark the contents of his wardrobe. When Clark left the city he left Malamud's pants with us, hanging in a closet, haunting the room. When he was in town he would happily recite stories about every American author you could imagine. He had met them all. He would sit in the kitchen eating Kellogg's Just Right cereal and ask how the book was going. I would tell him that he wasn't allowed to ask me how it was going and I wasn't allowed to ask him to relate his fiction to his life. Then, after I told him that, I abandoned all the rules, broke down, and described in detail exactly what I was writing about him. He helped me out with references and stories, but I know that he respected the critical act, and although he teased me imperiously about my subservient role as his Boswell, he also expressed regret at not having a full-time job as a professor so he could hang out at home and read and write, just like I was doing.

By 1987 I had finished the book on Blaise. No one was rushing to give me a huge advance for it. My rent was high. There were child support payments to be made. ECW kept struggling against debt, the story of its life. We had been publishing books for close to a decade. Although we were able to secure a government loan guarantee in 1986 from the Ontario Media Development Corporation that allowed us to borrow $70,000 new dollars, that was only a temporary solution to the problem, which was negative cash flow. Neither of us had ever taken a salary from the business. I dreamed of the day that I could have a regular paycheque for being a publisher. I was nervous about all those documents I had signed. If we screwed up, they could just come and take away the few assets I had managed to accumulate since the divorce, which had basically wiped me out. We had tried to find money to finance our grandiose projects in so many different ways: as editors, packaging books for other companies; as distributors; as ceaseless grant-getters; as vanity publishers; as sellers of rights to whatever we owned; by pleading with various corporations for a little funding. We were searching for a business model that would work, even looking to L.L. Bean for some marketing tips. I was impressed with their unconditional money-back guarantee and thought that if we offered the same deal our books would become irresistible. Who would not buy a book that they could return, no questions asked? Our 1985-1986 catalogue carried the Bean-like guarantee: "We will refund the cost of any book you purchase from us if you are not completely satisfied with it."

Nice guarantee. Customer service was what it was all about, right? We even invited our customers to call us collect on what we called our "Library Hotline." None of this seemed to help. We would have to make some changes. Should we cut back, try to pay down the debt? That wouldn't really work, since the debt was too big to be paid down through sales of our existing titles. Should we delay titles? Well, that was already happening, due to the fact that we were having trouble paying our printing bills. Maybe we should hatch a new multi-volume project. Maybe we should think about our past errors and find a formula for a series of critical books that would sell like hotcakes. After all, we needed something to keep us busy.

We looked around, did some thinking, looked for models that might work for us. Since 1984 I had been editing a series of books called Masterworks for Twayne Publishers in Boston. I had pitched them the idea of the series back in 1982, when I was still at Maine, and two years later they had accepted the concept and were ready to roll. The series was made up of critical books devoted to specific works of literature. A book on *The Scarlet Letter*. A book on *The Canterbury Tales*. Over the years the series expanded dramatically and, by 2000, I had edited more than 175 books in the series. Why not take the same concept and apply it to Canadian classics? This was the idea that led us to create the Canadian Fiction Studies series—short critical books on well-known Canadian novels. The first title—on Laurence's *The Stone Angel*—appeared in 1989, and it was followed by 35 other titles over an eight-year period.

The concept and design of the series was the result of some hard-learned lessons. These books were slim and relatively inexpensive to produce. The cover designs were standardized. We issued them in cloth and paper, going for the library and high school markets. After a while the series achieved a reasonable sales momentum, bringing in some much-needed cash. Another factor that helped to increase sales was our decision, soon before the series was released, to transfer our distribution to the University of Toronto Press. This eliminated many of the headaches Jack had been forced to deal with over the last few years, especially with the scholarly titles, which were taking up a lot of space.

Still, we remained primarily an academic publishing company. What could we do to break out and get a bigger piece of the market? This question was part of a larger one: What could we do to get a piece of *any* market? We started thinking about the concept of product tie-ins. Jack was mulling over the idea of a tie-in business that would operate in movie theatres. He imagined a chain of small boutiques in the theatre lobbies. The boutiques would sell items related to the current movie showings, with the stock changing as the films changed—the *Gremlins* dolls, the *Ghostbusters* soundtrack, biographies of the stars, the novel upon which the movie was based, and so on. How could we lose? There would be a captive audience emerging fresh from those films, ready to buy the products we would put in front of them the second they were in the lobby. We even had a great name: CinePlus.

Maybe the idea was terrific, but we knew how much capital it would take to get it off the ground. Rather than fantasize about new bank loans, we hit on the idea of approaching Garth Drabinsky, the force behind Famous Players theatres. No doubt he would listen to our pitch and then work to make the idea we had brought him profitable to Famous Players and ECW. To our astonishment we managed to get a meeting with Drabinsky. Determined to make a convincing presentation, we had a miniature model of the CinePlus boutique done up, along with a detailed business plan. When we finally got into the boardroom with Drabinsky he seemed preoccupied and aloof. He listened impatiently to our presentation and told us he would get back to us. Not too long after that, he turned us down, for no particular reason. Did he think the idea was useless? If so, why? Was he not impressed with our track record ("ECW Press grossed $240,000 in 1983 with a profit of $36,000")? Later we learned that he did not think it useless at all: in 1986 we read a story in the *Globe and Mail* about Drabinsky's plan to set up a chain of movie boutiques. How slimy can you get?

Well, let Drabinsky have his boutiques. We would pursue other paths. We had always wondered why our critical monographs didn't sell like hotcakes. What did Coles Notes have over us? Certainly not design, or the quality of the criticism. What could we do to get all those students lining up to buy our books? We realized that companies like Coles and Monarch had captured the market for non-Canadian titles, but why couldn't we do the same thing for CanLit? That was a promising idea, but without trade distribution we weren't going to get into the chain bookstores. Wait a minute. The whole Coles Notes concept was based on the idea that students didn't want to read; for them, reading was a waste of time. Why read *Macbeth* when you could read the Coles Notes on *Macbeth* in an hour? If this was true, why not create a product that would accommodate the students' laziness in the extreme? Why not create a type of Coles Notes that could be heard, rather than read? A series of notes on tape? With notes on tape, the student wouldn't have to read a word. He or she could just slide a cassette tape into a Walkman, press play, and find out all about *Macbeth* while travelling on the bus, playing frisbee, or going to sleep.

Armed with the insight that many literature students didn't really like reading, we put together a proposal for the Notes on Tape series and commissioned some academics to write trial commentaries, which we then had recorded by a professional voice at a studio in Toronto. That cost money. This idea was so hot, we figured, that it was dangerous to tell anyone about it. We hired a lawyer to help us protect the idea. More money. We had some nifty packaging designed and sent out dozens of letters to New York literary agents. More money. We realized that we needed a big publisher to bring this idea to market, and that in order to find that publisher we were going to need an agent. Our letters didn't get many responses, but one well-known agent—Julian Bach—did invite us to meet with him in New York. More money. Bach represented several big-name American authors. His office walls were decorated with framed covers by the dozen and it was all a bit intimidating, but Bach was unassuming and open. We discussed the idea and he said he would get back to us soon. We left with our fingers crossed. On the way out we passed Alice Walker, Bach's next meeting.

While we were waiting to hear from Bach I had a brilliant idea. One of the professors I had worked with on a book for G.K. Hall was Ken Atchity, a specialist in classics. Atchity was a go-getter. I got the sense the first time I spoke with him that he would not be in academia for long, and, sure enough, he wrote to say that he had left his university for Hollywood, where he would be pursuing a new career in the film industry. He was working with a talented group of people who were looking for product. Although Notes on Tape was not Hollywood material, I tossed the idea out to Atchity and he said it had potential. Massive potential.

Why didn't we come down to meet him and his team in L.A.? No problem. Before you could say "MasterCard" we had secured two tickets and booked ourselves into a motel close to the fabled Beverly Hills Hotel, where we were going to have lunch with Atchity and his crew. After the seven-hour flight we checked in and headed over to the hotel. Very elegant. Much wine was consumed. I started to worry about the bill. The guys around the table didn't seem to have much interest in us. Weren't they there *for us*? Apparently not. There was some pleasant chatter. I tried to turn the conversation toward Notes on Tape, and got some nice bland smiles. After lunch, we all shook hands. Jack and I walked around Beverly Hills, gazing at mansions. The next morning we flew home. I never heard from Atchity again until 2003, when he wrote to me in his new capacity—as a literary agent.

In the end, Julian Bach turned us down, and the series went nowhere. Coles Notes soon announced a notes on tape series, as did a number of other large publishers involved in the student note business.

Although we still had a substantial bank debt, which we had personally guaranteed, it seemed that maybe, just maybe, things were getting on track. We were making progress on completing the big money-sucking series, we had suspended publication of the Canadian Literature Index, we had embarked on the Canadian Fiction Studies series, and we had become better at applying for, and receiving, various grants. Yes, the clouds seemed to be clearing. There was only one little problem that had nothing to do with us. A recession was on the horizon, a big recession. By 1989 banks around the world were getting hit by a rash of bad real estate loans and rising interest rates that made them very nervous about lending money. They were looking around for signs of any weaknesses in the loans they had already approved. It didn't take them long to focus in on us. One day, just when I was feeling particularly optimistic about the future, the phone rang. It was Jack. He had just received a message from our bank. They had called our loan. We had been given seven days to pay it off. All of it. Or else.

CHAPTER SIX

I didn't have much in the way of what the bank wanted most: tangible assets. My divorce ten years earlier had cost me a house and the better part of my savings. I was making child support payments every month and living in a rented apartment. It was tough to save any money. I did own a seven-year-old Toyota, some furniture, and a barbecue. I assumed the bank would take them. But that would be a little joke. They would want more. Much more. We owed close to $100,000, not to mention all kinds of other outstanding payables and the salaries of our employees in Toronto and Montreal. Worse, we were pushing our credit card limits, having used those cards to get cash advances to pay off suppliers who were threatening to sue us or shut us down. There were no other assets for the bank to grab from me. I imagined they would take my salary directly. What was that called? Garnishing my wages. *Garnish*. To me, a garnish had always been a pickle at Schwartz's deli, or something to decorate a nicely presented dinner plate. Now it took on a different meaning. I pictured burly bailiffs at the door, letters from McGill's legal department, movers carting off my saggy bed and sofa, and the Greek landlord ringing the bell, demanding the overdue rent.

If things looked bad for me, they looked a lot worse for Jack. He still owned a house in Toronto. The bank could seize it. We discussed the situation briefly, but there was not much to say. Jack knew it would be up to him to run to other banks, hoping against hope that he could convince some loan officer to give us the line of credit we needed to pay off our debt at the other bank. I knew he felt desperate, cornered, resentful that the task had fallen to him, as had so many of the other business tasks, given the fact that ECW's head office was in Toronto. When he got that way it made him even more reserved than he usually was when it came to handling bad news. There were no expressions of panic, no moment when he wondered out loud how we ever got into this situation, no sense of impending doom. It was as if the possible outcomes had been processed and the course of action pragmatically determined.

Emotional expressions of personal failure or anxiety were generally left out of the equation. This prompted people to see Jack as a cynic, or as a cryptic, private person. He could be that way. But more important, he was proud. He had built up this business from nothing, trying every trick in the book, and then inventing some, to keep the wheels rolling. Sure, we had leveraged ourselves to the hilt, but all in the belief that one day there would be some kind of financial reward for all this activity. I think Jack believed that every challenge or disaster taught you some kind of invaluable lesson that went into the cerebral database that became his publisher's mind. There were no books about how to do this. It was all trial and error. Mostly error, in terms of financial gain. Yet here were these shelves, lined with books produced over a decade. There was a sense of history on those shelves. Thousands of decisions. Some kind of goal had been set, some territory mapped out, and we had gone far into that territory.

Jack would call me after his appointments with a succession of bank managers. It was no, no, and no. Then there was a different, more hopeful call. It looked like Jack had convinced the manager of a local CIBC branch that we could eventually turn a profit and handle our debt. In addition, Jack had convinced his father-in-law to guarantee the loan. The manager warned Jack that NSF cheques would not be tolerated, and gave him a sage bit of advice: "If you don't want to bounce cheques," he said, "don't write them." Why hadn't we thought of that? This struck me as another example of a simple business principle that had to be learned the hard way. If the bank saw cheques bouncing they would be quick to dump the account, but if people just didn't get paid, those people would either be pissed off and have to wait, or it would take them months to start suing us, and maybe we could pay them then. Or maybe by the time they sued us a new grant would have come in and we could use that to pay a bill that was six months old.

It took months for the new credit line to become operational. There was a lot of paperwork, credit checks, legal documents, and negotiations with our old bank. For close to six months we had literally no cash flow and were unable to write cheques, since the banking arrangements had not yet been finalized. One thing the new bank did not seem to know about, or care about, was our trophy collection of credit cards. Our card holdings had been steadily expanding over the years. We used the cards for all kinds of business expenses, including gas. Jack made it a policy to jump on every credit card offer that came through the door, no doubt in the belief that one day we would need every last drop of credit that could be squeezed out of the universe. He had a drawer of cards, many of them from strange banks, like Wells Fargo. Who had a credit card from Wells Fargo? I also built up my collection, using the address of my parents' condo in Florida to apply for cards issued by US banks. I loved the idea that when it came time to getting an advance on my credit line from one of those cards, it would be in fat American cash. So what if the annual interest rate was 23 percent? Soon we discovered that in addition to having regular credit cards you could also get cards that were connected to a credit line. After they gave you one of those babies, they wanted you to use the line to its max. We got quite a few of those. Obviously the people issuing these cards had not checked us out. Why would one company give me a credit line of $35,000 when I already had outstanding lines with other companies totalling way more than that? We had a common principle when it came to these cards: as soon as we received one, we would call the bank and ask for an increase in the credit limit, which most seemed only too happy to provide.

Somehow, during the months it took for our new bank to get the paperwork in order, we managed to keep producing books, at a more hectic pace than ever. Debt be damned. We were rolling out individual monographs taken from the ongoing volumes of *Canadian Writers and Their Works*. Because each one of those volumes contained five essays, they each produced five individual monographs, which we expected to sell to those libraries that couldn't afford to invest in the entire series. Libraries were always interested in books on canonized writers like Margaret Atwood or Robertson Davies. However, most of them drew the line when it came to Rosanna Leprohon and Agnes Maul Machar, and even the monographs on contemporary authors such as Josef Skvorecky or Roo Borson didn't do too well. The loss we took in publishing those titles offset the profit we might have made in publishing only the more popular ones. However, for a few years we saw real cash flow from *Canadian Writers and Their Works* as more and more libraries came to understand its multi-volume design. We were still rolling out the *Annotated Bibliography of Canada's Major Authors* series, 12 years after we delivered our six-foot-high stack of paper to Peter Martin Associates, which had long since gone out of business. And then there was the Canadian Fiction Studies series, with almost ten books in production in 1989.

There was coherence in those series, but when it came to individual titles there was a lot of experimenting with different kinds of books and markets. David Kent, whom Jack and I had known since graduate school, persuaded Jack to put out an anthology of Christian poetry in Canada. I had nothing to do with this, but Jack must have thought it would sell to, well . . . Christians, or church groups, or whatever. Then there was a video interview with Margaret Laurence, which Jack had commissioned through a contact he had with a film producer. Since I was used to thinking in terms of product expansion, I imagined this video as the prototype of what would inevitably become a series of videos about famous Canadian writers, for use in schools across the country, of course.

The fact that I knew so little about the anthology of Christian poetry, or the video, or, in fact, about several of the books appearing under Jack's direction, said a great deal about a fundamental shift that had taken place in the company. We were moving in different directions. Ever since the press was founded I had lived away from head office, running my own operation out of Maine and Montreal. I had a full-time job as a prof and all the responsibilities that came with it. I was also doing research and writing my own books and articles. My plate was full. But so was Jack's. He had been building ECW's infrastructure for 15 years. He had set up our distribution agreements, worried about warehousing, dealt with the lawyers and bank managers and insurance agents. He was teaching at Centennial College, but his aim was clearly to phase himself out of that position, which he did manage to do, gradually, over the next ten years.

What Jack really wanted to do was to be a publisher and to know every facet of the industry. He became involved in federal and provincial committees devoted to publishing issues. He read every book on publishing he could find. He particularly liked memoirs about publishers and editors, many of whom had made startling decisions or come back from the brink. He started visiting other publishers around the country, looking at different business models. He'd had to deal with the phone calls from creditors—regularly, day after day, year after year. The pressure was relentless, but he seldom complained.

Although my name was on all the company documents and I had signed the same bank loans as Jack, he was on the front line, catching the flak. Every once in a while the difference in our involvement in the company would flare up into disagreements about how the responsibilities of managing the company were divided. Jack would make lists of all the tasks he was handling and compare them to mine. I always came up short. Partly this was because Toronto was the centre of the publishing universe. Most of the industry players were there. The lawyers were there. Not to mention the bank, the office on Coxwell, the warehouse, the distributor, the typesetter, the designers, and more. Meanwhile, I was out there in Montreal, teaching classes on Canadian poetry while Jack handled most of the frustrations involved in running the business on a day-to-day basis.

One of the biggest investments Jack made—both in terms of time and money—was in our typesetting and design operation. We had been jobbing out books to various typesetters and designers over the years until 1984, when Jack got together will Paul and Bette Davies, who were doing cover design and typesetting out of their house in Oakville. Paul was an eccentric polymath. His expertise was all over the map, and none of it was conventional. He had been involved in computing for a long time and understood the ins and outs of typesetting. He was a champion marksman. He owned guns. He had studied physics. He understood motorcycles. He could give you a lecture on algebraic equations, and he wanted nothing more than to return to school to learn Latin. Jack and Paul forged a strong relationship, made stronger by Jack's patience with Paul's eccentricities. In 1985 they submitted a grant to the Department of Communications to obtain funding that would allow ECW to set up an in-house typesetting system. The application was successful, and by the end of the year Paul was typesetting most of our books. Jack began to envision ECW as a provider of type and design to other publishers, which is exactly what happened. ECW invested heavily in purchasing the equipment and supplies that would allow Paul to run ECW Type and Art, a part of the company that eventually created significant cash flow, mainly due to Paul's ability to handle complicated typesetting jobs for reference and legal publishers. The company contributed the rent for Paul's Oakville home-office, which was packed with expensive computers and printers. Obviously, Paul's role in the company was crucial. He was typesetting and designing most of the company's books, including the covers, and he was also doing third-party work. Jack tried hard to accommodate Paul's needs and to keep his equipment current. Paul clearly loved Jack. If he went on a trip he would send Jack postcards with a single word—"Hi!" (I'm away, but remembering you always.)

The third-party typesetting business looked promising at the start. By 1987 Paul was doing complicated jobs for Butterworths Canada, a subsidiary of Butterworths UK, which was part of an even larger international publishing conglomerate owned by Reed International. We thought the connection would lead to strong American and European publishing contacts. Butterworths' bread and butter was law books of all kinds. They were pumping out reference series and annual guides at a feverish place and simply couldn't handle all the typesetting inhouse. Jack established an ongoing relationship with Andrew Martin, who was running the Canadian operation. Early on, Andrew suggested that Butterworths might be interested in buying ECW. We had long been dissatisfied with the distribution services provided by the University of Toronto Press, which had been handling all of our titles since 1986, and eventually Jack approached Andrew about the possibility of Butterworths assuming our marketing and distribution, which the company agreed to do in 1989. With the typesetting for Butterworths ongoing, and the new distribution agreement, it seemed that we had finally hit on a business relationship that would bring us some much-needed cash.

Because Paul played a central role in this relationship, Jack found himself meeting with him often, and spending long hours in Oakville going over proofs or discussing a variety of projects. That kind of investment only served to accentuate the differences between the Montreal and Toronto offices. Jack would discuss the typesetting business with me on a regular basis, but it was hard to be involved in all the projects, which changed from day to day. It was clear that the polarization of the two offices was increasing. I think that in a bid for power within the company, Paul played us off against each other. When ECW published its 100th title in 1989, Paul did up a special flyer to celebrate the fact, and signed it: Jack David, Paul Davies, and Robert Lecker. Somehow, I had been bumped to third in line and now it looked like the business had three partners. That little power play, and others like it, pissed me off. If I got fussy or demanding about a particular typesetting job or a cover design, Paul would say I was impossible to please and let Jack know. Jack tried to stay out of the fray, but inevitably he was caught in the middle, mainly because he had the primary relation with Paul. Over and over again he would be forced to mediate between us, which was an unfortunate position for him to be in, and one that was bound to weaken the primary relationship between the two publishers. Besides, I knew that Paul was a great typesetter with an innate understanding of the structure of the typographical page, but I thought his sense of cover design was overly conservative, which didn't matter so much as long as the kind of books we were publishing were primarily academic. However, as it turned out, our future did not lie in academic books, and the more involved I became in pursuing non-academic designs, the more Paul and I ran into conflict.

This kind of tension was a problem, especially because Paul was a key player when it came to Butterworths. The sheer volume of typesetting that Paul did for them meant that his role was key. Jack tried to further interest Butterworths in buying all or part of ECW. After all, why pay all that money for production to another company when you could just buy that company and fold it into your own organization, saving overhead and other costs? Butterworths was already distributing our titles. Now they could have our production as well. All they had to do was pay us a bundle. Jack spoke to Andrew Martin about the possibility, and he was, in fact, interested. Our hopes rose. If they paid us enough we could kiss our mega-debt goodbye and work for Butterworths on salary. One worry was that because they were a foreign company Butterworths could not buy us outright. They would have to own 49 percent but have a controlling interest. Andrew made the pitch to his head office in London. They bit. Over the next few months we had to present them with reams of figures about sales, grants, debt, and all of the niggly details that a purchaser needs to have in order to complete a buyout. We figured we would walk away with about $700,000. But the deal went sour. It got nixed by head office, which, as the story goes, was uneasy about our reliance on grants. This was a heavy blow, especially for Jack, who had spent so much time preparing the papers in response to Butterworths' due diligence requests. Maybe some day there would be another offer to buy us. However, nothing was on the horizon, and the debt was as pressing as ever. There were few options. For the time being we had to return to our ongoing relationship with Butterworths as our distributor, and as the best client of ECW Type and Art. However, after the failure of the sale, how long could that relationship be expected to last?

Whether it was sheer impatience with my dealings with Paul, or resentment caused by my distance from Toronto and all the solitary work he put into the Butterworths deal, or a general sense of discrepancy between his goals for the company and mine, Jack made a crucial decision that fundamentally changed the nature of the company and its direction. Toward the spring of 1989 he told me that he thought we should develop our lists separately, according to our individual visions of what the company should publish, and which titles would make it most successful. Of course the ECW backlist as it stood at that time was not the product of constant agreement between us about which projects to pursue. Jack had developed individual relationships with many authors over the years, as had I, and some of the books reflected those relationships. But for the most part the backlist had been the product of consensus and joint discussion—the various multi-volume series, the critical books supported by grants, the books by Hugh Hood, John Metcalf, and Leon Rooke, or quirky books that for one reason or another we both felt had a chance of success, and even the journal, which I had been managing out of Montreal.

Jack was proposing a radical departure from this model. Now it would be up to us, individually, to sign new books and to work out the design for each. Production would also be handled separately, through the individual offices. Jack also said he had no interest in pursuing the journal, since it had become so preoccupied with theory that it was no longer much fun. He was happy, he said, to let me run it as I saw fit, so long as we kept getting grants. Maybe Jack's intent in separating our responsibilities was to show me how removed I was from the centre of the action, or maybe it was to even out the workload. Or maybe his decision was simply the product of his profound anti-corporatism. I know he always believed that people worked best when they made their own choices, took responsibilities for their actions, learned from their errors, and did what they liked doing. I protested against this change. Jack replied that it was simply a refinement of a process that was already in place, since we were already dealing with authors and production on an individual basis, even if the books involved were part of larger series, and since we sometimes disagreed about which books should be signed.

I saw the seeds of conflict. Implicitly, the new arrangement would put us in competition with each other. It would widen the gulf between Montreal and Toronto, making it less and less necessary to speak about joint efforts. It would create two ideologies within a single company, inevitably weakening the company image, which would end up lacking focus, derived as it would be from two disparate visions. Worst of all, it threatened to undermine the basic relationship that had forged the company in the first place—the relationship between me and Jack. Now the relationship would be territorial. And there would be no way of doing what was always essential in publishing, as in any other business: testing and questioning one's ideas with a trusted partner, or a group. Up until this point, we had always talked through the projects together, tried to poke holes in each other's arguments about the merits of a particular project or book. But now it would be sink or swim on your own. If you screwed up, you would have no one to blame but yourself. The decision made it inevitable that two partners who had always worked together would end up competing with each other, however unconsciously, and that the employees would inevitably be touched by that competition, creating schisms within the company. What disturbed me most about this scenario was not really the risk of screwing up—I knew that there would always be titles that didn't work—it was that I would be alone in facing the disappointments and failures as well as the successes, since they would not be the product of any kind of communal action. It wasn't like I was working in a big office surrounded by others to whom I could turn with my ideas and disappointments. I had one employee—Holly Potter—who had started working for the press shortly before this turn of events. Holly was a perceptive and sympathetic friend with an inimitable sense of humour. She helped me in every aspect of my involvement with the journal and the press, but she was not a replacement for Jack.

I deferred to Jack because there seemed to be no other choice. He had made up his mind. Neither of us had any kind of leverage on the other. We had equal shares in the company, which had been registered as an Ontario corporation, and, since 1986, we had a buy-sell agreement in place that made it clear we were the company directors, with equal weight. When a partnership is truly a partnership, that kind of arrangement is fine. But if there comes a time when one partner is in fundamental disagreement with the other, little can be done to resolve the situation, since neither has any kind of deciding power. The only alternative would be for one partner to offer to buy out the other's share, but this was clearly an impossible option at the time, since there was no money around, and no bank was going to lend us any.

So I went along with Jack's plan to acquire and develop our titles independently, even though I had misgivings from the start. It wasn't the kind of change that instantly turned day into night, or night into day, depending on your perspective. We were hardened deal-makers and were always thinking about how we could sell the rights to our projects, get weird grants, find people to support various ventures. There was always the question of how to manage the continually ballooning debt, or discussions about who might lend us more money. There were lots of buoyant moments, amusing twists and turns, deals to be hatched and discussed, shared victories, laughter, hopes. At one level, we were still very much in this together, united by our history and the sense that one day, finally, something big would happen that would make us some cash, relieve the ever-present debt. We speculated about how much the company would be worth to somebody who truly understood its value. We waited for the call from the wealthy buyer who wanted nothing more than to invest in a powerhouse of CanCrit. Nothing changed overnight. Even though I would now be operating on a much more individual basis, it would take time to acquire new titles, time to get them into production, time to gauge the result.

This shift in my role as a publisher forced me to confront some basic literary questions, which started out as business questions: Why were some authors so popular with academics while others remained on the periphery? What kind of criticism got read, and what kind got ignored? Was there any kind of interface between literary criticism and the broader market for books on popular culture? Would it be possible to further develop a publishing program that capitalized on the Canadian canon? Why did there seem to be so little debate about this canon, when it was obviously something that could put money in the bank or cause the bank to come knocking on the door? It was nice to think of the canon in Dr. Johnson's terms as something that had "pleased many and pleased long," but it turned out that if you were a publisher you had to think in much more precise and immediate terms—like, why should I invest in a book about Christopher Dewdney when very few people will actually buy it, even though Dewdney is such a great poet? Or, how is it that Sinclair Ross got so famous in CanLit circles when in fact his fiction is so crushingly dull? What did Jack McClelland know that I didn't know when he signed up that book for the New Canadian Library series?

These questions started me thinking about the relationship between what I was doing as a publisher and my life as a CanLit prof. I had been teaching Canadian literature for more than a decade. By doing so, I had in many ways supported the existing canon, and, through ECW's various reference and critical books, I had further reinforced the canon. But I had seldom thought about it. Every once in a while someone would complain about the authors we had decided to cover in one of our series, or one of my students would ask why there were so few people of colour represented in Canadian literary anthologies, or why experimental writing didn't seem to show up much in those anthologies. I began to sense that my Canadian literary tastes had been formed with very little in the way of self-examination. I also sensed that there was a prevailing consensus in the Canadian academic world about an existing canon. Which is not to say that there weren't all kinds of non-canonical figures in that canon. Even some of the most overtly subversive writers (I think of people like bill bissett, Dave Godfrey, Dionne Brand, or Hubert Aquin) had somehow managed to find a place in the canon. And there were several academics who were championing particular authors who seemed to operate outside the canonical frame, or who were interested in examining issues from non-canonical perspectives, especially feminist perspectives.

So the Canadian literary canon that I had somehow come to possess and promote through ECW and in my teaching was by no means etched in stone; there were all kinds of exceptions.

Still, as an editor who saw hundreds of submissions to the journal and who worked with hundreds of academics who were devoting their professional lives to CanLit, I was struck by how much the study of Canadian literature was driven by an overriding consensus about which living authors were worthy of study, or about which dead ones were candidates for resurrection through the publication of special editions or collections of essays devoted to their work. When I looked at the canon that I was reinforcing, it seemed clear that, especially in terms of Canadian fiction, the canonized material tended to be more conservative than experimental, more in keeping with the values of conventional realism than with the subversive aesthetics aligned with postmodernism. Sure, ECW was happy to promote writers like Michael Ondaatje and Robert Kroetsch, but they were the exception rather than the rule. Most of the fiction writers who were covered in the *Canadian Writers and Their Works* series were realists at heart; they seemed to be valued for their ability to evoke time and place, to create rounded characters who operated in recognizable settings. How did it turn out that way? Here we were, in 1990, and American fiction was dominated by a postmodern movement that had taken root 20 years earlier. Meanwhile, Canadian fiction seemed to be going in the opposite direction, valorizing writers who were fundamentally realists or modernists. There were some other contrasts as well. The rise of American feminism had led to a wholesale reassessment of the American literary canon and the values it had entrenched. Feminist critics insisted that many texts that had been excluded from the male-dominated canon would have to be revisited, and they also made it clear that this task would not be easy, since many of those texts had simply disappeared from view. It would take time, and research, and rehistoricizing in order to introduce this lost writing into discussions about canons and canonical value. But in Canada, there were few parallel inquiries, especially in the early 1980s. Although Shirley Neuman and Smaro Kamboureli had edited *A Mazing Space*, a ground-breaking collection of essays on Canadian women's writing in 1986, and although Barbara Godard had followed this a year later with another edited collection of challenging essays entitled *Gynocritics/Gynocritiques* (which we published), there was little effect upon the established canon, in the sense that most Canadian criticism continued to focus on the established writers. And even though feminist collectives in Quebec and

English Canada (notably Tessera) posed crucial questions about the canon, gender, and literary history, their intervention had an impact on theoretical values that did not significantly influence the CanCrit industry, which remained focused on producing books and articles on recognized figures. After all, the canon was the canon because it replicated itself, not because it was open to challenge and change.

Some publishers had the courage to issue books by women that had been ignored or allowed to go out of print, but there was nothing in Canadian literature that could compare to the massive revaluation that was going on in the United States. It seemed to me that one reason for this contrast originated in a Canadian need to reinforce a sense of time and place. Could it be that the emphasis on realism, so dominant in the Canadian canon, was a displaced form of nationalism, another way of validating the country that produced it? That question prompted me to consider the relation between canons and the idea of nation. Maybe literary canons somehow embodied national ideals. Maybe the texts forming a canon represented a grammar of consensus, values that were shared but not named, subsumed as they were in literary structures, styles, and forms.

Looking back on my own involvement with the canon, I realized that in many respects it had been mobilized by my own nationalism, a nationalism that had taken hold in my student days at York and that had been nurtured by a continual investment in Canadian literature, through the journal and the press and in the classroom. Part of this was a response to growing up in Quebec and seeing the effects of the events leading up to the election of René Lévesque and the Parti Québécois in 1976 while I was still at York, one year before Jack and I founded the press. We never discussed the election, or its results, or the Quiet Revolution, or the thousands of people who left Montreal, certain that their futures would be imperiled under a separatist government. Yet, however unspoken our beliefs, we shared a strong sense of nationalism. My move to the United States heightened my nationalism. And when I got to McGill, I realized that my job was to teach Canadian literature in a political environment that, outside the allophone and reduced English communities of Montreal, often seemed overwhelmingly anti-Canadian. Teaching Canadian literature in Montreal was not the same as teaching it in Toronto. But I was no politician. The tools I had at my disposal were literary.

I wanted to believe that despite the threat to national stability I saw around me, on a daily basis, there was still a way of finding community and consensus. I turned to the Canadian canon, perhaps even developed ideas about the Canadian canon, as a construction that would release me. Perhaps it was a dream. I began to read up on canonical theory and started to understand John Guillory's notion of the ways in which canons were a kind of cultural capital. I studied Charles Altieri's work and became interested in the way he was willing to challenge the assumption that canons were necessarily the outmoded vehicles of repressive patriarchal values. What became clear was that countries in the process of inventing themselves were much more prone to celebrate the relation between canon and nation, while countries that saw themselves as already invented—especially the US—were ready to deconstruct their canonical identities. They had the self-confidence that would allow them to sever the connection between canon and nation, a prerequisite to renewing that connection so that it could be destroyed, and renewed again. Well, it seemed to me that you couldn't take a real shot at the canon or begin to deconstruct it until you had identified the object of your attack. I started to think about naming the Canadian canon, sketching out some ideas about what made it unique. This inquiry gradually took over my interest in individual authors. For the next five years—right up to the second referendum in Quebec in 1995—I remained preoccupied with canonical value.

Most of the critical writing I did during this period focused on the canon. What became clear, from the time I published my initial essay on the subject in *Critical Inquiry* in 1990, was that although few Canadian critics had examined on the canon, they had a lot invested in their versions of it. The *Critical Inquiry* article set out the basic argument that the Canadian canon was the fundamentally conservative product of the academic institution that had brought it into being, and that it represented, through its emphasis on relatively conservative realist fiction, a displaced form of the nationalist values at the heart of the institution that had constructed it. This was followed by other articles in which I argued that there could be no effective dissent or subversive activity directed against the canon until we recognized the existence of such a canon, for, failing that recognition, there was no basis for dissent. Ironically, the identification of a canon—however conservative that canon might be—was actually the means of empowering those forces that would engage in its destruction. How could you undermine something that had not yet been named?

Naturally these ideas met with some resistance. In an attempt to present an opposing view, *Critical Inquiry* approached Frank Davey to write a response to my piece. Not surprisingly, he found my model of the canon to be exclusive, monolithic, one-sided, and ignorant of some of the challenges that had been directed at the established canon, mainly by people who shared his interest in experimental poetry, feminism, and critical theory. Good, so the debate was on! Further testimony to my assertion that once you got out there and named the canon, dissenters were sure to appear, guns blasting. It didn't matter who was right, because of course there was no right or wrong. What mattered was that we finally had some debate, and the very fact of that debate gave life to its subject matter.

I didn't mind Davey's condescending attitude towards my essay. (Well, maybe a little.) I expected it. He had been a professor at York and no doubt still saw me as a student. He had territory to protect, having worked hard to establish himself as a critic determined to question the status quo and to champion the experimental, especially experimental poetry, no matter how incomprehensible it might be. The journal he founded, *Open Letter*, was a testimony to anti-canonical action. He was, after all, the guy who had written "Surviving the Paraphrase" and who had been taking shots at the thematic critics for years. He was a West Coast man at heart who had been forced to come east, and I'm sure he resented some guy from Montreal talking about the Canadian canon as if the West Coast did not exist. And I probably wasn't theoretical enough for Davey. Whatever motivations there were behind his critique, I still respected Davey's intelligence and what I saw as his commitment to Canadian literature, even if we were following different paths. Quite the opposite kind of critic was Tracy Ware, who decided he would try to trash my argument in a paper presented at the annual Canadian conference for English professors. He got up and delivered a 20-minute attack on the wrongness of my ideas. I sat in the audience, wondering what I had done to warrant all of this close attention. Good for my ego, and good for Tracy's *c.v.*, but generally speaking, the people presenting papers at these conferences were reluctant to take chances. The ferocity of Ware's attack was quite unusual. Yet it didn't rouse the audience to engage in any productive debate about the issues at hand. There were some carefully worded comments, a question or two, and then everybody left the room and went for a beer.

This was symptomatic of the general sense of apathy that had crept into CanCrit. It was also an indication of the territorialism that characterized the profession. The myth was that a group of open-minded and enthusiastic professors could get together to share ideas and test their assumptions. The fact was that the professors had become increasingly self-conscious about their turf. People specialized in Margaret Atwood, or queer studies, or early Canadian poetry. The more they specialized, the more they seemed cut off from their colleagues, which was ironic, because the whole idea behind publishing articles and going to conferences was to share ideas, but how much could you share if you had decided to narrow your area of specialization to the point where only a handful of people recognized the names of the authors you were talking about? Canadian criticism seemed to have become an isolating force, rather than something that brought people together. And the Canadian canon seemed to be something that was connected to professional advancement, and, in my case as a publisher, also to the possibility of financial reward. It was by no means innocent.

My preoccupation with the canon inevitably spilled into the classroom. My students, especially the graduate students, were subjected to courses on Canadian criticism that explored the politics of the canon and the CanLit industry. In one course I inflicted *As for Me and My House* on them, as well as the proceedings of the Future Indicative Conference, and the special issue of *Open Letter* devoted to Robert Kroetsch, no doubt possessed by some crazed notion that they would be as involved as I was by the ways in which critics spoke and how they conducted their business. I found it incredible that that the University of Ottawa Press would publish the proceedings of that conference on theory. Not because the contents weren't fascinating. To someone whose career was devoted to this stuff it was captivating reading, not only because some of the papers were genuinely insightful, but more importantly because they showed just how rarefied and obsessive the discussion of Canadian literature had become. I'm willing to bet that aside from library sales, which might have accounted for 200-300 copies, not more than 50 individuals invested in this book (excluding my students). It was a book for a private club.

If my students groaned at the essays they were forced to read in *Future Indicative*, they moaned at the experience of studying *As for Me and My House*. Let's face it. This is a very tiresome book. When it was first published in New York it was quickly dismissed by reviewers. Many of the reviewers assumed that Sinclair Ross was a woman. The book soon went out of print. No one paid any attention to it for years, until it was resurrected in the New Canadian Library series by Malcolm Ross. Because the novel had been out of print for so long, Jack McClelland was able to buy the rights for a song. What turned the book into a Canadian classic was its pedagogical value as a text that could be used to illustrate unreliable narration. It was Bill New who first energized the discussion of the novel in these terms, and dozens of critics following him were eager to explore Mrs. Bentley's unreliability and the many ways in which her narration made it impossible to get any true sense of her long-suffering husband, who lived under her narrative thumb.

I don't know how many times I have taught this novel. At one point, I think I believed it was a valuable book, even though I always encountered resistance to it in the classroom. I wondered what kind of sex the Bentleys had, if they ever had it. Images came to mind that were profoundly depressing. I would ask the students what they thought. Every year they told me the same thing: they thought the novel was boring. *Sooo* boring. I talked about Mrs. Bentley's repressed sexuality. The students laughed. I explained that the real excitement was all contained in her closing words ("That's right, Philip. I want it so.") because those words made the whole story ambivalent and called everything we believed about Mrs. Bentley and Philip into doubt. I explained New's argument. I talked about Wayne Booth and the idea of unreliable narration. This did capture their interest a bit, but it didn't change their view of the novel, which failed to move them, despite its lofty place in the Canadian canon. How could it be that such a bad novel had received so much critical attention? More to the point, how could it be that none of this attention seemed to have filtered out to the general public, which remained completely unaware of this canonical gem in their midst? Thousand of students were subjected to the story. Dozens of articles had been written about it. Careers had been established by individuals who had devoted a big part of their professional lives to its interpretation. Yet if you found yourself talking to an educated person outside the university, even someone passionately interested in Canadian literature, the mention of the novel simply evoked a puzzled stare. It was a pedagogical and critical creation, of no interest to the public. I imagined myself as a TV reporter interviewing people on rue Ste-Catherine in downtown Montreal: "Can I take a moment of your time to ask you about one of Canada's most famous novels?" Not a single person would have heard of it, unless they had been forced to read it in a course on CanLit.

After I realized that the Canadian canon had little to do with the public's perception of which books really mattered, I decided to write up the perverse story of the canonization of *As for Me and My House*. I knew that my opinion would ruffle feathers, particularly the feathers of those who had extolled the virtues of the novel or who were heavily invested in the sacredness of the New Canadian Library series. McClelland had even managed to create a committee called the Canadian Classics Committee, which would be charged with identifying the greatest Canadian novels of all time (most of which were published by McClelland & Stewart). How could someone even think of challenging the authority of this novel, which the Classics Committee had already pompously pronounced "Indispensable for the appreciation of Canadian literature"? When I presented my paper at a conference in San Francisco people in the audience got angry. They thought my manners were bad. It was impolite to challenge the value of such an iconic text. Who did I think I was? Later, privately, and outside the conference room, they took me to task for airing CanLit's dirty linen in a foreign country, as if any controversy surrounding the book should be kept at home, in the CanCrit laundry basket. Bad Canadian manners. Bad boy.

Presenting papers at conferences did not always work out well for me. I knew that one way of approaching these papers was simply to see attending conferences as a means of obtaining subsidized travel to interesting places. Sometimes I'd see my fellow academics writing their papers on the plane, or speaking from hastily assembled notes written on scraps of paper or even scribbled on napkins. I was too structured to make that kind of leap, so I always got started well in advance, working over my papers so they could be delivered in the allotted time. Then the presentation day arrived. I would head off to the designated room, often to find three or four people in the audience, with another three or four facing them at the front of the room, scheduled to present papers along with me. It did seem strange to have such a small audience whose members often didn't recognize the text I was discussing and it was difficult, in the question and answer period, to generate any real sense of exchange. Of course I got used to this and came to accept the fact that if there was going to be an exchange of ideas it would often take place at a conference reception, simply because the time allowed for presentations had to be limited. But still, the question nagged: why did I fly halfway around the world to talk to three people? I gave a talk to *two* people at Duke University. They flew me down and wined and dined me at an apparently swanky restaurant that served sliced raw hot dogs at the salad bar. Why was I there? What was I doing in Christchurch, New Zealand? Why was I raising a glass with German academics at a resort hotel in the Black Forest? Who were these people in this conference room in Santa Fe? Why was I on a scenic boat ride to a Native reservation near Seattle, pondering the paper I would deliver the next morning? What would I say about Canadian literature if I went to Goa? Or Japan?

Sometimes attending a conference in an exotic location or teaching a class in a foreign country could be a sobering experience. In 1992 I was invited to give a series of lectures on Canadian literature at the University of São Paulo in Brazil. My hosts were unfailingly generous and polite. I could see what they were up against in their desire to cover Canadian literature in their English courses. It was very difficult for them to obtain texts. There were no bookstores in Brazil that stocked English-Canadian titles, and the cost of purchasing and shipping books from Canada was prohibitive, given their limited budget. So the professors got one copy of the material they wanted to use and photocopied it like mad. In Canada they would have been busted for copyright infringement in a second, but anyone who saw how difficult it was for them to obtain the material legitimately would certainly have excused them. They had to overcome the severe budgetary restrictions that made it impossible for them to use legitimate texts, and they also had to overcome the limitations of their own library (and others throughout Brazil) which had essentially stopped buying new titles during the period of military rule, from 1964-1985.

Because that period saw the publication of so many titles crucial to the "explosion" in Canadian literature during the late 1960s and 1970s, the library at São Paulo was missing many central books and periodicals. And it wasn't only those publications they were missing. During my first lecture, when I was trying to present an overview of Canadian literature from a regional perspective, I could see that most of the people in the audience looked confused. I stopped the lecture to ask if something was unclear. Many hands rose. Yes, what I was saying was very unclear, because practically no one had any knowledge of Canadian geography. Where was Vancouver Island? What were the prairies? Why was Charles G.D. Roberts so preoccupied with this place called Tantramar if it was just a little marsh? I asked the professor who was hosting my visit whether it would be possible to get a map of Canada, so that I could provide a visual reference to the regions I was discussing. She went off to the library and returned with a small, outdated map. Newfoundland was not even on it. That was all they had. Despite this kind of restriction and the enormous difficulties they faced in accessing primary and secondary material, the teachers I met in Brazil remained enthusiastic and committed. They had been bitten by the CanLit bug.

Sometimes it took a trip like that one to put other conferences into perspective. A year before my visit to Brazil I went on a wonderful trip to Italy, which was marred only slightly by a few small issues at the conference itself. It was one of those first-rate conferences, funded largely by the Canadian government and organized by the International Association for Canadian Studies, a swanky outfit in those days. The conference itself was held in Torre Canne, a small town near Brindisi. The Italians were always hospitable. When I arrived at my hotel room there was a nice bottle of local virgin olive oil waiting for me, along with a bottle of wine. The conference area itself was social in the best Italian way: there was an espresso bar, a regular bar, and lots of people sitting around smoking and having a good time. This was Italy, and this was how it should be. Several senior Italian professors moved among the crowd, trailed by beautiful graduate students, who were fondled regularly by the Italian profs. When it was time for each conference session to begin the conference organizer left the espresso bar and rang a little bell, signalling that it was time for everyone to move off to the conference rooms. He rang and rang, but no one budged. Thirty minutes after each session was supposed to start the participants began to wander into the assigned rooms, amidst much back-slapping, cigarettes, and laughter.

My paper was scheduled for ten in the morning. Obsessively punctual, I showed up at the appointed room five minutes ahead of time. It contained about 200 seats, but there wasn't a soul around. I paced the hallway, waiting for the bell to prompt my audience to get moving. Nothing happened. I waited 15 minutes. No one. I couldn't stand it any longer. I decided to find out what was going on. Maybe I was in the wrong room? I found the conference organizer sitting at the espresso bar, laughing it up with a buxom graduate student. When I asked what was happening with my session he seemed momentarily affronted, but then he regained his sense of humour, took a sip from his cup, and said "Vengo! Vengo!" I'm coming.

A few minutes later he got up and rang the bell. Three or four people emerged from the throng of professors. Eventually they made their way down the hall and took seats at the back of the room. The panel of paper presenters sat down behind a table on a raised platform, looking out over the absent crowd. I was supposed to be third. Sometime during the first presentation I heard some loud giggling and the sound of a door opening. The room was suddenly flooded with about 50 pre-teens, young kids chomping on gum and snickering while they crinkled packages of snack food that was spilling on the floor, crunching under their Nikes as they rumbled into skidding seats. I could hear the gurgle of straws sucking on empty pop cans. At least a dozen of them were fiddling with their Walkmans, adjusting their headphones and dropping cassettes. A can hit the floor, oozing Coke. The chairman of the panel leaned toward me and whispered in my ear: "Some local students, invited just for the sessions this morning. They will be very interested in your talk!" Really? They couldn't sit still. They laughed and moved the chairs around and squirmed in their seats, popping bubbles and looking everywhere but at the poor profs sitting at the front of the room. This was a test. Be professional, I told myself. You are a visitor in this country. I stood up and delivered my paper on "Representations of Value in Canadian Criticism" to a restless gaggle of adolescents who had been given the morning off school. At best, I was an irritating distraction, a silly figure at the front of the room in a sports jacket, reading some kind of paper in a language they couldn't understand (if only I had dressed more like Terry Goldie, a CanLit specialist who routinely showed up at conferences wearing thong-like bikini briefs and sandals). After the presentations, the panel chairman turned to the assembled masses and asked, in Italian and English, whether there were any questions. Surprise! None of the students had any questions for me, and the three conference participants who had been in the audience at the start of the show had quietly slipped out during the first presentation. Even the woman who had presented the paper before mine left the hall as soon as she finished speaking. Well, I had been professional. That's what counted in this kind of situation. I left the room and did the right thing. I got myself a nice glass of wine. And then I had a hefty scotch. After all, it was lunch time.

This kind of experience provided ample evidence that conferences should not be taken too seriously. They were basically social gatherings, designed as much to bring people together as they were to share ideas. ECW had been exploiting the social side of Canadian conference-going for years. In the beginning we got the idea of sponsoring a party at the annual meeting of learned societies, informally known as "The Learneds," which were held at a different university each year. We always attended the conference when the CanLit sessions took place. Our plan was to host a party that would bring together our authors, raise the press's profile, and recruit new talent. The problem was that these parties tended to be expensive, especially because we insisted that our prof-clients have as much to drink as they wanted, as well as good food, because if ECW didn't stand for generosity and quality, what Canadian publisher did? I would consult with caterers and planners months in advance over the wine selection and the hors d'oeuvres. No Cuvée Rouge for ECW. Live music was essential. We designed unique invitations every year to make each party seem distinctive and researched the perfect spot for these events—the Killam Library at Dalhousie University, the Winnipeg Art Gallery, or the Cecil Green Park mansion at UBC, where waiters in starched white jackets served a selection of reds and whites while our guests indulged in seafood and roast beef carved to order on the terrace. We had also hired a string quartet. At the height of our belief in the promotional power of conferences we chartered three buses to bring our partygoers from the University of Guelph (no reception rooms good enough for us there) to the chic restaurant and inn at the Elora Mill, about 20 minutes away. We catered to 125 people who heard readings by our specially invited authors: Roch Carrier and Robert Kroetsch. These parties cost us a bundle, even though we had managed to split many of the costs with the Association for Canadian and Quebec Literatures (ACQL) or the Association of Canadian College and University Teachers of English (ACCUTE), organizations whose members were often our authors. Eventually we had to abandon these annual events, not only because of the cost, but also because we gradually lost interest in the Learneds, which had started to focus more and more on presentations by eager graduate students who would roll out the post-structuralist jargon without the least self-consciousness until it became unbearable.

I wanted to find a different way of approaching CanLit, especially in the classroom, where I could see how quickly the students turned away from the more self-indulgent forms of theory. I had the luxury of being able to teach a full-year course on the development of Canadian poetry, which forced me to confront the poetry canon. Once again I found myself pulled to the writers who were most tortured by their craft, the authors whose poems seemed to be about the impossibility or the inauthenticity of making poems in the first place. Language, they knew, was suspect, coloured as it was with values that could never be detached from history, or politics, or place, or the particular features of a writer's life. They also knew that metaphor could no longer be seen as an innocent literary device. This was the realization that made a poem like Leonard Cohen's "How To Speak Poetry" such a pivotal work. Cohen asks: "What is the expression which the age demands?" The answer is clear: "The age demands no expression whatever."

The critics understood this too, sensing that their own language was suspect. However, the poets seemed to have a more genuine way of expressing their growing distrust of language and art as instruments of truth. I saw the distrust emerging early on, even in some of the Confederation poets, especially Duncan Campbell Scott, whose Piper of Arll knows he has to find the courage to play a different song, and I found it in A.J.M. Smith's "The Lonely Land" with its profound distrust of harmony, its attempt to make dissonance a form of beauty, against all odds. I saw it in Margaret Avison's "Strong Yellow, for Reading Aloud," a poem dedicated to undoing her students' unquestioning belief in poetic truth, and in John Newlove's "That There Is No Relaxation," with its repudiation of "shining lines." I kept returning to Gwendolyn MacEwen's tortured relation to her own poetic craft, her drive towards prelapsarian consciousness, the preliterate world she knew it would be impossible to find because metaphor had made the return impossible, as she discovers in "Eden, Eden" and many other poems. Most of all I saw it in Michael Ondaatje, poet of the extreme, a man obsessed with the inadequacy of everything he wrote, making beauty out of the pressures of anxiety and doubt. A poet whose terror of language draws him towards an inescapable fear of words and an equal fear of silence:

There is my fear
Of no words of
Falling without words
Over and over of
Mouthing the silence

I could see the aesthetic problem that Ondaatje was dealing with translated into critical terms. I knew that at one level criticism meant nothing. No words could really do justice to the moment a poem came together in your mind, no critique could really convey the way a good poem permanently altered your vision, made it impossible to see things the same way ever again. But if you pulled back from the criticism you also pulled back from some kind of engagement with the art. You had to have some kind of conversation with it. There had to be some way of speaking that seemed genuine. The problem the critic faced in finding an appropriate language was the same problem the poet faced in dealing with the inadequacy of words.

Unfortunately, I found few critics who were able to help me out with the problems of voice. The Canadian critical landscape was filled with a number of very earnest voices, most of them sound but plodding, or it was overpowered by the theorists who were doing their best to make sure everyone understood how wrong they had been in their ideas about the way literature worked. It was around this time that the eagerly awaited fourth volume of the revised *Literary History of Canada* appeared. Well, maybe that is an exaggeration. It wasn't as if people were buzzing in anticipation of the critical tome's imminent release, but I was excited, if only because this new volume would deal with the history of Canadian literature between 1972 and 1984, the years that marked my own entry into the field. Published in 1990, the contents of the *Literary History* were necessarily a bit dated, but I turned eagerly to the section on theory and criticism to read what Barry Cameron would say about the developments during the years that ECW had come into its own.

The first warning sign of what had happened to Canadian criticism in those years came with Cameron's opening disclaimer, where he announced that his chapter would be "ideological, self-reflexive, and post-Saussurean." Uh-oh. It's not that Cameron was wrong. When he argued that "the writing of literary history systematically forms the objects of which it speaks" he was right on, and he was also correct to observe that writing literary history was as much about the critic's own struggles with language as it was about various authors' similar struggles. What bothered me was the tone of the chapter, the way it conveyed a condescending smugness—Cameron's sense that he was so far ahead of the critics he was writing about, that he knew something they didn't, and that he had a way of using his post-Saussurean vocabulary to show just how sophisticated he was.

What was the subtext here, as we profs like to ask? The subtext was that criticism had been replaced by theory, that theory was something highly specialized and somehow distant from the appreciation of literature, and that the study of literary history was something that happened in a rarefied space that could be inhabited only by the select few who knew the codes. This attitude appeared again and again in the literary theory that emerged in the 1990s, and Canadian theory was by no means exempt. But there was a problem. If you needed to be such a specialist to get into the club, where did that leave the intelligent undergraduate student who was passionately interested in Canadian literature? It left that student outside. And what did it do for the ambitious graduate student who wanted to enter the profession? It forced that student to learn the codes, or at least to make gestures in their direction. All of this meant that the way in which theory became practised had little to do with the relationship between literature and daily life. In fact, critics like Cameron were quick to question the assumption that there was any relation between literature and something called real life. In this context, it was hard to understand how these theorists managed to retain an interest in Canada.

Cameron disdained the idea that literature could function "as a means of national identification and a force for national unity." I had a different idea. If my students couldn't understand what the hell I was saying because I was so post-Saussurean, what good was I to them? If I couldn't talk to them about Canada as something distinct and identifiable, why should they enroll in a course called Canadian literature? The study of Canadian literature did not have to be a rah-rah session in front of the flag. But what it could be, productively, was an examination, through literature, of how different writers had imagined the country at different times. And it could also look at the problems they faced in representing their country if they felt that such a representation was no longer possible. Postmodernism did not destroy the idea of nation. It simply raised the question of how nations could be redefined in contemporary terms and in relation to all kinds of new questions about how countries were imagined. In this context, critics such as Benedict Anderson in his *Imagined Communities* were of far more use to me than Homi Bhabha, the high-powered post-colonial theorist whose convoluted sentences left people scratching their heads.

Caught in the midst of the rise of Canadian theory, I became preoccupied with the idea of connecting with my students, no matter what it took. While Cameron was arguing that "within a Canadian context, post-Saussureans argue that the form and contents of Canadian literature derive from discursive practices" (just the name—post-Saussureans—made me think of Darth Vader), the students were listening to Tracy Chapman and INXS's "Suicide Blonde." No post-Saussureanism there. I kept asking them to bring in their CDs. Rap was still in its early phase, so I could still get most of the music. At the end of each term they completed anonymous evaluations of their professors. They usually wrote nice things, except for the ones who said I should be fired immediately for being pompous or way too dull. Then there were the students who used the evaluation forms to give welcome advice: "Lecker should go off to a mountain retreat and just chill."

I wanted to figure out a way to connect with the students through the kind of books I was doing with ECW. But we were still essentially an academic publisher, doing critical books and reference series, with the occasional odd item thrown into the mix. The journal remained a scholarly production, although I tried to liven it up a bit with full-colour covers by Canadian artists. That was a far cry from doing books that the students might connect with. In fact, ECW was about to enter another major transition, even though I could never have predicted it at the time. One look at the kinds of titles we were producing showed just how many scholarly bases we were trying to cover. In 1990, with the National Library of Canada, we copublished Freda Waldon's *Bibliography of Canadiana Published in Great Britain, 1519-1763*. It was not a hot seller. There was that kind of book, and then there was an introduction to Farley Mowat's *The Dog Who Wouldn't Be*. I just couldn't escape the CanLit stuff. My daughter Emily had just entered high school, and she came home with a reading list of recommended Canadian novels. Every title and author was spelled incorrectly. And they didn't recommend a single ECW title! I fumed. Then I wrote a nasty letter to the principal that I never mailed because Emily would have killed me. So this is what CanLit had become in the hands of high school teachers. Obviously they couldn't be counted on to fight the good fight.

By the end of the year we had all kinds of titles scheduled for release in our Canadian Fiction Studies series and were planning yet another new series—the Canadian Biography Series—which would be short biographies of well-known Canadian figures from all walks of life. The breakaway from the constraints of publishing only about literature was just around the corner. That was the way it was in publishing. Your best book was coming out next season and that would be the book that would turn things around. You just had to hang in there a little longer and finally there would be some relief from the debt, the incessant phone calls from printers, the disgruntled authors looking for their royalty cheques, the poet from Kentucky who was badgering me to publish her book about pet roosters. We were always on the brink of success. We would wangle a grant. Snag some kind of rights or distribution deal. The phone would ring.

Not too likely. It was 1991. Jack and I had been at this game for more than 15 years. There were 81 projects under production or development. Three years earlier there had only been 38. We had never taken a salary. We owed more money than ever. The credit cards were maxed. I was teaching big classes and sitting on all kinds of committees at McGill. There were graduate students to supervise, and lots of undergraduates who wanted to contest their grades, hand in late papers, stop in for a chat, ask about the readings, or consult me about various crises in their lives. Then there was the whole editorial business with Twayne and G.K. Hall, which had grown by leaps and bounds. By 1991 I had edited more than 70 volumes in the Masterwork series, a task that required me to correspond with dozens of authors and to write detailed reports on each of the books I was recommending for publication. The same held true for the two other series I was editing for those companies: Critical Essays on World Literature and the Twayne's World Author Series for Canada. I would get up early in the morning, read the books and write reports. This was a joke. It was 4:30. Why was I awake? Then I would head off to McGill for a day of teaching and advising, interspersed with calls from ECW authors. I would cut out large blocks of time for all the ECW stuff, but it was unusual for me to be able to find a full day. I was writing my own articles, usually on the weekends, and was having trouble keeping up with all the research and teaching preparation. There were dozens of papers to grade, theses to read, conference papers to write. I was constantly worried about debt. Sometimes I felt panicky. I couldn't sleep. When I did sleep, I always had the same dream: I'm in a car, careening down a road, and all of a sudden I discover that the brakes are shot. I wake up just when the car veers totally out of control, just before the fatal crash. I thought about guys my age, even runners like me, who dropped dead from heart attacks. That wouldn't be so bad. Or a massive stroke. That would be okay. But there were all those other problems I didn't have time for—brain cancer, Lou Gehrig's disease, Parkinson's (my father's affliction), Crohn's—a whole list of diseases that I stayed awake imagining, as if by imagining them I could hold them at bay. (Could you really get Parkinson's if you were actively *thinking* about it? No, because those diseases always crept up on people when they least expected it, so if you did expect it at any moment, the disease would know that, and would stay away until it had a chance to surprise you. Obviously the trick was to *always* be thinking about it, and about all the other diseases that could sneak up and get you.) Often, when I was supposed to be writing my editorial reports and figuring out how to lose more money in the stock market, I found my hand wandering to the fat *Merck Manual* sitting resolutely on the bookshelf, a constant brick-like reminder of just how much could go wrong with me in the next few seconds and certainly in the next few days. I would drive down to McGill, listening to R.E.M., thinking about CanLit, thinking about Twayne, thinking about Jack and ECW, thinking about the phagocytic system and "Primary Nonspecific Immunodeficiency Disorders" or the distinct possibility of "Fistula in Ano."

I didn't share my various neuroses with Jack. In fact, we seemed to be sharing less than ever. Back in 1988 he had sent me a postcard with a Joey Waldon illustration of an unshaven guy with a belt around his neck and this caption: "It finally got to where Bobby began missing his belt loops." The original caption did not say "Bobby" but Jack had whited out the original name, whatever it was, and stuck in mine. On the back of the card he wrote "SLOW DOWN." So I guess he was sensitive to what was going on. I think he sent me the card after I had gone with him to hear a reading by John Metcalf and Alice Munro at the University of Guelph in November of that year. Jack picked me up at the Toronto airport. I could hardly keep my eyes open during the drive. As soon as the reading started I fell asleep in the auditorium.

Jack's card was a friendly reminder that I was pushing it. By 1991, however, the messages he was sending were no longer quite so friendly. In June of that year I opened my mail to find a letter from Jack that began with these words:

> With the impending completion of CWTW and ABCMA, and the signing up of virtually all of the CFS authors, much of what we started out to do is approaching completion. The nature of the company has changed substantially, and—compared to the 1980s version—will probably be unrecognizable in a couple of years. At the same time my financial and work contribution to ECW has not lessened, and although we tried last year to equalize the efforts each of us was putting out, I don't think that has happened in fact. I would therefore like to make you an offer for your part of the company under our buy-sell shotgun agreement.

The letter went on to detail the terms that Jack proposed for the breakup. I could keep the journal if I wanted it. The company would pay me a certain amount over five years. Jack would offer Paul a small equity position in the company. I was stunned by the letter, angered, bewildered, and fearful about its implications for my personal and financial future. I also felt sidetracked by Paul, whose apparent value, in Jack's eyes, was clearly superior to mine. Jack argued that this step was necessary because I wasn't "fully involved in the game as it is currently being played," that my role was primarily in acquisitions, not in the daily affairs of the business, as if there would even be a business if no good acquisitions were made.

There were other aspects of this offer that troubled me deeply. Ever since I had been editing books for Twayne and G.K. Hall Jack had insisted that my editorial work for those companies somehow fell under the ECW wing. In other words, if I worked for another company, ECW had a claim to the fees or royalties that I earned from that work. I couldn't understand the rationale behind this argument, since, by logical extension, any money

I made should flow to ECW. Why did it matter whether that money was earned by writing, or editing, or teaching? Did ECW have a claim on my McGill salary? Did it have a claim on the meager royalties I made from my own critical articles and books? I didn't think so, but for years I had been handing over the money I made from my editorial work to the company. Not a bad source of revenue, since some of those editorial projects had done pretty well, and new titles were always appearing. Now Jack was saying that as part of his buyout offer, ECW would relinquish its claim on the Twayne royalties, as if it had any legal claim to begin with. I had given that money to the company in the hope that it might help prevent bankruptcy. Jack even allowed that I might continue to acquire manuscripts for ECW, "but I doubt that you'd want to see that happen." This did not sound like my partner speaking. The assumption of ownership over something he didn't own. The condescending generosity that would allow me to work as a freelance acquisitions editor for the company that I had cofounded, the non-recognition of what I had brought to the company that had kept it alive, and, most of all, the way in which the letter came at me out of the blue. I had always respected Jack as an upfront negotiator who would listen, and try to be fair. This was not the man I had known for 15 years.

I don't know whether Paul had a role to play in Jack's decision to make this offer. I did know that the work with Butterworths was gradually dwindling, and perhaps this made Paul more eager to secure his position in the company before it was too late. Or perhaps Jack had just had enough of the dunning phone calls, the endless worries about money, and the sense that he was there, holding the fort in Toronto, and doing it all alone. I didn't see this. I saw myself building series that would make the company prosper. I saw myself running a journal that would own a big chunk of CanCrit and that would pay off like good real estate one day (which it did). I saw a troubled company churning forward, and I felt deeply involved in its every move, frustrated by my distance from the centre of the action.

Whatever my feelings, something had to be done. Because we had a "shotgun" buy-sell agreement, I could have invited Jack to make me a formal offer to buy me out, and then turned around and forced him to accept exactly the same terms he had offered me, which meant that I could have taken over the company, and left him out in the cold. Of course, I considered this, but it was not realistic. I would have to give up my job at McGill and move to Toronto, since the business could not really have been operated out of Quebec, which, at the time, did not have nearly as much grant money for publishers as did Ontario. Besides, I wasn't ready to give up teaching, and I didn't want to live in Toronto.

I'm not exactly sure how we worked through this crisis. We talked. I tried to be honest about my feelings and concerns. It was agreed that I would take on additional responsibilities, in order to lessen Jack's load. In particular, I became responsible for the bill paying, and wrote all the cheques. Now the creditors started to call me instead of Jack. The storm seemed to pass, for the moment. We worked it out. But I was shaken, and I knew that in the coming years I would have to find more time for this company, even if there was no more time. There were new courses to teach, a book of essays I had edited on the Canadian canon was about to appear, and there was a whole new series—the Canadian Biography Series—in the making. And there were the ever-present challenges of avoiding bankruptcy or the calling of our multiple loans. By 1991 we owed $160,000 to the bank and another $90,000 on various credit cards and lines of credit. Yet we were planning to double our production, from 16 to 30 titles in 1992. For the first time I found myself working on books that were not connected with literature at all. Biographies of Pierre Trudeau, Alex Colville, k.d. lang. I started thinking about politics, music, art. The books rolled out. Our 1992 catalogue opened with a letter to librarians announcing that the previous year "was our most successful year ever." Thanks to those librarians, who seemed interested in our academic titles, some of the books had done reasonably well. There was still a ton of debt, and lots of bills, but there was energy moving us forward, a renewed belief that our new series would be the best one yet. Then we got lucky. One of the titles in that new series took off. And when a title takes off, it always opens a door. In our case, what lay behind that newly opened door was a market we had hardly touched. That market had a familiar name: America.

CHAPTER SEVEN

Our 1992 catalogue announced the first few titles in our Canadian Biography Series—short books on the lives of Alice Munro, Dorothy Livesay, and Stephen Leacock. The whole conception of the series was oriented towards school and library sales. We advertised the "durable binding" and "easy to read typeface" used in these books, but in fact we hoped the books would be quickly destroyed by the hundreds of students who would undoubtedly line up to find out all the gritty details of Livesay's life. As far as we were concerned, the more damage the students did to the books the better. The libraries would be forced to reorder. For the sake of uniformity (and cost-cutting) we used a template-like cover design, changing only colours and the picture of the book's subject. The layout was as boring as you could get, but I think we achieved the ineffable look of consistent dullness associated with library and reference books of the time.

If regular people wanted to read these biographies that was fine, but we still didn't really think of ourselves as trade publishers, although there were several trade titles on our backlist. The main thrust of our activity was still Canadian criticism intended for the library market. In 1992 we were able to announce the completion of the first 20 volumes in the *Canadian Writers and Their Works* series. That only took us a decade. Meanwhile, the journal kept pumping out issues. With the grants it received and modest subscription revenues, *Essays on Canadian Writing* more or less broke even, and every once in a while we got nice little cheques from various publishers who used the journal material in essay collections and reprints. We also seemed to be able to manage a few poetry titles a year, mainly because, again, the federal and provincial grants covered the publication costs, even if most of the poetry books only sold a meagre few hundred copies. However, any profits we were able to bank were quickly offset by our commitment to publishing money-losing reference works, so long as they had something to do with our suicidal mandate: Canadian literature. Why else would we support a 1,000-page bibliography of English-Canadian short stories "with 20,000 citations and 11,000,000 characters filling 1,000 pages of 9-point type" (as one of our flyers boasted), or a 400-page annotated bibliography of A.M. Klein, or a 600-page bibliography of theatre history in Canada, from the beginnings to 1984?

There was always some rationale for undertaking these projects, which caused endless headaches for everyone involved and required bundles of cash for their expensive printing and binding. There might be a government grant that would partially offset the cost. Or maybe the author had a research fund that could be diverted to us. Perhaps there would be some esoteric program run by some obscure government agency that would cover part of the cost, so long as we filled out a bunch of application forms and sweet-talked the bureaucrats and waited six months to find out if the funding would come through. But the bottom line was that no business could really make it this way. In our idealistic moments we imagined that Canadian high school, public, and university libraries would have to purchase copies of these essential reference works. A new vision started to emerge: ECW didn't really originate in a journal called *Essays on Canadian Writing*. No way. It stood for *Essential* Canadian Writing, and sooner, rather than later, we hoped the libraries would get that point.

They didn't. In fact, library budgets were being cut back. We could sell a few hundred copies of some of the more expensive reference books, but almost never more than a thousand of any reference or critical title, and in order to break even we were going to have to do a lot better than that. It was the old story about the limited nature of the Canadian marketplace. If you could sell 300 copies of a reference book on Canadian literature in Canada you were sure to lose money or possibly break even with some kind of external support. But if you published the same kind of reference book on American literature in the US and sold 3,000 copies, you could definitely make ends meet, and probably walk away with some profit. The market just was not there when it came to our central product. And American libraries had little interest in our list because most of them didn't know our books existed. They hardly knew that Canada existed. We had no American distributor, and our limited promotional mailings to American libraries only resulted in small sales. Then, all of a sudden, things changed.

In 1992 we released the fourth title in the Canadian Biography Series—the first biography of k.d. lang. At that time our trade titles were being distributed in the United States by General Distribution, the company we had signed up with after the Butterworths deal went sour a year earlier. We were just getting to know General and its president, Jack Stoddart. Athough Stoddart clearly had big plans for Canada there was not much action through General in the States; they would fill orders that came their way, but there was no sales force to speak of and no effort to push the Canadian titles in any concerted way. Several months after the lang biography appeared something strange happened. Orders! There were lots of orders for that book, coming through General. Then, things got even more interesting. Jack had a talk with David Wilk, who was running an American distribution company called InBook out of East Haven, Connecticut. InBook catered to a number of small, independent publishing companies, many of them oriented to feminist, lesbian, gay, and alternative lifestyles. InBook's clients had picked up on the lang biography and were wondering why it was so hard to find copies in the United States. Wilk invited Jack to a meeting in East Haven, where InBook had its warehouse and offices. He wanted to distribute the book in the US, for real. Although I was sceptical, Jack made the trip. According to Jack, InBook central was a bustling place, with crates of books coming and going. Wilk had big plans for InBook. He was ready to sign with us for the k.d. lang bio distribution rights, and he expressed interest in taking on other books on a title-by-title basis. We signed. All of a sudden, we had an American distributor.

The first thing InBook encouraged us to do was to redesign the book's cover. Punch it up, they said. Make the picture of k.d. bigger, use more colour. They were thinking about the trade market, and talking to a publisher that had little experience in trade publishing. It was a different world. The redesigned cover wasn't much of an improvement, but it put lang front and centre. Sales started to take off. The book was no bestseller, but we sold thousands of copies and had to reprint to meet demand. Who was buying this book, and how did the word get out? Although we had published the biography because of lang's Canadian roots, never really thinking about how she was one of the first lesbian pop stars to really come out, she had a massive following in the American lesbian network, and that network talked up the book, which got it mentioned on lists of popular gay/lesbian titles, ensuring a continuous flow of orders from what was, for us, a most unlikely source. Feminist discussion groups also zeroed in on the title. Clearly this was an untapped market. And just as clearly there were some big lessons to be learned here about how to sell books: identify a niche audience, figure out how to reach it, and give it a product it wanted. There was nothing startling about this discovery. The big difference was that we had always set our sights on relatively small niche audiences—Canadian academics, fans of Archibald Lampman, or diehard followers of Frederick Philip Grove. But the niche we had now discovered was huge, and, unlike Canadian professors, a good part of that audience was more than ready to spend money on books about the entertainers and writers they admired. What we also began to see was the massive power of the Internet, even in its relatively undeveloped early stages. It was the Internet discussion groups that had allowed lang's fans to spread the word. From this point on we always used the Internet to target fan bases and discussion groups in order to generate interest in specific titles.

It didn't take long for us to focus on publishing niche-related titles. That shift forever changed the direction of the company. If you're a publisher sitting on a sizeable backlist with lots of titles that continue to sell, year after year, you can afford to make some mistakes, follow your ideals, pursue a publishing program that is focused and consistent. You may even have the luxury of being able to reject all kinds of submissions in the interest of maintaining the high standards for which you are known. However, if you've got yourself into a ton of debt by publishing books about Canadian literature for 15 years, and your back is against the wall, and all of a sudden you see some money rolling in, you might just think about changing your program dramatically, embracing the source of that newfound cash.

That's what ECW did, in part, and the decision to move in that new direction permanently altered the company, taking it down the road of trade publishing and into all kinds of niche markets very far removed from CanLit. One year I was editing a scholarly journal and publishing bibliographies of Robertson Davies and books about the theatre of James Reaney. Not too many years later I was still editing that journal, but ECW was publishing books about *The X-Files*, Muddy Waters, George Clooney, extreme martial arts, Godzilla, and the Dave Matthews Band, along with Canadian novels, poetry, and a smattering of literary criticism. That kind of shift is bound to be wrenching and filled with surprises. I liked that. I liked the idea that the phone could ring and I didn't know whether it would be a prize fighter or a professor on the end of the line. But every once in a while on that trade publishing road, I had to ask myself why I was so enthusiastic about publishing a photo-filled biography of Jennifer Lopez, or why I found myself wanting to sign up a history of Christian rock and roll, or what made me invest in a book about the very worst of pro wrestling when I had never watched an hour of wrestling in my life. I would be preparing a lecture about postmodernism and Robert Kroetsch's fiction while I was thinking about the design of a full-colour, glossy book on the Dixie Chicks. I would gear up for a seminar on the Canadian long poem, intoxicated by the incredible sense of longing and absence in Michael Ondaatje's *Tin Roof*, while I was worrying about the lawsuit Ondaatje was threatening to launch against ECW over our upcoming unauthorized biography. I knew that ECW's image was changing once we started to get e-mail regularly, around 1994. Every once in a while I would open a message that was meant for the people at Extreme Championship Wrestling, the alter-ECW. Was that my other side? Was that the company I might have founded if I had never become Dr. Delicious? Jack always joked that the most successful book we could do would be called *ECW by ECW*. The wrestling fans would eat it up, even as they wondered why this history of their favourite sport had so much to say about some heavy-duty chick wrestlers called Dorothy Livesay and Alice Munro.

The big changes didn't happen overnight. Publishing is slow. You decide you want to move in a new direction, pursue a different audience. That decision itself can be made fairly quickly. But then you have to research the topic, find out how big the niche really is, how addicted the fans are, whether they are addicted and rich, or addicted and poor, in which case nothing will really move them to put down cash for a book. And even if you know the niche is there, you have to figure out how to reach it. Once you've decided that you are indeed going to publish a book about Melissa Etheridge you have to find the perfect writer, someone who is truly plugged into the community you are appealing to, but preferably someone without an agent, because the agent will usually demand too high an advance, making it difficult to turn a profit. Then there is the business of actually getting the manuscript out of the author by the due date, editing it, securing photos, clearing permissions, figuring out how to design the book, typesetting, proofing, printing, praying, and spreading the word. All of which meant that we might have been thinking more like trade publishers in 1992, but we didn't have a viable trade publishing program with solid US distribution until 1995.

Still, the shifts were palpable. On one level, we continued to pursue the Canadian market by trying to develop reference series that would have wider markets. Jack was working on a guide to MBA schools and a guide to law schools that would appear on an annual basis. The Canadian Biography Series began to embrace all kinds of popular Canadian figures—Wayne Gretzky, David Cronenberg, Peter Gzowski, Pierre Trudeau.

Jack believed there was a pretty big market for books about famous Broadway plays, so he commissioned titles like *The Making of My Fair Lady* and *The Making of Gypsy*.

We had also been studying the way other publishers who dealt with literary criticism handled their product lines. My experience with Twayne and G.K. Hall had taught me that once libraries recognized a series they would usually place a standing order for every volume, an observation that led us to continue betting on multi-volume series like the Canadian Biography Series and the Canadian Fiction Studies Series. But we were also influenced by the publishing strategies developed by Gale Research, a Michigan-based company that had been using ECW material for years. Gale specialized in slicing, dicing, and recycling literary criticism. They would collect material on a major author and put out a special volume devoted to his or her work, then they would use some of that material in another volume on great American writers, then they would use it again in their collection devoted to contemporary fiction, then they would use it a fourth time in their history of American literature, and so on. Back in the early days of ECW we had the impression that Gale was just a big, unthinking machine, with thousands of employees scowering the critical landscape like vultures, looking for scraps of criticism they could bring together and regurgitate in endless forms. Was there really any thinking going on at that company, or was Gale propelled by a pack of editorial cannibals, pumping out product?

I decided to test the thesis that there was no critical intelligence at work there. In 1976, *Essays on Canadian Writing* had put out a few slender issues and was not yet listed in the various periodical indexes that would direct people to our content. What would happen if this little startup magazine told Gale that it wanted to review an entire Gale series? I liked the idea of trying them out with a request to review their Contemporary Authors series, which ran to 64 massive volumes, each of which was about 500 pages long. I figured we might as well ask for the entire Contemporary Literary Criticism series too—another measly six volumes. The total request was for about 35,000 printed pages. I sent out our standard book review request form, asking them to please send the 70 books as soon as possible. Our deadline was tight. I tossed the letter in a mailbox and forgot about it. Then, about two months later, there was a call from a trucking company. They had a delivery to make to our 100 square foot office at York. Sure, bring it up. What arrived, in about 15 heavy boxes, was both complete series. Well, I thought, I had better review this. I gave the 64 volumes two pages in *ECW* number 6, and Jack gave the critical series another two pages. Four pages devoted to 35,000 pages, in a journal with a subscription base of about 200. Even before the reviews were published we had hustled every volume down to a used bookstore in Toronto, which paid us a couple of hundred bucks for the whole shebang. Just enough money to keep Visa at bay for another month. Anyhow, Gale deserved to have all those books disposed of in that way: they had referred to us as *Essays in Canadian Criticism*. Obviously there was no rigour to *their* editorial methods.

This was the Gale I remembered when we started some of our own series in the years to come. How could Gale's slice-and-dice approach be adapted to ECW? In some ways we had tried this approach by publishing monographs that were self-contained excerpts from the *Canadian Writers and Their Works* series. By the time our big series were finished, however, we began to think more seriously along the lines of the Gale model. The only difference was that, unlike Gale, we could not afford to buy material from other publishers, so we had to cannibalize our own. Since George Woodcock had provided introductions to all of the *CWTW* volumes, we could recycle that material into a book and give it the Woodcock imprimatur: *George Woodcock's Guide to Canadian Poetry*, or *George Woodcock's Guide to Canadian Fiction*. And because each of those *CWTW* volumes included a biographical essay, we could pull those out and create spinoff titles like *ECW's Biographical Guide to Canadian Poets*. Whatever would sell.

After dealing with Gale for years, encouraging them to buy as much material from us as possible, we were surprised to receive a call one day from Bob Elster, a Gale executive who had been given the responsibility of setting up Gale Canada, a division of the giant company that would focus on the Canadian library market. What soon became apparent was just how little the company knew about the state of reference material on Canadian literature. I had several conversations with Elster in which I tried to give him the lay of the land, always pointing out that ECW had charted the territory, and suggesting that we could help Gale achieve their lofty objectives, which had been set out by Gale's super-giant parent company, the sprawling Thomson Corporation, which had been relentlessly swallowing up every library and reference publisher it could get its hands on. Elster seemed like a pretty casual guy, but I suspected he was under enormous pressure to meet Thomson's expectations when it came to numbers. I imagined him sitting around a table with the Thomson honchos, who would spell out exactly how many units of this and that would have to be developed and sold in order for Gale Canada to stay in business, and in order for Elster's reputation within the corporation to stay intact.

We had been developing ideas for all kinds of new series that would be of interest to Gale. One was a multi-volume reference work, modelled on *Canadian Writers and Their Works*, that would be called *Canadian Painters and Their Works*. There had never been a library reference series devoted to Canadian art, and it seemed like an idea that would appeal to librarians. We already had a detailed proposal in hand for this project and had lined up a series editor, as well as possible contributors who would write on the 100 or so artists covered by the series. We were also kicking around the idea of developing similar series on athletes, politicians, musicians, and so on.

After discussing various projects and what ECW could offer Gale, our conversations turned to a familiar theme: what could Gale buy from ECW, and how much could we get out of them, and how soon? A couple of months later Elster suggested that maybe Thomson would just buy ECW outright. Fabulous. I fantasized about the purchase price, which would obviously be substantial. For them, buying ECW would be like picking up a bag of peanuts with some loose change you found in your pocket. And besides, we were the competition. It made sense for them to absorb us, so they could have the terrain to themselves. The best part of this was that Thomson was a Canadian corporation, so the Foreign Investment Review rules didn't apply in this case, as they had in the failed Butterworths deal, which would have involved some fancy footwork in order to skirt the regulations. No, this time it could be fast and clean. All that had to happen was for Elster to convince the higher-ups to pony up the cash.

If only it were that simple. Thomson wanted numbers, spreadsheets, reports, title analyses, legal documents. We had already prepared a lot of this material for Butterworths, at terrific cost to Jack in terms of time and labour. Now he returned to the Butterworths file, updating it, amassing reams of paper, grumbling about Thomson's never-ending requests for more and more data. This went on for weeks while we held our breath, waiting for the offer that would finally release us from the debt that never seemed to disappear. Obviously Thomson's interest in ECW meant they saw the tremendous potential of our various series. They understood that, properly marketed by a company with their huge resources, those series would just take off and produce the profits we had always dreamed of. And if Elster managed to acquire ECW on behalf of Thomson it would be a big feather in his cap, proof that he had done his homework and found just the right company to further the goal of making Thomson even richer.

Yes, things were looking good. Very good. Until a little e-mail mishap occurred. By this time we were using e-mail on a regular basis. Jack and I had been going back and forth on the Gale deal for weeks, with Jack complaining about the endless paperwork involved. I knew that he didn't like Elster, whom he found evasive and inefficient. Like Jack, one of the things that bugged me most was people who said they would do something and then delayed, or found a way to get around their commitment. Well, we didn't have to love Elster. We only had to sell him the company. One day during the process, when Jack was particularly ticked off, he sent me a message saying what a dud he thought Elster was, complaining about his foot-dragging. The only problem was that instead of sending this little missive to me, he mistakenly sent it to Elster himself, thereby ensuring the swift end to our dealings with Thomson and Gale Canada.

Now that we had screwed ourselves, I wondered where Thomson would turn its sights. Would it gobble up some of the university presses? There wasn't much in the way of other opportunities if what they really wanted was to get at the library market for Canadian literature. But here was the surprise: after about six years of poking around in Canada and checking out the terrain, Gale Canada quietly closed its doors and Elster moved somewhere else in the organization. However, what they had managed to produce under the Gale Canada imprint bore a striking resemblance to some of the ECW proposals—series with names like *Contemporary Canadian Artists*, *Contemporary Canadian Musicians*, and *Contemporary Canadian Biographies*. But the fact that they pulled out after publishing these series suggested that even Thomson, with all its resources, could not make a Canadian office self-sufficient, probably because the titles developed by Gale Canada just didn't generate enough sales to warrant a separate office. If Thomson couldn't make it how could we, with our persistently limited resources and our inability to advertise the titles effectively?

The failure of the Gale deal inevitably made me even more cynical about the nature of our business. Even under the best circumstances, it seemed impossible to sustain a publishing program devoted to Canadian literature and criticism. I tried to keep my cynicism out of the classroom and to remind myself that I had gotten into this because of the Canadian poets and fiction writers whom I admired, not because I wanted to get rich quick on CanLit. But every time a deal went sour, I couldn't help but review the time I had devoted to CanCrit, and I couldn't help but wonder where professordom might have taken me if I hadn't spent all those years getting further and further into debt.

I was imprisoned by that debt. The irony was that, in my personal financial life, I had avoided debt at every turn. I hated owing anybody anything. The business, on the other hand, always seemed to require cash to fund tomorrow's project—the project that would finally make a dent in the credit card balances or help to pay off our multiple bank loans. We did speculate about the ultimate exit route if those projects failed and the bank called our loan again. We would just fire everybody (all three employees), shut down the offices, cancel virtually everything, and put out three or four books a year. As new grants came in we would apply them to the loans, along with the sales revenues from our backlist. It would be illegal to use the grants in this way, since they were awarded to cover future publication, not existing costs, but you have to do what you have to do, and besides, was the Canada Council going to sue us if we went out of business?

Although we had acquired some backing provided by the federal government through loan guarantees provided to publishers, I never believed that if the bank kicked us out, the government would come rushing in to save us. They would probably get around to saving part of us, but then the picture would get murky. For one thing, we had personally guaranteed these loans. I didn't see the bank waiting patiently for the federal government to cover them after they had decided to terminate us. That was fantasy land. No, they would go after us directly and settle with the feds later, if in fact the government program did what it was supposed to do in terms of backing us. No one knew how it would work, since no one had never been called upon to support any other publisher in default. Even if they did get behind us, I knew it was not going to be clean. My credit record would be affected. Whatever assets I had would probably be frozen until things got sorted out. There would be stress. I would owe lots of money to somebody; that was certain. What choice was there but to carry on, in the hope that the ship could gradually be turned around as we developed our trade list and left behind the CanCrit publishing program that had always defined us?

I knew that the huge amounts we owed also stressed out Jack. From time to time he would express deep concern about how the bank was treating us or how the feds might or might not come to our aid. He was always sniffing around for new sources of cash. Eventually he got us in with the Federal Business Development Bank, after convincing them that, sure, we could handle the payments on the big loan they were about to give us as well as all our current payments because we had a great business plan that was going to cause a big pop in revenues over the next few years.

I didn't understand how Jack managed to convince the bank that this would be the case. He had a set of magic cash flow projections that he played with every time he met with a bank officer. The numbers got shifted around according to what the banks needed to see. If they wanted lots of revenue in six months Jack's spreadsheet made that happen. Did they want to see even more money a year from now? No problem. Jack just pumped in more figures. When the banks asked Jack to explain how we could possibly make that much money just six months from now he was entirely prepared to deliver a detailed description of each upcoming title, our various advertising campaigns, our staff incentive programs, our exploding typesetting business, our recent biography of Leonard Cohen, our infatuation with the Sabon font, and on and on until the bank person began to slump and glaze over. Please shut this guy up and get this paperwork off my desk. Then the paper would disappear into some bank pipeline leading to the department called Risk. Inevitably someone from Risk would call with a Question. Jack would give them an Answer, but I think he preferred, first, to soften them up by talking about some new CanLit venture in painstaking detail, until the Risk person was prepared to hear any answer, anything, if only this monologue about Sinclair Ross or Canadian culture would mercifully stop, once and for all. Then they would go away again. Who ever knew that a prodigious commitment to Canadian literature would have such a profound impact on the busy people who made money happen?

The bank managers and the people from Risk were always being switched around and sent off to new branches. You could be introduced to a credit manager one month and the next month someone else would answer her phone. Or the old voice message would still be there because the new person had just started and hadn't recorded a new message yet. Once in a while you would get a real tough nut who took a hard look at our figures and realized how ridiculous it all was and decided to put us on notice. If they got really snarky Jack would write letters to their superiors, outlining our unique contribution to Canadian culture, stressing the federal government's loan guarantee, and asking that we be treated with more respect. Astonishingly, this usually worked. Someone higher up would call up the snarky person and say "Look, these guys are just peons and the feds will cover their ass when they go under, so why not just be nice and give the bank a good name?" Then the snarky person would call up and make some arrangement, and we knew we were okay until his inevitable replacement showed up a few months down the road, at which point the whole show would start again.

Since it became more and more difficult to keep my views of the CanCrit industry out of the classroom, I decided that I should try bringing it right into the classroom, in a formal way. In 1993 I gave a course called "The Politics of Canadian Literature." The course description makes it sound like the main focus would be on the Canadian canon, and that was true. I had been writing about the curious process that allows one novel or poem to gain precedence and power while another is marginalized and forgotten. I wanted to test some ideas with the students. But I was probably more interested in power, in the people who seemed to be running the CanLit show. The students didn't share my interest. It's not that they couldn't appreciate the fact that literary politics played a large part in the construction of the Canadian canon. It's just that they came to see that literary politics inevitably came down to literary personalities, and that in order to really get into the debate it was also necessary to know those personalities. Students could read a book-length interview with Robert Kroetsch in *Labyrinths of Voice*, but how many could really be expected to be more enthusiastic about that interview than about reading Kroetsch's novels and poems? Even the understanding that Kroetsch thought the long poem was like lovemaking didn't seem to have much impact. They knew absolutely and totally and completely that the long poem was not like lovemaking. They could read Frank Davey's *Canadian Literary Power* and even find a whole chapter of the book attacking their beloved Professor Lecker, but unless they were really grounded in the theoretical issues and unless they understood Davey's own need for power they were just not going to get into this. They appreciated Linda Hutcheon's clear explanations in *The Canadian Postmodern*, but ultimately the postmodern issues Hutcheon raised were not connected with their daily lives. They could talk about historiographic metafiction and irony, but this wasn't where their passions lay. They knew that theory was important and intellectually interesting. Still, they liked a good story.

Sometimes it was a little too easy for me to get caught up in the political infighting and to forget about some of the reasons I had come to Canadian literature in the first place, without any knowledge of the canon or the critics. And often, just when it seemed that I had gone over some edge and could never get back to that original sense of the poetry and fiction, something would jolt me back to a kind of naive awareness of what drew me to CanLit. It might be hearing a recording of P.K. Page reading from her work, or looking at old anthologies of Canadian literature in the Rare Book Room and wondering about the era in which their editors lived, or it might be meeting a contemporary writer in the flesh and quaffing the few beers it took to wash the cynicism away.

The end of the course on the politics of Canadian literature also marked a turning point for ECW. I may have been thinking about Page's sensuous, mysterious lines, but I also had to start thinking about our first exhibit at BookExpo America, the huge book show organized annually by the American Booksellers Association. The show took place in June of each year, most often in Chicago or New York. My first visit was an eye-opening experience. Publishers who could afford them took booths that lined long lanes in cavernous display halls. The place was piled high with thousands and thousands of titles. The design of each booth was crucial, since so much depended on attracting the attention of potential buyers over a three-day period. Gaudy and tasteful displays drew attention to the current bestsellers, while publishers explored every imaginable gimmick to lure bookstore buyers to their booths.

Walking into the exhibition halls was like entering a carnival full of lights and sound, with signs and book covers assaulting you at every turn. Then there were the personalities who had shown up to promote their books. At the end of one aisle I could see Annie Sprinkle, the porn star, distributing autographed cards with her photo on them and yukking it up with curious bystanders, explaining why her new autobiography was just such a penetrating read. She was standing, almost nude, next to a wizened little guy who had published his own book about extending life through the wonders of cruciferous vegetable juicing. He sat forlornly in a tiny booth, fondling his juicer. Around the corner Tim Zagat, the Donald Trump of restaurant guides, was handing out hundreds of copies of his latest survey of New York dining spots. He loved his generosity. He loved his pin-striped suit. He loved his manicure. Four women walked by in tight black leather and latex outfits with Catwoman hoods, brandishing whips, their laced-up boots and tops emblazoned with the title of a new S & M manual. Down another aisle, Roger Ebert, sur-rounded by publicists and handlers and security agents, was signing copies of his just-released movie guide. Another publisher was offering cupcakes and brownies to promote their latest dessert cookbook. The cookbook author, an anorexic-looking woman with graying hair, scurried around a makeshift kitchen looking worried. A lot of the conventioneers tugged small wagons or toted complimentary canvas bags stuffed with free offerings—books, toys, candies, pens, dolls, t-shirts, CDs, coupons, badges, little bags of M&Ms. The biggest publishers would take up hundreds of feet of real estate, their aisles carpeted in wall-to-wall shades that matched the special furniture and lighting they had imported for the occasion. You could line up for free t-shirts promoting a new book or a famous author, or get one of the advance copies publishers gave away by the truckload. The smaller publishers did the best they could, putting money into posters or special eye-catching book displays. It was a book orgy.

InBook encouraged us to have a presence in the section of the hall they had booked for their client publishers. We shared the cost of a booth with Quarry Press, which was run by Bob Hilderley. We paid $1,500 US for five shelves in a booth that was about six feet wide. Three of those feet were ours. The upcoming titles we displayed were still the oddly mixed products of a company in transition from scholarly to commercial publishing. A biography of Leonard Cohen and another on Tony Hillerman next to a study of A.J.M. Smith's metaphysical poetry. A gay/lesbian guide to travel in Canada sitting beside a 600-page study of patterns in the writing of Alice Munro. Surrounding us were the other booths of InBook publishers. We were a happy crew. To our left was a press that specialized in books about extreme sex and bondage. I saw several titles expounding the pleasures of using medieval-looking devices and machines, with detailed illustrations. There was another on the benefits of strangulation and orgasm, and another showing gruesome, unedited photos from homicide investigations. "We've done very well with this," the publisher told me enthusiastically. A little further down was a press run by militant feminists in black Goth outfits who specialized in covert political action. Against men. Their fingernails were really long. They seemed quite friendly, but I was watching my back. Across the aisle was the booth run by Giant Ass Publishing, and next to them a company devoted to comic books and gay graphic novels, hosted by three all-American looking guys wearing creased khakis and button-down shirts. They stood next to the people from Firebrand Books, whose titles included the very successful Dykes to Watch Out For series. On our right there was a substantial booth displaying a range of how-to books on bomb making and urban guerilla warfare. We were right at home.

Well, not really. The hundreds of displays around me provided concrete evidence of how much we had to change to enter the world of trade publishing. These covers used big, bold colours. Their titles could be seen from miles away. They had captivating images that drew you towards them. And the publishers were trying hard to brand their products, to create an identity that book buyers could recognize easily. What was our identity? It was hard to explain to people who stopped by the booth, which made the need to create a commercial identity seem all that more important. InBook contributed to this sense of urgency, not only by encouraging us to enter the publishing scene at Book Expo, but also by insisting that we present our upcoming titles at their bi-annual sales conferences, where they would question the titles, our marketing plans, or the design of our covers, which they wanted bolder, more commercial, much more in your face. I could already see that this would pose a problem, since we were working with a handful of designers, most of whom were committed to producing the kind of reserved, sometimes elegant covers we used on our scholarly books. In particular, I could see the potential conflicts with Paul Davies, who was still doing most of our cover designs. Paul was a great typographer and a man of many skills, but I just couldn't seem to convey my sense of how I wanted the covers to be radically different in the future. No matter how I tried to push for bigger and brighter, there was always disagreement about position, size, colour— the whole look and feel of every cover. We would fax samples back and forth, the faxes making it even harder to distinguish what colours we were talking about, or how a design might look when it got into print. Eventually I would get colour proofs that looked dramatically different from what I thought I would be seeing. And inevitably conflicts multi-plied as I tried to sort out why the cover I was looking seemed the opposite of the one I had in mind. We had no way of viewing or transmitting digital images at that time. The technology was just opening up.

It wasn't only the difficulty of designing those covers that pointed to the perils and tribulations of entering the trade publishing world. Those sales conferences we attended were always a major source of stress. InBook scheduled them in Chicago twice a year. We had to show up with our cover designs for each title that would be in the InBook catalogue, and we had to be prepared to say why they were special and would sell like hotcakes. For years we would arrive at these gatherings with covers in the rough, or even with simply an image that we hoped to use on the cover, even though the deadline for completed covers had passed. Despite the surface enthusiasm of the many sales reps who had assembled in the overheated hotel conference room to hear two days' worth of presentations by a wide range of independent publishers, I always sensed, especially in those early years, that they thought we were a pair of amateurs. Who were these Canadian dudes with their books about Northrop Frye and their gay/lesbian guide to Canada? How was I going to make a book on Leonard Cohen sound good enough for them to sell, let alone a biography of Frederick Philip Grove?

How could my presentation possibly compete with those of the more radical InBook publishers, who stood at the front of the room, speaking with conviction about their latest offering on creative bondage or winning sex methods? One year, I heard a publisher talk for her full two minutes about why her company was about to publish the second, revised edition of a highly successful book on vaginal fisting. She described the competing titles in detail (there were several!), stressed the authority of her publication and the author's credentials, and added that what made the new edition really special was the presence of full-colour photos. I imagined it as a kind of kinky coffee table book. The publisher fielded a number of questions. There seemed to be a lot of enthusiasm for this title among the reps. Next to that, what did ECW have to offer a jaded book buyer in Miami or L.A.? How could those reps possibly get excited about selling a few thousand copies of our titles when they could put their efforts into vaginal fisting? And how could I ever do justice to our titles in a measly two minutes? "More than enough time to make the case," I was told. But by the time those sales reps who were listening to my two minutes got to present our titles to *their* clients a month or two later, especially the chain store buyers, they might have ten seconds to make the case. And those buyers could make or break your season. As the large chains displaced the independent bookstores from coast to coast, it became harder and harder to publish titles that might appeal to particular regional interests, just as it became more difficult to introduce new writers.

There were a few strong independent stores left, but for the most part our sales reps had to appeal to a handful of buyers or wholesalers who would evaluate a title on the spot and decide whether it would live or die. Inevitably this bred cynicism among the reps. They knew that the buyers had to turn over stock. You might have the greatest new novelist in the world, but that writer was not going to get shelf space unless you could assure the buyer that there would be significant money expended on marketing and promotion. And that money just wasn't there for the small, independent publishers. Eventually, the exceptionally talented young writer who was first published by a small press willing to take a chance would end up with Random House, which had the budget to get that writer's book on the shelves. At one point I proposed that ECW spend a substantial amount of money to buy one square foot of national space next to the cash registers at one of the chains ("product placement"), only to be told that that kind of real estate was owned by the big guys and that ECW didn't have the money or the presence to get in on that land, no matter how good the title. Besides, I learned, the space had long ago been booked on a permanent basis. Within that kind of system, there was very little room for innovation by small and medium-sized houses. The reps knew this and encouraged the smaller publishers to develop lists that would appeal to the all-powerful chain store buyers. There was no joy in this formula. The reps I was addressing might make a living by working with those buyers, but it couldn't have been much fun. Understandably, they were a cynical bunch who thought about books in terms of dollars and units and shelf space and megabookstore nomenclature (as in, "What section of the store will this go in?" or "There's no section for this title"). I can only remember one or two instances when one of those reps said they had really enjoyed reading a book. In fairness to them, however, reading books was not their job, nor did they have time to study their clients' titles in great depth. Their skill was in sizing up a book immediately and in understanding whether or not it would fly. Reading had nothing to do with that.

I often returned from these sales conferences feeling torn and depressed. We had no money to pay for our trips there, or our two hotel rooms, or the upscale restaurants I liked to frequent while we were away on these business trips ("It's a valid business charge," I told myself as our debt continued to climb). I would be scouring the local Zagat guide for the most interesting place to have lunch while Jack pointed to a grubby-looking diner and said, "Time to fill the tank." Later I found out about priceline.com, the online travel agency that auctioned off hotel rooms at ridiculously low prices. We found ourselves checking into the most luxurious suites in Chicago and New York and then meeting in one of our rooms to discuss the absence of cash. I thought about our conversations when we met on these trips and realized that we were both together and apart. We could talk about the sales reps, exchange gossip, fill each other in on the latest deal or plan. There would be some chuckles. But I could see that our worlds had begun to drift apart. Each of us was developing titles independently. Jack would tell me a bit about a few of his upcoming projects and I would think some were good and some would be a disaster. I'm sure he thought the same when I told him what I was working on. Yet he was fiercely proud, and once he had set his mind on a plan it was hard to slow him down. He believed that a person should be given the freedom to make his own mistakes and to learn from them, which is great if there aren't huge financial consequences, but lousy if it means you're going to lose your house. I knew he thought I was messing up on some of my titles but his determination to abide by my decisions almost always trumped his impulse to intervene. I adopted his principle. I'd look at a title he had just signed and would think it was going to bomb, but I shut my mouth and crossed my fingers, hoping it wouldn't.

Jack was always calm on the outside, but I think he was churning within. He kept going over and over the reasons why various titles had sold and others had failed. As time went on, he applied the results of his analyses with a vengeance. He would support the publication of poetry and fiction because it gave the press a good rep and because the grants would more or less cover the cost of production. ("It's a wash.") However, his real interest was in developing titles that would make money but had no value to him personally. I was slower to give up my interest in academic titles but inevitably I started to embrace the general cynicism of the industry. In 1992 I was still involved in completing the Canadian Fiction Studies series. When we ended that series a year later, we had put out 33 titles. They were mainly academic. Two years later I was publishing biographies of Alex Colville and Michael Ondaatje. They were a bit more tradey, but still academic books in disguise. By 1996 I got the point: I was signing contracts for biographies of Melissa Etheridge, Shania Twain, and George Clooney, along with a book on financial management by Brian Costello, a Canadian money-management guru. I didn't give a damn about George Clooney. Why was I doing this? Jack was cranking out huge books filled with hockey and baseball statistics, biographies of Muddy Waters and King Clancy. All of this next to the final volumes of the *Canadian Writers and Their Works* series, a large-print biography of Lucy Maud Montgomery, a biography of Margaret Laurence. George Clooney and Margaret Laurence? You had to wonder. And why were we publishing large-print books for the blind? (They got grants.)

The development and production of these titles was a constant source of anxiety. Between 1990 and 1994 we churned out more than 100 titles on revenue that was never enough to meet our expanding production costs. We negotiated with the printers for more time. We played with the cash flow statements so the bank would stay out of our hair. We kept looking for support money on every title—a grant, an institutional purchase, a bulk sale, a new credit card, a hidden credit line, a scam. Somehow we were driven forward by the idea that this was all going to work out in the end because we were getting better at this, weren't we?

I think our unstated reasoning was that if we just stayed the course and learned from our mistakes and broke into the American market things were bound to get better eventually. That was all good, except that I didn't have one job, I had two. As soon as I finished teaching my courses, holding my office hours, supervising graduate students, and fulfilling my responsibility to various departmental and faculty committees I ran over to the ECW office a few blocks away, wolfing down a bagel en route. I'd find Holly swamped in production issues connected with the journal and the books. The phone was ringing, there was a stack of mail waiting to be answered, filing that needed to be done, and my desk was a chaotic mess. The loon letters were piling up. I could feel the pressure building. I had maybe four hours to work. I couldn't think straight with that mess in front of me. There were often a dozen calls to be returned. I had to concentrate on issuing new contracts to authors. But I was also thinking about the deadlines I had to meet for new covers, the grant renewal application that was due for the journal in a week, the catalogue copy that had to be written, an ongoing disagreement with Paul about a specific design, and the impending arrival of an egocentric author who thought his book was our entire list. Then there were the new titles to be researched, ideas to be tested, financial commitments to be made.

It was a tidal wave. My head was buzzing. I wanted to call up Jack and say I needed relief, but how could I do that when he had long ago decided to spend most of his time with ECW while I had committed myself to McGill, to my own academic writing, and to all the administrative and teaching responsibilities that come with a university position? I wasn't about to give that up, and I knew that deep down I loved the teaching, the exploration of new ideas, the sense that even in the busyness of it all McGill would offer some kind of haven, a place where ideas still counted, where it was still possible to sit down with a group and talk about language, the Canadian long poem, a recent Atwood novel. Not to mention the fact that McGill provided an actual salary. So I didn't often call Jack, maybe because I sensed that he would have little sympathy. My loyalties had been divided. His were pure. No wonder I couldn't put the time into the business that he did. What right did I have to complain about my workload when he was handling the bulk of the administrative tasks connected with the press? I knew that was true, but it did not feel like it was true. It felt like I was trapped, alone, charged with the responsibility of carrying my weight, signing successful new titles, showing that I was playing my role in improving the company.

By the time I'd worked my way through the jungle on my desk I could feel the anxiety deepening about the rest of the day. I had no free time. My partner was getting distant and aloof and probably thought I was screwing up the business. Hours would pass in a moment. I was surprised at how often I found myself sitting alone in that ECW office feeling jumpy and nervous and sweating. I imagined my publishing decisions gone horribly awry, pictured failed projects that I had placed such hope in, thousands of books returned to the warehouse and the company debited for the return. I had to get out of there. I had to get some exercise. It was the only way I could find some time away from the grinding sense of guilt and frustration that seemed to haunt me from hour to hour. I was enslaved to this business. It started out as fun but now it was not fun. I would head over to the track, running lap after lap as I tried to regulate my breathing and keep my mind clear. I could find a few clear patches, but then the evening ahead would rear up. I wanted to spend some time with Emily, who was now 15. I wanted to sit and do nothing in front of the TV except sip a scotch and watch the news. I wanted to cook a nice dinner with Mary and have an hour of downtime. Complications arose. I was still acquiring and editing books for Twayne and G.K. Hall. By 1994 I had acquired about 250 titles for a variety of series. For each book, I had to find an author, coach him or her through the writing process, get the final manuscript, and write up a final report recommending publication. There was no way I could get through that volume of material without reading at night and in the early morning so I could write up reports on the weekend. I hated the work even though it allowed me to read commentary written by some really first-rate scholars. There seemed to be no time that I was not writing a report. I'd squeeze in 50 pages of a study of *The Great Gatsby* at night, and then early the next morning I would try to read a few of the essays in the collection on Kafka, which was sitting next to another collection of essays on Ayn Rand. I could more or less keep my head above water by writing and reading for most of the weekend, except that I still hadn't dealt with the problem of how to be with Emily, when to grade those 75 papers that were looking at me from the corner of my desk, how to keep my body from falling apart, or when I was going to prepare my lecture on the development of modern Canadian poetry, even though the lecture was in two days.

I'd run five miles. Leave the club. Go home. The usual household stuff was happening. The Quebec Association for the Handicapped was calling to request a donation. The property tax notice had just arrived. Up 12 percent. Why was my back so sore? One of the radiators had sprung a leak. There was a message from the dentist's office, reminding me of my appointment tomorrow. I felt a tingling in my arm and a burning pain in my chest. No doubt it was a heart attack. Because I knew it was a heart attack, because I got there before it had a chance to strike, it backed off. This strategy can be bothersome, especially when it reaches a peak. But I would rather be driving around town imagining that I am having a stroke than actually having one, wouldn't you? And I would rather be sitting in front of the TV, having a scotch and thinking about liver cancer than actually getting liver cancer, right? In the end, without imagining it, I would usually pass out around 11 so I could get up the next morning at four, the usual start to another anxious day.

One thing was sure. Things were changing fast. By the summer of 1993 I was getting ready to go on sabbatical. In the fall, we learned that Mary was pregnant, expecting in the summer of 1994. At home, I was working on *Making It Real*, a book about the English-Canadian literary canon while Mary continued to copy edit for the press. At the office, I was fielding more and more calls about books related to music and sports and popular culture. I was okay when it came to bridging the gap between writing about Canadian literature and signing contracts for books on Canadian artists like Alex Colville or the mystical Alexandra Luke, Canada's first female abstract painter. But I had a tough time focusing on the ins and outs of the Canadian canon when I was worrying about how ECW would handle the design of our new line of gay and lesbian day calendars, an upcoming book on Melissa Etheridge, and another on the abstract art of Quebec painter Claude Tousignant.

My interest in Canadian painting had always been related to choosing images for the various covers of *Essays on Canadian Writing*, an activity that gave me pleasure for years. My parents had always collected art and their house was filled with good paintings. They also collected Inuit carvings, and at one point had started an Inuit art export business, selling to people in Fort Lauderdale, where they owned a condo. My father did deals around the pool. I didn't know much about the art world when I was growing up, but when my father died my mother expressed a willingness to take a bolder step into collecting Canadian art, and we started to make a few purchases. In the process of building this small collection I learned about painting and the arts in Canada. I loved the subtle radiance and warm glow of Suzor-Côté, the magical and tumultuous images in the early oils of Edmund Alleyne, the provocative experimentation that marked the work of Alexandra Luke, the stark existential simplicity of Betty Goodwin's convoluted, tortured figures. Then, moving into more contemporary painting, I discovered the incredible encaustics of Tony Scherman. I would stare into the deep strata of Scherman's canvases, stunned by the realization that he was teaching me to see paint in a whole new way, bit by bit, in all the lines of distress and rebuilding that made up the narrative layers of his complicated, polyphonic canvases. I loved the sensuality of the paint itself and got drawn into the swirling, tumultuous world of Michael Smith. Then, one day when I was visiting the Galerie de Bellefeuille in Montreal, I came across a magnificent canvas by Tom Fenniak, surely one of Canada's finest painters. Jacques de Bellefeuille, whose gallery houses many of the arts works I lust after, started introducing me to a number of figurative painters he represented. There was a door opening here. The irony was that I managed to purchase a number of the paintings bought through my father's estate, even though the conditions of his will made it impossible for me to use any of that money to offset my personal debt. I was surrounded by beautiful images that I was essentially warehousing for my mother, but I had to remain conscious, all the time, that these were investments that would be sold in an instant if her circumstances demanded it.

My growing interest in Canadian painting prompted me to search for new works to grace the covers of each issue of the magazine. Every one of those images led me into a different community, put me in touch with artists and their representatives, and in every instance I found them generous to a fault, happy to see their works appear on the cover of a scholarly magazine, mainly because it looked so good, with its glossy four-colour reproductions. I would visit studios and see works in progress. I had a long list of paintings I lusted after.

One day, when I was trying to get permission to reproduce an image for an upcoming issue of the journal, I came into contact with James Campbell, one of Canada's most eccentric and knowledgeable art critics. There seemed to be absolutely no aspect of abstract art that Campbell had not touched. He had read everything. He had written dozens of monographs and catalogues for a variety of galleries in Canada and the US. Here was a man who was seeing these painting in an entirely different way. On many occasions, as our friendship grew, I tried to imagine what it would be like to see through those eyes, to get the depth of association and awareness that Campbell brought to every painting or drawing that was presented to the massive headlight of his brain. He took me into strange worlds, showed me how to appreciate the glorious beauty revealed by canvases that first struck me as hideous and grotesque. He made me understand the power of simplicity, the tension inherent in starkness, the magnificent pressures lurking in works of profound asymmetry and darkness. He was secretive, obsessed, overflowing with information, and forever addicted to the world of art. He also collected all manner of quirky artefacts and boasted the largest collection of hot sauces I've ever seen. ECW published a book of his essays, *Depth Markers*, along with his introduction to a beautiful book on the abstract art of Claude Tousignant, one of Quebec's most accomplished painters. We also published the dark and fetishistic *Mr. Chilihead*, an account of the life of a man who is ruled by his quest for hot peppers and the pleasures of capsicum pain. James encouraged me to pursue that pain. Although he went into hiding from time to time, falling off the map, I always enjoyed seeing James again when he returned to the world, burning with enthusiasm for a new work, a new idea, or ready to take me to yet another artist's studio, an inevitably rewarding journey that often turned into a visual orgy that left me feeling intoxicated and wanting more.

I remember the day we were printing the Tousignant book. James and Claude didn't trust the printer to do perfect justice to the mono-chromatic range of Claude's paintings. They insisted on being present at the printing plant in Quebec's Beauce region when the signatures rolled off the mammoth press. We drove out through the Quebec countryside, James and Claude in high spirits. The plant seemed to have anticipated their visit. There was a special facility there, like a hotel suite, designed specifically for people who had to camp out while their books were being printed. Apparently this was not such a rare thing after all. James and Claude set themselves up in the room. James pulled out a box of Cuban cigars. Claude readied his bottle of Lagavulin. They lit up and poured themselves shots, looking for all the world like two of the happiest kids you'd ever seen. By the end of the day, the ashtray was piled high and the Lagavulin was low, but they were satisfied and ready to return to the city.

Just being in rural Quebec for this little printing expedition reminded me of separatist politics. I had always associated rural Quebec with separatist fervour. It was all those people at the printing plant who were going to vote Yes when it came to the next referendum. This wasn't just idle speculation. In September of 1994 the Parti Québécois swept to power under the leadership of Jacques Parizeau, promising a referendum the following year. I wanted to use my sabbatical to get some writing done, to finish my book, but all of a sudden there was this huge threat on the horizon. The daily newspapers were filled with talk about plans for secession, how the country would fall apart, how federalists would be treated in a sovereign Quebec. I know that the issue affected people across the country, but it had to be especially intense for anglophones living in Quebec, mainly because the threat was so local and the issue of our future rights was something that came up again and again.

Mary and I discussed potential strategies in the event of a Yes vote. Could we remain in a sovereign Quebec? I couldn't see how I could possibly stay in a new country that had rejected my former one, especially when every single aspect of my career was connected with the link between country and identity. Canada made me. It was the force that got me into pub-lishing. It was the country that produced the literature I talked about every day. How could I write about the Canadian canon—which itself was an expression of some kind of national consensus—when the country was on the verge of collapse?

I wanted desperately to keep my job at McGill. If we chose to leave, commuting would be the only option. Besides, the idea of continuing to teach Canadian literature at McGill in the event of separation would be an act of resistance, I told myself. Then I realized that it would embody about as much resistance as teaching American literature in Canada, which is to say, no resistance at all. We considered the proximity of Vermont. But how could we live in the United States? Ottawa seemed the logical option. But that would mean a long commute, several times a week. And Ottawa was not Montreal. The town of Alexandria was just over the border in Ontario, 45 minutes away. But we didn't want to end up in a rural village surrounded by fields and the 401. All of a sudden my future was threatened. I didn't know where we would end up. My sabbatical year, which had begun with Claire's birth in July, was gradually becoming a year of tension. Mary was exhausted, caring for a perky infant who refused to sleep; I was worried about finishing my book before I returned to teaching in September; and now the prospect of political upheaval coloured my thoughts each day.

I can see how much the impending referendum affected me while I was writing that book. In the preface to *Making It Real* I made explicit reference to the referendum, and wrote that "in such a political climate, no one who writes about Canadian literature can pretend that they are engaged in an apolitical activity. No one can pretend that it is possible to speak about Canadian literature without interrogating the country." I complained that Canadian critics had failed to engage in this kind of interrogation "at precisely the time that such commentary might have contributed to the national debate about Canada's future."

In retrospect, I see that I was questioning the very utility of literary criticism, wondering about its ability to effect political change. I wanted to believe that an interrogation of the canon could contribute to the examination and formation of critical communities. I had this idealistic sense that the more you talked about a nation and its literature the more you increased the value of your subject. I was embracing Charles Altieri's idea of the canon as a body of literature that should be examined as the repository of national ideals. I understood the problems inherent in Altieri's position, its fundamental conservatism, but I wanted to find a safe place, a bulwark, a discourse that made me feel at home, even as I understood that this would be to construct a false myth, to deny difference, to act as if there was constancy and permanence rather than fragmentation, shift, and flow. To admit that the boundaries of the canon could change, that the consensus it embodied could fall apart and yield to new forms of intervention, was essentially to admit that the borders of Canada could also change. So I knew, intellectually, that Quebec could go its own way. But I also knew that in accepting that idea, no matter how much I viscerally resisted it, I was also accepting the idea that the Canadian canon was a sham, a construction invented by critics to make it possible for them to do their work.

The months leading up the referendum coincided perfectly with the trajectory of my sabbatical. By the time I returned to teaching in September of 1995, the referendum was only a month away. The polls were predicting results that were too close to call. I read the papers with a mounting sense of dread. How could we have arrived at the point that this was happening all over again? I was teaching in Maine when the first referendum went down in 1980; strangely, it had had little immediate impact on me. Now, however, I had to listen to Jacques Parizeau's endless condemnations of Canada. Not a day went by without some Parti Québécois minister talking about the way Quebecers had been oppressed. What upset me most was the rhetoric of separation, the way the PQ talked about how they would achieve their objectives after a Yes vote. If Canada didn't cave in and just agree to the separation they would make a unilateral declaration of independence and simply break away on their own. I was no history student, but I knew where unilateral declarations of independence had led other countries in the past; usually such declarations produced civil unrest, violence, and sometimes even civil war.

The PQ did little to reassure people that this would not be the case. Instead, they talked about the creation of their own quasi-military force. They blithely assumed that the federal government would just hand over the keys to its various agencies in Quebec, that the transfer of power would be orderly and democratic, after the initial shock. There I was, teaching a course on the development of Canadian poetry, publishing a magazine called *Essays on Canadian Writing*, and finishing up a series called *Canadian Writers and Their Works*. Would I end up as an editor in exile? How could I walk into a class the day after a Yes vote and pick up the syllabus at the point we left off, two days ago, when Canada had still been whole? My professional investment in Canada seemed pathetic in the face of this wave coming at me. I was counting down the days, certain that if the Yes side won my life would be forever changed, feeling more and more desperate and powerless as the vote approached.

On the evening of the referendum we invited some American friends over to watch the results. That was a mistake. I wanted it to be a kind of social evening that ended in a celebration. Although the polls still showed a very tight race, it looked like the separatists were heading for defeat. Our friends thought the whole spectacle was amazing. Thinking of the American model, they could hardly believe that this was all being taken seriously, that the federal government might actually consider letting Quebec go, or that a province (which they equated with the status of an American state) could simply up and leave. It was unthinkable. Well, it may have been unthinkable, but it was unfolding on the television screen before us. I had visitors. I wanted to be social and welcoming. But all I could do was focus on the results as they started to pour in.

Almost immediately the Yes side took a big leap ahead, much bigger than any poll had predicted. What was happening? My heart was pounding. I felt choked. Those numbers couldn't be real! The whole thing was going down. I wanted to be alone. I wanted to hide and pretend this wasn't true. Now a commentator was explaining that these initial results were not surprising because the rural vote was coming in first, and rural Quebec was massively behind the PQ. (I remembered my trip to the Beauce.) The real test, he said, was the cities—Montreal and Quebec. For another agonizing hour we sat there, watching the results teeter back and forth as the Yes side gradually lost its huge initial majority. The No had a slight advantage. Now the Yes had pulled ahead again. Then new numbers shot up: the No was marginally back on top. The polls had closed but it was still too close to call. I felt like I had been on an emotional roller coaster ride that was never going to end, high one moment and in despair the next. Finally it did end, but on a very precarious note: the No side had won by less than one percent. I watched in morbid fascination as Parizeau prepared to face the media and acknowledge defeat. Then he stood in front of all those cameras and blamed his narrow loss on "money and the ethnic vote." I looked around the room. Our American friends could hardly believe what they were hearing. No one could believe what they were hearing. The night was over. I was sad, relieved, exhausted, in a state of disbelief. Canada was still my country. But something huge had changed. Something had been broken. Some level of trust had been sundered. I went to bed, feeling a rising sense of pressure. I knew I had to do something. Say something. Write something. I stayed awake and started planning.

CHAPTER EIGHT

The disastrous outcome of the referendum seemed to go hand in hand with a disastrous year at ECW. But anyone looking at the company from the outside would never have had this impression. In spring 1995 we put out a large library catalogue that consolidated our titles in biography, bibliography, reference, and criticism. It was a hefty list, one that gave the impression of company solvency and substance. At the same time we were starting to issue annual trade catalogues that focused on commercial titles. There were lots of books being produced. Too many. Despite the outward appearances, there just wasn't enough money for all of this activity.

Although Jack and I had been discussing our perpetual cash flow crises for years, the months leading up to the referendum were particularly difficult. We couldn't pay the bills. Paul Martin's budget cuts had affected everyone, and matters were made even worse when Mike Harris introduced his own round of draconian cuts in Ontario. The bank was on our case. Jack was getting angry calls from creditors on a daily basis. There was little he could do. Soon after the Quebec vote we met in Montreal to discuss our options. We went over the figures again and again, vowing to slash this and that expense, looking for any cost that could be eliminated. No matter how hard we tried, there was no avoiding the single most sensitive issue that was contributing to our expenses: staff salaries. In Toronto, Jack had developed a deep bond with Don McLeod, whose daily contributions to the business were invaluable. Don had been with ECW since 1987. He had a background in library science and was originally hired to do freelance research. A year later he was working pretty much full-time at the ECW office and handling everything from bookkeeping to advertising to editing. He had been through the worst times at ECW and at one point things got so bad that he worked for almost two months without being paid. Jack felt an unwavering loyalty to Don, who had seen the ups and downs of the business up close, and who had undoubtedly witnessed the emotional toll our financial problems were having on Jack. In Montreal I was working closely with Holly Potter, who was holding the show together and helping me look more organized than I probably was. I relied heavily on her expertise and her sense of diplomacy when it came to dealing with some of our crankier authors.

Because so many of the administrative aspects of the business were centred in Toronto, it seemed logical that if there were to be staff cuts they would happen on the Montreal side. However, Jack knew that I was working flat out, and that if Holly left I would find it almost impossible to carry on alone, given my responsibilities at McGill. Jack was still teaching at Centennial College in Toronto, but he was gradually pulling back from teaching and spending a lot more time in the ECW office. In what was probably one of the hardest and most generous sacrifices he ever made, Jack agreed that we would have to let Don go, while Holly's hours would be cut back. By the first week of November we had delivered the news. With that delivery the whole mood of the company changed. Jack was alone in the office, assisted from time to time by his wife, Sharon. I'm sure there was resentment at the fact that I had managed to retain Holly, and I know that the physical distance separating the two offices during this critical period also contributed to a growing sense of alienation.

By the end of 1995 I was in an emotional pit. It looked like this time the business really was going down the tubes. I was losing weight. Probably cancer. As usual, I kept wondering where the money was going to come from when some bank or creditor finally busted us. But what was really driving me crazy during this period was the ongoing behaviour of the Quebec government, which had just put us through the torture of the referendum and now refused to bring closure to the results. They had always said that a win for their side would be 50 percent plus one vote. Well, the federalist victory was close, but not nearly as close as that. The federalists had won by more than 50,000 votes, and that wasn't counting all the No ballots that had been destroyed, or ruled ineligible, or lost by unscrupulous and partisan vote counters. Yet the separatists vowed to hold another referendum when the timing was right. The process would only be over when *they* won. The profound hypocrisy of this position, spewed out by government officials at every possible opportunity, made me feel like I was living in a permanent political limbo.

To make matters worse, each day brought new revelations about some of the assumptions underlying the pronouncements made by people speaking for the separatist cause. I became convinced that as a

Jew and as a federalist anglophone I was a kind of second-rate citizen in the eyes of the PQ (but not in the eyes of the Quebec people, who are among the most accepting and tolerant I have known). It was because of Jews like me and all the other "ethnics" that the separatists had narrowly lost their fight. Sure, Parizeau had been forced to resign and give way to Lucien Bouchard, but the PQ rhetoric continued to stress racial and linguistic superiorities. It was the rhetoric of resentment, the chauvinism of whining losers and bullies, the bad breath of a government that extolled the values of democracy when it looked like they might have power and then ignored those values when their hold on power began to slip away. Meanwhile, the PQ would not back away from its commitment to pull Quebec out of Canada through a unilateral declaration of independence, a UDI. Even if they didn't pursue that revolutionary and dangerous route, I wondered how they could imagine establishing a new country in which half the population was against separation. It would never work. Besides, they knew that even those who had voted Yes were responding to a fudged referendum question: at least half of the Yes voters were under the impression that Quebec would have an economic and political association with Canada. So how stable could an independent Quebec really be if it was founded both on fantasy and contempt for the rule of law?

What was the anglophone press in Montreal saying about all this? Precious little. The *Gazette* was being run by a group of spineless pacifiers who were consistently reluctant to rock the boat. How was it possible that PQ representatives could spout their ethnocentric values and threaten a UDI while that newspaper just sat back? And none of the national papers seemed to be concerned about the issue either. For people in Toronto the referendum was over. The flames had died down. It was no longer a crisis. But for federalists in Montreal, the razor-thin referendum results and the nonstop separatist threats kept the issue front and centre, a matter of daily concern. The bottom line was that we were living in a state of perpetual uncertainty. Even though the referendum was officially over, the separatist government refused to say it would not hold another, who knew when. The sword of Damocles had been lifted, but no one knew when it might fall. Separatism had been turned into a perpetual waiting game conducted by politicians who issued threats.

The more I fretted about the issue, the more I began to wonder what role I could possibly play in the political tensions that were swirling around me. One day I got a call from David Black, a former student of mine with whom I'd kept in touch over the years. David was an in-your-face personality, to say the least. He may not have been the world's greatest student, but he had chutzpah like no one I had ever met. He had survived his teen years by some miracle, after testing his mortality by doing crazy things like driving on the highway at 220 kilometers per hour, just to see whether the car would get airborne on the curves. Fearless, passionate, he hated the separatists. He was also pretty well connected. His father is Herbert Black, the Montreal-based metals trader and bon vivant who controls the American Iron and Metal Company and whose art investments are legendary. David had met up with a Montreal business-man by the name of Gary Shapiro, who had started a grass roots lobby group to advance the cause of federalism and stop the uncertainty. Gary was working with another business guy—Jean Brière—who was a committed francophone federalist.

I went to one of the group's initial meetings—they called themselves the Quebec Committee for Canada, or QCC—and I was hooked. Here was a group of people who had decided to take some action. Over the next few months I became centrally involved in the QCC. The group was "underground" in the sense that no one outside it had access to strategy meetings or plans. Essentially the QCC worked to undermine the PQ's power base and to show that their refusal to admit defeat was creating a climate of uncertainty that was hampering business and sending Montreal into decline. The QCC tried (successfully) to draw the attention of American journalists to the situation in Quebec, believing that the PQ was much more concerned with American impressions of their actions and knowing that the separatists would be sensitive to any news coverage that suggested they were not defenders of democratic rights. At the same time, the QCC undertook a number of publicity campaigns designed to undermine PQ credibility—anything to get them out of power as soon as possible. We placed huge posters in bus shelters throughout Quebec, showing pictures of Montreal in decline, with the heading "Stop the Uncertainty." We took full-page ads in the *Gazette* and *Le Devoir*, saying the same thing and imploring the government to recognize its defeat. Every week we met to draw up plans. In a few months the membership of the group had swelled into the thousands. Who knows where the money came from to print up those bus shelter posters? Who knows where we got the cash to pay for those ads? Who knows who paid for the million postcards we sent out to households all over Quebec, conveying the same message as our full-page ads? Hmmm.

As it matured, the QCC became involved in the partition movement, and was the driving force behind the votes in favour of partition held in municipalities throughout Quebec. We knew that the PQ hated these municipal votes and, as the movement snowballed and more and more communities voted to secede from a separate Quebec, we began to sense the desperation of the separatist politicians, who always had trouble arguing with the partitionist logic. If Quebec could separate from Canada, communities within the province could unilaterally separate from Quebec. For two years (until we could see the PQ headed for certain defeat) the QCC executive committee met weekly to plan specific actions. We often had visitors who probably would rather not have been seen in our company—people like the US attaché to Canada, or strategists for federal political parties, or radio and television personalities who were openly or not so openly behind the federalist cause.

We would cheer when we made a hit or got some coverage in the papers. Even the *Gazette* mustered the courage to ask us to meet with their editorial board, and finally we got to sit down with Daniel Johnson, the former premier of Quebec and at that time the leader of the Liberal opposition. Four or five of us went up to his office. While we were waiting for Johnson to meet us, we noticed that the Canadian flag was nowhere to be seen although the *fleur de lys* was everywhere. As soon as we got into the meeting with Johnson, David Black asked him where all the Canadian flags had gone. Wasn't his the party that had ostensibly fought against the PQ in the referendum? Weren't they the last hope for federalism in Quebec? Were they or were they not Canadian? Like so many other federalist politicians at the time, Johnson had obviously caved in to the soft nationalists in his party, and he was one of them, lacking, as he did, the courage to display the Canadian flag, just like the PQ, who had studiously removed the maple leaf from the National Assembly buildings in Quebec.

Was there any way that I could use my own training as an academic to out the deep hypocrisy underlying the PQ's post-referendum stance? Hadn't I been arguing, for years, that academics had removed themselves from public debate? I had been trained to do research, yes, but all of that research was literary, looking for sources, or critical articles, or archival material. Could that training be turned toward some kind of political research and commentary? Could my writing find a larger community outside academia? I decided to examine various Quebec newspapers and government press releases containing statements by PQ representatives in order to see whether any kind of consistent pattern emerged. I started poring over the newspapers, paying particular attention to some of the small-town papers, which often recorded the unvetted pronouncements made by local MNAs and other PQ officials when they visited various ridings. A pattern began to emerge. I began to see that the PQ was endorsing a view of linguistic and ethnic supremacy that was responsible for the ongoing violation of democratic principles and human rights. And I began to understand more about the PQ's plan to secede from Canada through a UDI—a tactic that would undoubtedly leave most of Canada ungovernable. Finally, I saw that the PQ had steadfastly refused to recognize the claims of the province's aboriginal peoples, who had made it clear that if Quebec separated from Canada, they would take their lands and separate from Quebec. Although the PQ were quite happy to contemplate the partition of Canada through a UDI, they didn't recognize the rights of other political entities to partition Quebec, another example of their malignant hypocrisy. It was a frightening picture.

As my research continued the shape of an essay began to emerge. I started to write, more quickly than I ever had, as the pieces fell into place. By May I had produced a 50-page document called "High Noon: Separatism and Revolution in Quebec." What would I do with it, now that it was complete? It was too long for any journal to publish and too short to be a book. Besides, I felt an urgency about what I had written. Book publication would take far too long. Frustrated by my inability to circulate the material through conventional means, I decided to typeset it myself, and to release it as a small monograph. My plan was to print up a few hundred copies and to send them to politicians and human rights organizations around the world. I also planned to distribute them to influential business leaders, various embassies, and of course a variety of newspapers and broadcasting venues. I did the printing, sent out the mailing, and expected nothing to happen, just like when I published my scholarly articles and no one would care. But this time I was wrong. Massively wrong. The shit hit the fan.

Early on the morning of June 12, 1996, just as I was getting ready to look over some cover suggestions for an upcoming issue of the journal, the phone rang. It was Carman Miller, the dean of Arts at McGill. He asked if I had seen the front page of Montreal's biggest French daily, *La Presse*. No, I hadn't. Carman told me that my picture was on the front page, under a headline that read "Un professeur de McGill mène une campagne haineuse contre le PQ aux É.-U." ("A McGill professor leads a hate campaign against the PQ in the United States.") I felt a wave of panic and nausea. What did this mean? Where would it go? Was my job in danger? I'd never heard of a dean calling a professor at home in the morning. Carman apologized for calling me so early. He just wanted me to be prepared for a tough day as other media outlets picked up on the story. Perhaps more important, he wanted me to know that although the university would not take a position on what I had written, it would stand, unequivocally, behind my right to free speech. I ran down to the corner store and got *La Presse*. My hands were shaking. How could I ever handle being put in the spotlight this way? I wanted to run away. I wanted to disappear. I felt like I'd been shot.

Over the next few months I came to understand just how crucial Carman's assurances were. Most academics who obtain tenure see it mainly as a form of lifelong job security, usually forgetting that one of the reasons tenure exists is in order to ensure that people can speak their minds about sensitive issues without fear of losing their jobs. Tenure serves an essential form of political protection, even though that form of protection is seldom tested to the limit, especially in North America. In my case, it was. A lesser university might have wavered in the face of the storm that was about to engulf me. But McGill never wavered. They never took a political position on my essay, but from day one there was not a single member of the administration that ever led me to believe the university would not fully defend my right to free speech. I was always treated professionally, fairly, and respectfully. In this way, the university earned my loyalty in a way that could never be measured as a response to salary increases, or rewards for meritorious teaching or service. It earned my loyalty because it showed itself to be big enough to stand behind the knowledge that truly free societies are founded on debate and dissent. I'm sure they were profoundly uncomfortable with all the media attention my article focused on McGill. Yet not one person ever suggested that I put a lid on it, or tone it down.

By the time I got to my office that day the phone was ringing non-stop. My e-mail account was flooded with messages. Ironically, the copy of my essay that had made it into the hands of the *La Presse* reporter was discovered in the US, no doubt one of the copies I had sent out to senators and members of Congress. Now the word was out in Quebec. I was inundated with calls from newspapers and radio and television stations. It was like a stone thrown into a pool: the initial splash, then the widening ripples as various media outside the province began to pick up on the story. *La Presse* reporters went running up to McGill to find out whether I had yet been fired for my hateful comments. They started at the office of the department chairman. He told them I had a right to express my political opinions. This enraged them. They ran over to the next building to see Carman. He told them the same thing. Even more enraged, they hustled over to the next building and the principal's office. He repeated the university's commitment to the protection of free speech. Obviously the university was not going to fire the hate-monger. The reporter who first broke the story was not happy with the dean. When he refused to condemn me, the reporter published a story saying that in fact he had. To his immense credit, Carman wrote immediately to *La Presse*, saying, "I do not condemn nor do I deplore Mr. Lecker's article. That would be a violation of his right to free expression, a restriction on the university freedom which is a fundamental condition of employment in a university, recognized and protected in all free societies. Not only is academic freedom essential to the dissemination of knowledge—which is itself the reason and function of a university—but it is also a basic right inherent in all free and democratic societies like Quebec." The firmness and generosity of that letter brought me close to tears.

For days the French papers carried versions of the initial story. They called to interview me. Reporter after reporter challenged my assertions. They tried to turn me into the hate-monger I was supposed to be. They tried to put words in my mouth and trip me up. But there was only one problem with their challenge. I had footnotes. I had the quotations. I had done my research. When they said I had made things up I referred them to the documents behind my assertions, and asked them to call me back if it turned out my information was false. No one called back. I had cut my teeth on verifying quotations for *Essays on Canadian Writing*. There was no way anyone was going to find an inaccuracy in one of my 82 references. No way. So what did they have left in their arsenal? The usual methods employed by hack journalists: attack the author without fully representing his ideas, or say he has attacked *le peuple*, when in fact what I was attacking was not Quebecers, but a hypocritical and reckless government that was threatening to lead *le peuple* into chaos by ignoring the rule of law. My essay was meant to help everyone understand what the PQ was trying to achieve. Of course the French press wanted nothing of that message.

Although I was branded a dangerous offender by the Quebec media, and although Lucien Bouchard publicly denounced me (my greatest claim to federalist fame), word about the essay continued to spread into the English media outlets outside Quebec. For weeks I was called to be on radio talk shows and was interviewed for television news stories. I never got used to this, especially the television. My eyes would always be darting around as if I were a hunted animal. My radio voice came across okay, but I could hardly reconcile the personality that emerged in those talk shows and interviews with the person who was publishing books on Alice Munro and Shania Twain or walking into a lecture hall to talk to hundreds of students about Archibald Lampman's approach to landscape and nature or Northrop Frye's concept of the garrison mentality. Even more surprising was the fact that none of my students seemed to know about my current incarnation as a hate monger, but perhaps this was not so surprising since they seldom read the papers or watched the news. (Their general ignorance of current events never ceases to amaze me.) I was a split personality, talking about mythopoeia or post-modernism in my Canadian poetry class in my professorial voice while inside I was raging about the abstraction of it all, tortured by how useless these intellectual exercises seemed in the face of what was happening to me on a concrete level every day. I was getting bizarre phone calls at home and at the office. Deranged federalists from all over Quebec tracked me down to offer their praise. A security company run by a federalist business man called to offer me a security system. There were all kinds of cranks calling the house in the middle of the night. Strange letters were coming through the mailbox. Was I worried? Very. I started checking under my car before I got in. I imagined the bomb placed there by some crazy whose mission it was to finish me off. Yet for some reason I refused to retreat. Every time one of those newspapers bad-mouthed me I wrote back. I particularly wrote back to the *Gazette*, which had refused to take an unequivocal stand about the risks associated with a UDI.

Just when I thought things had pretty much peaked I got a call from Dianne de Fenoyl at *Saturday Night*. They had heard about the essay and were wondering if I could send them a copy. The next day Dianne called back and said that even though their special July-August 1996 "Tabloid" issue was on the press, they wanted to include a condensed version of my piece. I knew this would create some kind of explosion, but I said yes. Why not? The whole reason behind circulating the essay in the first place was to get it some kind of exposure. But I had no idea how shocking it would look when the issue of *Saturday Night* appeared a week or so later. It had a gross cover with lots of tabloid-spirited headlines like "Queen schemes to rule Chuck and Di from beyond the grave" and "Family Shocked: Mom poses nude at Eighty!" along with "HOT FLASH . . . SEX IN THE DESERT." Running across the top of the issue was a banner that read "Exclusive: Robert Lecker's explosive essay on the coming chaos in Quebec." The essay itself was adorned with photos of Montreal graffiti saying things like "eng<u>lishit</u> Go Home!" "ENGLISH

DEAD," and a picture of a man hanging from a gallows next to the word "ANGLOS."

This kind of exposure ratcheted things up. I got a call from an assistant producer at CBC TV who wanted to put me on Face Off, the nationally televised program devoted to spirited debate about political issues. They were going to fly me to Toronto along with Josée Legault, a professional journalist and committed separatist who had been writing about the situation in Quebec for years. We were supposed to duke it out on national television. I met Josée on the plane. She is a most pleasant person who is used to being in front of cameras and having microphones thrust at her day and night. By the time we got to the CBC studios in Toronto all I could think about was how on earth I was going to do battle with this formidable and intelligent opponent who had trained in the trenches for years. The producer of the show was one of the most aggressive women I've ever seen. She yucked it up with Josée who was obviously a regular visitor and shot glaring glances at me while I cringed in a beauty parlour chair as a makeup technician powdered me up. I was intensely aware of the shininess of my nose and bald head, both of which seemed to be causing her problems. She was cursing under her breath. A few minutes later we were brought out to the set. I felt faint with nervousness. I kept smelling the thick makeup on my face.

I was surrounded by five huge cameras that looked like cannons, all pointing at me. The producer looked grim. She started counting down from ten. The show began. The moderator looked happy, way too happy. The gladiators were present and accounted for. I was in the ring. I imagined the hundreds of thousands of people—maybe millions of people!—who were about to watch me screw up as I was mauled by a separatist pit bull. I could see them sitting in their living rooms from coast to coast, looking at me and shaking their heads. There would be no pity. No one could rescue me. I tried deep breathing. Why was I here? Who was I? I felt like some kind of impostor. I could hardly concentrate on the job at hand, which was to smash Josée and everything she stood for. But she had no such problems. She charged over me as if I were a crumpled box in the gutter, an annoying little object in her path. She was a verbal assault weapon. The bullets never stopped. I tried to talk but sounded lamer and lamer when I managed to get a word in edgewise, which was about once. We stopped for a commercial. This was hell. I was sitting on a high chair that swiveled back and forth. My hands were wet with sweat. I imagined the chair spinning faster and faster, out of control, spiralling me down to the floor. The cameras were sure to follow.

I gulped water, trying to centre myself. Josée winked at the cameraman and talked jauntily about the resto she would be visiting later than evening in Montreal. I completely folded. After the debacle was mercifully over I could hear the producer raking some underling over the coals for the enormous error of putting me on the show. "Where THE FUCK does this guy come from?" she was screaming. "Who THE FUCK is he?" "There was supposed to be *friction* out there. *Friction!* Do you know what that word fucking *means*?!" The underling was whimpering "I'm sorry. I'm sorry" while she looked at me with disgust. They gave me a Face Off mug and sent me packing. Josée and I flew back to Montreal. Just another day on the beat for her. For me, a total wipeout. I got home and looked in the mirror. I'd forgotten about the makeup. My shiny nose was peaking through it, the real me behind the mask.

Over the next few weeks I did everything I could to stay away from television cameras. It was September, classes were just starting, and I had to get my lectures together. There were all kinds of ECW books on the go. The flurry of activity resulting from the news coverage and the *Saturday Night* article meant that I was way behind on many titles. Jack was amazingly understanding about all this. I knew that one thing we shared was a commitment to the idea of Canada, a commitment that was the original force behind our interest in Canadian literature. Although I don't think he completely understood the extremes confronting federalist anglophones in Quebec during this period (who could, if you weren't living those extremes?) I know he sensed how important this battle was for me. Instead of criticizing the toll it was taking on my involvement with the business he stood back and let me do what I had to do. He often seemed amused by some of the shenanigans I got caught up in. Maybe inside he was wondering how far this was going to go, and when I was going to get back to the real world. But he always lent an ear and appeared to be generally sympathetic.

One afternoon, just as things were calming down a bit, I got a call from a local radio station. They had read my work and wondered if I would be willing to host a radio talk show. Me? A radio talk show host? After the Face Off bust? I expressed misgivings. Come down to the station, they said. We can hook you up with one of our regular hosts— Gord Logan—and he can teach you the ropes. So I headed off to this radio station and met Gord, a seasoned professional. They were thinking of putting me on air for an hour, three days per week. I would have my own researcher, and the topic of the show would be Quebec politics. I could take that in any direction I wanted, and the researcher would help me book guests and coordinate the call-in aspect of the show. I said Yes. Who knows why. Something different. So three days a week at six in the morning I headed off to the station, making an immediate pit stop in the bathroom as soon as I arrived, a constant case of nerves. The show started at seven.

Radio timing is nothing like lecture timing. It has a completely different rhythm. The rhythm becomes especially important on a call-in show. If you get out of sync with the caller you can start talking over his or her voice and the whole thing wobbles out of control. Gord taught me how to pace my voice, how to slow it down, and how to listen for the good bits when people started ranting, as they inevitably did. I would set up interviews with specialists across the country—economists, political scientists, historians—and often invited well-known politicians into the studio. I remember meeting a shy Mario Dumont, the leader of the Action Démocratique party in Quebec, and getting to ask him firsthand whether he supported the PQ's threat of a UDI.

There was lots of fun and moments of hysterical laughter. Because I had no formal training in radio broadcasting I also had no idea that one should tone down such laughter on the air. Also, it was not wise to get too angry with invited guests who didn't share my point of view. Gord taught me to respect my on-air visitors. Then, when the mike was switched off, he would curse at them when they deserved it. I got the hang of this after a while, but I also got tired of the calls, most of which came from bored people with severely limited points of view. The show reminded me, every week, that there was another side to me that I hardly knew, the side that was talking into a microphone in a small, soundproofed room, addressing a multitude of unseen listeners. I couldn't help but remember the lines from Alden Nowlan's "The Broadcaster's Poem":

> So one part of me
> was afraid another part
> might blurt out something
> about myself so terrible
> that even I had never until
> that moment suspected it.

Sometimes separatist callers would get through and threaten me. That always put me in a bad mood. Besides, preparing for each show was a ton of work. I could never just walk in cold. I had to know as much as possible about the person I was interviewing. I had to find out who specialized in different topics related to Quebec politics. By the end of every show I was exhausted, and the day was just beginning. Now it was eight in the morning and I had classes to teach, students to advise, and a welter of ECW troubles brewing at the company office. After four months, I gave it up. But they still say I have a nice voice ...

With the radio stint behind me I was starting to look forward to a bit of a break over the Christmas holidays in 1996. I would have a chance to rest up, focus on a number of the upcoming spring titles, and explore some new book ideas that I thought would bring ECW some much-needed cash. A few days after classes ended I was picking up my mail and noticed a curious light-green envelope in my box. I cringed at the thought of what this one might contain. Most of the bad mail, I thought, was behind me. But as I picked up this hefty envelope and looked at its rich design I knew that it would be a different kind of missive than any I had received in the past. In gold embossed lettering I read: "On Her Majesty's Service."

What did Her Majesty want with me? The envelope contained a lengthy invitation to visit a special retreat called Wilton Park, a by-invitation-only conference facility run by the Executive Agency of the British Foreign and Commonwealth Office (FCO). Every year it brought together writers, academics, government policy makers, and represent-atives of various NGOs for a series of small conferences that covered some of the key political, security, and economic issues confronting the world. I was being invited to participate in a special conference on places that the FCO felt might experience an upsurge of violence due to political instability. Some of the countries on the list were no shockers: Congo, the Palestinian territory, Sudan, Sri Lanka. And then came the real surprise: Quebec. The conference organizers asked if I would present a paper on the ramifications of a potential UDI in Quebec and participate in the general discussion about global violence with conference members from other countries.

How in the world did Quebec make it onto this list? Although the PQ had steadfastly refused to recognize the perils inherent in its own threat of enacting a UDI, it seemed clear that a number of political observers and policy makers in other countries—particularly the UK—were aware of the imminent risks. This amazed me. I couldn't imagine what form the conference would take or what role I might actually play, but it seemed to be similar in format to an academic conference—one that would be unlike any I had ever attended. Anyhow, violence aside, it sounded like fun. I would fly to London and then be met by a Wilton Park representative who would take me to the conference site, described by the organizers as "a modernised sixteenth century English country house in beautiful surroundings in the middle of the English countryside." For security reasons I would not be told in advance about any of the other conference participants; they might be PQ representatives, Canadian parliamentarians, or high-level politicians and activists from a number of war-torn countries.

I accepted the invitation and booked a flight to London at the end of February 1997. As soon as I boarded the plane I recognized someone who had to be a fellow conference-goer. It was David Payne, the notorious Brit who had gained Canadian citizenship and then become a separatist, winning election to the Quebec National Assembly as a member of the Parti Québécois. Many considered Payne to be a sorry excuse for a politician and a traitor to boot. He spoke with a British accent, extolling the virtues of separation and the importance of French linguistic purity in Quebec. Whenever the PQ needed someone to prove that the English were not oppressed in Quebec they trotted out Payne, as in: "Look Anglos! He made it! You too can be a successful separatist! You too can support laws that restrict your freedom of speech!" I went up to him on the plane and introduced myself. He mumphed at me and asked if I was heading over to Britain to kick up more shit. I think he said "shite." I tried to be polite. But I told him he'd better be ready, since I was about to speak in depth about Quebec's plans for a UDI and to generally spill the beans about the PQ's repressive acts.

A Wilton Park representative met us in London and drove us to the conference site in Sussex. It was truly a beautiful place, with old buildings and a sense of solid British tradition that conveyed authority and purpose. I had a nice room in a modernized building next to the conference house. Everything was run according to a tight schedule. Soon after my arrival we were brought together in a large meeting hall and told the rules: the exchange of ideas was to be civil; the identities of conference participants could not be revealed while the conference was in progress; no papers delivered at the conference could be copied or distributed outside the conference itself. I stood there sipping a glass of wine and glanced around. There were representatives of every shape and colour, some of whom huddled in clusters, surrounded by men who looked like body guards. The most nervous person in the room was one of the leaders of the LTTE or the Tamil Tigers of Eelam, the militant terrorist organization that was at war in Sri Lanka. Holding a perfectly civil conversation with him was another activist from Uganda, a big black man who spoke in a booming voice. The next day the LTTE man distributed pictures of buildings they had bombed.

I got the sense that there were serious tensions around me, although it was hard to decipher the signals, or to figure out who was angling for what. But it was bizarre to see these high-stakes politicians sitting around the big conference table, speaking in cultured tones about genocide and torture and a host of pending disasters. Next to them, I seemed like a fly, a shortish professor of English with tenure at a world-famous university who was worried about his civil rights in Canada, one of the most stable and democratic countries in the world. Which it was. And is. But I had to remind myself that I had been invited here for a reason, and I had to keep that reason front and centre in my mind as I listed to the stories of violence and abuse and failed attempts at relief that were swirling around me. The reason was that if no one identified the problem early enough, people would just assume that everything was normal, and then, if there was a problem, it would be too late to act.

I began to realize that even though I was in the profoundly privileged position of living in a peaceful country where there was high respect for individual rights and freedoms, that position was being threatened by a political party that flouted the rule of law. It was precisely because no one thought anything bad could ever happen in Canada that it was so important to point out that it could. So I did my best and gave my paper. Payne showed up to say I was delivering a pack of lies. We got into a heated argument. The person chairing our session had to break it up.

I returned to Montreal determined to get even more involved in some kind of political activism through publishing. All of the media exposure brought me into contact with a number of journalists and writers who were loyal to the federalist cause. Some of them offered solace. Gwynne Dyer, a friend from before the time I got involved in issues related to Quebec, told me that it would all blow over soon and not to worry too much about the negative press. I met Josh Freed, a respected Montreal journalist, at a party at Gwynne's place and he could hardly bear to speak to me. I had rocked the boat at a fragile post-referendum moment. I was upsetting the peace. I met Tommy Schnur-macher, a very popular radio personality who never gave the separatists a moment's rest. Tommy wanted to have his say on post-referendum politics in Quebec. He was incensed at Lucien Bouchard's remark that Canada was not a real country. I offered him a contract on a book that would mockingly be given the title of Bouchard's comment. Over the next few months I decided to widen ECW's involvement with books about the current political situation in Quebec. That decision was an eye opener.

There were two specific books I wanted to publish and I was certain they would make a big splash. One would be a translation of a book by Guy Bertrand that had already been published in French to screams of indignation in the French press. Bertrand was a famous lawyer and a former separatist who had renounced his separatist leanings and gone over to the federalist side. His book made a number of the points I had discussed in my own work. Bertrand was particularly worried about a UDI. Ironically the Canada Council provided the ex-separatist with a grant to cover the cost of translating his work, and I struck a deal with him through one of his representatives. I never spoke directly with Bertrand. I was proud of publishing the book, but the man himself was a different story. When it finally came time for our launch I went up to Bertrand and introduced myself as his publisher, expressing my enthusiasm that we finally had a chance to meet. He gave me a limp hand and ignored me as he scanned the room, looking for his next power play. He was wearing thick makeup and his hair was dyed jet black. (Ever the man of the moment, Bertrand decided to become a separatist again a few years later, although he may be a federalist again by now.) He would eventually claim that the judges on the Supreme Court of Canada were involved in a pro-Jewish consipiracy. Has he no shame?

The second idea I had about a book on Quebec politics concerned the fate of the Native peoples. I was fascinated by the arguments in favour of partition they had raised in numerous interviews and documents. Their position was simple: they were a people, a nation. If the PQ could claim that Quebecers were a people, a nation that could decide to separate from Canada, then the Native peoples could also claim (with much more historical force and authority than the PQ) that they were a nation and that they could unilaterally separate from Quebec. The Native argument—developed most articulately by the James Bay Cree—struck a chord because it not only demonstrated the narrowness of PQ thinking (and its warped conception of the "nation" of.Quebec) but also because it opened the door to the fascinating idea of other communities with distinct identities unilaterally separating from an independent Quebec. Eventually the partition movement became one of the central forces accounting for the PQ's defeat by Jean Charest's Liberals. It appeared that most Quebecers did not want to see the province chopped up into several little territories.

The Cree took this issue of partition very seriously. They had published a massive study on their right to self-determination called *Sovereign Injustice: Forcible Inclusion of the James Bay Crees and Cree Territory into a Sovereign Quebec*. It may not have been a snappy title, but it was an incredibly detailed document about the legal ramifications of a UDI, both in terms of the general population and specifically in terms of the Cree and their territory in Quebec. The book contained 1,700 footnotes and pages and pages of legal citations. The Grand Council of the Crees had published this study for distribution to lawyers, policy makers, and government representatives. However, they wanted a simpler and more accessible version of their arguments to be available to the general public. I suppose because of my writing on the ramifications of a UDI, they contacted me and asked if ECW might be willing to do the trade version of *Sovereign Injustice*.

I had been moved by the plight they described in that book and felt deeply sympathetic toward their arguments. It struck me as an honour that they would trust ECW with this project; I'm not really sure why they approached us. What I do know is that they were a very careful and deliberate group of people with an excellent legal team. When I finally managed to arrange a meeting with a number of Cree representatives to discuss the project, I began by making a little speech about how *Sovereign Injustice* had struck an emotional chord. They had no time for my heartfelt empathy. They were practical, determined. When would the book be done? How would the project be managed? How could they be certain it met their legal requirements? We worked through the project and finally released the title as *Never without Consent: James Bay Crees' Stand against Forcible Inclusion into an Independent Quebec*. We had a launch for the book and I met Cree Grand Chief Matthew Coon Come, the man responsible for fighting the multibillion-dollar Great Whale hydroelectric project to a standstill and then engineering a revenue-sharing deal with Quebec for all future natural resource projects on Cree land. Coon Come had been bothering Lucien Bouchard from the moment he became premier, and in response to the separatists' referendum he had held a Cree referendum in which 98 percent voted to stay in Canada if Quebec separated. He later intervened in the federal government's Supreme Court of Canada reference on the separation issue, ensuring that Natives would have a say in any post-referendum negotiations. Somehow, my extremely modest and temporary involvement in Quebec political issues had allowed me to sit at a table next to this man who had devoted his life to bettering the condition of his people and the Native population of Canada. Like the Cree representatives I had met before him, he was serious, determined, and extremely well spoken. Oddly enough, after working with the Crees, I felt that in some ways they would be better defenders of federalism than any of the federalist politicians who had emerged before or during the referendum debate.

Although most of the books I signed up in connection with the Quebec situation had a fairly local impact, I was also increasingly drawn to titles that would have a much wider popular appeal, particularly in the States. I felt that if the company continued to publish books in popular culture we would eventually fill a niche. A quick look at the 1996 distribution arrangements for various ECW titles showed a company in transition. We were using General distribution for trade titles in Canada and scholarly and reference titles in the United States while we continued to use the LPC Group (which had bought InBook in 1997) for our US trade titles. When it came to international orders we were still in limbo, having signed a distribution arrangement with a company in Cardiff, Wales, for our academic material, and in 1993 we signed on with a company called Turnaround in London to distribute our commercial titles in the UK. It was clear that the future would have much more to do with trade books than with reference or scholarly titles, so the relationship with the trade distributors became more and more important over the next few years.

After 1996 most of our successful titles were in the areas of sports, entertainment, and popular culture. Jack had produced a book on David Duchovny of the *X Files* that sold well. Buoyed by the reception of the Duchovny book, he went on to publish another on Gillian Anderson, and then he really opened up the door with a wide variety of sports books, a number of biographies of film directors, and the first of what would be a long list of books on professional wrestling. (Jack had seen that wrestling fans loved their heroes and had the money to buy all kinds of titles connected with the sport.) To add to the mix, he came out with a book called *Girl Show*, an illustrated retrospective of adult entertainers in the carnival world. I was doing books on *Buffy the Vampire Slayer*, George Clooney, Shania Twain, Radiohead, Melissa Etheridge, and the Dave Matthews Band. A number of these titles were written by members of the ECW staff, which had grown in the years after Don's departure. The new hirings were partly made possible by new government grants that supported internship salaries, or by other government programs that supplemented the employee's wage. Jennifer Hale, who worked in the Toronto office, wrote books on *Buffy* and *Xena* under the pseudonym Nikki Stafford, while Michael Holmes, our poetry editor, agreed to write the Shania Twain bio.

Every once in a while I would be struck by the weirdness of these titles and my connection to them. How did I ever get to the point that I was seriously looking for an author to write a book on Regis Philbin and why in the world was I doing a book on Shania Twain? Obviously the desire to succeed in publishing at all costs was perverting me, forcing me to embrace titles that might be lucrative but which held little interest for me personally. It was a kind of prostitution, and I was doing it all the time. Worse, there seemed to be no end in sight to this cynical approach. The pressure was on to find titles that would sell, and we had got ourselves into a mentality that dictated a list of acquisitions based on the existence of rabid fan bases and niche markets. In this context, an academic study of, say, Phyllis Webb, might be a poor seller, but at least it might have some kind of intellectual integrity. There were a number of trade titles that I pursued out of real passion (I loved the music of the Dave Matthews Band and Tom Waits and would have done anything to publish a book on Trent Reznor if the competition wasn't so stiff), but I really had to wonder who I was when I saw ECW books on Jennifer Lopez and Tim Horton sitting on my desk.

Sometimes the pursuit of a music title would lead me into surprising meetings or experiences. After I heard James Di Salvio and Bran Van 3000 play in a local Montreal club, I became convinced the group would become massively famous and that ECW should do the Bran Van book before someone else did. I set up a meeting with Di Salvio, met the band, and learned a lot about where hip-hop and DJ culture was going. We never did the book, which was a good thing, because the band didn't take off as I expected, even though I still think their CD, *Discosis*, is amazing.

Jack liked to work with experienced Toronto writers on successive titles, especially when he knew the author would deliver the goods on time. He also liked the idea of using Canadian authors for the books, mainly because they were eligible for funding under the Canada Council's block grant program, which meant that a number of the titles would get a little extra kick of government cash, assuming they were eligible. I signed foreign authors more often than Jack, encouraged by my belief that if I found the best writer for the job, whether in Toronto, or L.A., or London, increased sales would follow, and those would more than compensate for the grant. Jack believed that we should always look for our writers in Canada first, not only because they would be eligible for grants, but for nationalist reasons as well. He was probably right, but my search for appropriate authors often took me in different directions.

Sometimes we would go the Canadian grant route, only to be cut off at the pass by the Canada Council, which realized that their eligibility requirements had not been quite stringent enough to disqualify us for funding on a particular title they deemed to be too commercial and popular to warrant us receiving government money. They liked biographies, if they were serious and literary, but they didn't like celebrity biographies, especially if they were based on cut and paste research. After they were compelled to fund our Shania Twain bio because it met the existing guidelines, they warned us that celebrity biographies (even biographies on famous Canadian celebrities) would never get funded again. If that was the case, would they fund a book on carnival strippers if it was written by a Canadian, and what about a biography of Muddy Waters, also written by a Canadian. Would it get a grant?

The more we pursued these popular titles, the more it became clear that the Canada Council was sending out some confusing signals about its mandate. Was it there to fund titles that would otherwise never see the light of day because they were sure to lose money, or was it there to support companies because they were doing a range of good things but still losing money and might soon be out of business? Ironically, the more the Canada Council put restrictions on the types of books eligible for funding, the more it drove us to find titles that would have a much broader appeal in the North American market. If there was no special reason to publish a biography of Shania Twain rather than a book on wrestling then we would choose the title that seemed to offer the most sales potential. If you wanted to benefit from government funding you had to tailor your project to the program requirements, which meant no guidebooks, or compilations of statistics, or sports trivia, or cookbooks, to name only a few of the genres excluded from the funding categories. As it focused its mandate over the years, the Canada Council increasingly refused to support critical books, arguing that they were not creative works, and therefore should be funded by SSHRC because they weren't accessible to a general audience.

Right there, in that decision, you can see the beginning of the end of CanCrit, and the reason why so many publishing companies have turned away from Canadian criticism over the past decade. If the history of Canadian literature shows us anything, it is that publishers will simply not pursue critical works that are ineligible for funding, and even if that funding is available, as it still is through SSHRC, a commercial publisher will not go through the laborious process of getting SSHRC support. Instead, they will turn their energy in other directions. Ironically, the Canada Council's decision not to fund critical books ensured that those books would never be creative and further ensured that academic critics would spend less and less time discussing Canadian literature, simply because their books would not get financial support from the main funding body or from most of the other funding bodies that were mandated to make culture more accessible to the public. The long-term result of the council's ruling was that CanCrit began to dry up in the mid-1990s, and this explains why there is so little of it today. Who suffers as a result of this? Mainly our contemporary writers, whose work does not get the critical attention it deserves, and which has generally been denied the kind of critical responsiveness enjoyed by an earlier generation of writers. In the end, grants became the force that determined whether Canadian literary criticism would be published or not.

The double-sided nature of ECW wasn't only the result of the choices made by two copublishers who had different ideas about how to keep the company afloat. It was also a response to the funding possibilities that had to be considered in virtually every decision. Our Janus-like image emerged most clearly in the spring 1999 catalogue. Jack and I had long been worried that the Canada Council would see all our trade titles next to our literary titles and decide that we had become too commercial to remain in the block grant program or would conclude that we didn't merit the extra funding that came with the Council's bonus points for being good cultural citizens. We needed to find a way to convince the Council that we were doing the kind of literary titles it liked to see. At the same time we wanted buyers to view us as a trade press, not just as a publishing house that put out Canadian poetry or short stories. The solution to this problem was to create two distinct catalogues that could be bound together but also separated when required. We printed a catalogue of our literary titles that was slightly smaller than the catalogue of our commercial titles. All we had to do for the Canada Council was to send them the interior catalogue, which had its own spiffy cover. For other eyes, we could either send out the combined catalogues, which had been saddle-stitched together, or we could separate them and use one or the other. So the cover of the trade catalogue for spring 1999 highlighted a biography of the band Radiohead, a book called *Slammin':
Wrestling's Greatest Heroes and Villains, Girl Show*, and one of our Secret series of travel guides; meanwhile, the inside catalogue featured the artsy

cover of a new novel by Tony Burgess. For the fall 1999 catalogue we repeated the process: the trade cover showed books on Godzilla, a biography of David E. Kelley, another bio on Gillian Anderson, and a collection of hockey trivia, while the inside catalogue featured Catherine Gildiner's literary memoir *Too Close to the Falls*. Somehow, I had reached the point where I was publishing an annotated bibliography of works by and about Stephen Leacock alongside a biography of Sarah Michelle Gellar called *Bite Me!*

The increasing emphasis on trade publishing took us both down some new roads, both good and bad. On the good side, it allowed me to pursue a number of my own interests, one of which was travel. I had long been frustrated by conventional travel guides and wanted to try something different. My idea was to produce an eccentric guide to Montreal, one that would celebrate all the great places the big guides by Fodor's and Frommer's and Lonely Planet missed. I hooked up with a professional writer, Tod Hoffman, and he agreed to write *Secret Montreal*. We developed a unique design for the book, which featured a cover photo by my friend Linda Rutenberg, who used a special technique to achieve a painterly and moody effect.

To my astonishment, *Secret Montreal* soon made it onto the local bestseller list. I was elated. Even though I soon learned that the local bestseller designation does not necessarily translate into great sales, I took it as positive feedback on the conception of the book in general, and I began to think of a series of guides that would be based on the same design. Over the next few years I signed up numerous titles in the series. In some cities, like Chicago and Toronto, the books did quite well, going into a reprint, but in other cities, especially New York, they failed miserably. I remember standing with Mary in a Barnes and Noble on Fifth Avenue, watching excitedly as a store clerk picked up a handful of the guides. "They're restocking!" she said. Finally, the books had caught on and were now selling briskly. But one second later I saw that in fact they were being taken off the shelf by the handful, the sudden death of the non-seller.

Still, I often enjoyed meeting the Secret authors, and sometimes there were great bonuses attached. For example, the author of *Secret New York*, Robert Sietsema, was the restaurant critic for the *Village Voice* and wrote for a number of other established publications that paid him to visit some of North America's finest restaurants. One day he called to say that he was coming to Montreal to do a restaurant roundup for *Gourmet*, and would Mary and I like to go out with him one evening to visit some of the high-end restaurants he would be reviewing. "What do you mean when you say 'some' restaurants?" I asked him. "Oh, we'll start early and visit three," he replied, as if this were the most natural thing in the world. A few days later we hit three stellar restaurants, tucking into full meals at each. (He generously gave our doggy bag of impeccable sushi to the taxi driver who was taking us to the next restaurant.) The extravaganza took six hours. We had wonderful sake at Tree House. We had a huge Fanny Bay oyster topped with pineapple-dill confit at Toqué!, the city's most renowned place. There was duck and foie gras. Sietsema ordered champagne. Several rich desserts appeared. No big deal. The next day he would be doing the same thing all over again, in Toronto. What a life!

Although the numbers never justified the Secret series, I kept it going, mainly because I believed that one day the phone would ring and one of the big travel publishing companies would offer to buy it for a million dollars. And every year when this didn't happen I would talk it over with Jack, who reminded me how much money the series was losing, along with the hugeness of the competition and the unlikeliness of success. I think he would have been quite happy to pull the plug, but he knew how personally invested I was in the look and feel of the series, and maybe, inside, he also believed we might one day get the call. So every year we said "One more year. One more year."

Perhaps one of the reasons Jack was willing to live with the losses on the Secret series was that we were experiencing strong sales on other titles. Some of the music titles, in particular, had done quite well. I had decided to find an author to write a Dave Matthews Band book after hearing an early CD, *Under the Table and Dreaming*, when I was browsing in a store in Florida. I put out a call for an author on the Internet and was swamped with inquiries. It didn't take me long to find someone whom I thought knew the story of the band as thoroughly as it could be told. After we signed the contract I met Morgan Delancey, the author, in Charlottesville, Virginia, where the band had come together in the early 1990s. The idea was that we would both look through the archives at the University of Virginia, where some of the band members had gone to school, to see if we could find any original information that could be used in the book. It was like one of the archival research projects I remembered from my own days as a CanLit graduate student, but instead of looking for details about John Newlove I was digging into files in the southern US, looking for stories about one of the best bands I had ever heard. While we were in Charlottesville we also stumbled onto a cache of photos that had never been published. I bought the photos and obtained the rights to use them in the book, which finally came out in 1998. It took off, selling close to 100,000 copies in a first and second edition.

When we were completing the Dave Matthews Band book I asked my students if there were any diehard DMB fans around, thinking I might find some helpful advance readers. Almost immediately I was approached by an energetic-looking guy who said he knew everything there was to know about the band. I invited him up to my office. The second he walked in he asked if he could just use my computer for a moment; there was something pressing he had to do on the Internet. Curious, and somewhat affronted, I said sure. He dumped out a bag of computer disks and inserted one into a drive. Up sprang what looked like the script for a play. But it was not a play. It was a record of his most recent adventures in an Internet chat room, where he had been busy assuming an identity and seducing women online. I could see that there was another side to this young man. In fact, given the number of disks he had spilled onto my desk, I could see that he had many sides. I watched closely as his fingers flew over the keys. The chat seemed crude, but one aspect of it I found exciting: the ability to create multiple personae and to play them out, anonymously, online.

David asked me if I wanted to give it a go. Before I knew it I was engaged in a chat with a person who professed to be 20 years old, and very interested in me. And why not? I was 23, athletically inclined, a student in Montreal, and my girlfriend had just left me. David said I needed a picture of myself, just in case someone asked me to post it. "How can I give you a picture of myself? I'm almost 20 years older than my chat room self." "No big deal," he said. "I'll just find a new picture of you on the net." After a few mouse clicks a picture of someone I'd never seen before appeared on my screen. "That's you," David said. Not bad, I thought.

I named myself Lamp Man, after Archibald. That night, when I got home, I crept into my office and booted up the computer, determined to explore my new identity. There I was, right in the chat room, and I was being approached by a number of chatters! Almost immediately one asked for my pic. I sent it off. "Man, you are hot!" came the reply. "Yes! I thought. Lamp Man *is* hot." Better still, I could be anyone. I could be several hot people. I could even be a hot woman. I started to think up her name. I headed back into the chat room, determined to find out more about this world. Only then was I able to pinpoint what it was that had been bothering me, somewhere in the back of my mind, since the moment I logged on. It was the spelling. These chatters were illiterate. None of them could spell. And their grammar was atrocious. None of them even grasped that I was named after a famous Canadian poet. I started to pick on some of the chat room denizens, challenging them to spell properly. Had they ever read a book, I asked, starting to get huffy. "Wht R U," one replied, "some redneck trash teachuh?" I couldn't confess outright, so I stood my ground. A lot of them seemed to find my comments offensive. Several typed "LOL." Another one said, "Lamp Man is a spelling Aunty." Then the illiterate chatters rose up and started cursing me en masse, telling me to get out of the room. They shut me out. The next time I saw David I asked him why they had all typed "LOL." He paused for a moment, and then said, "It stands for Laugh Out Loud." Very funny. This was not the life for me.

David had been to dozens of Dave Matthews band shows. When I learned that they would soon be performing in Ottawa I asked him if he had any tips to offer that might get me closer to the stage. "Sure," he said. "Just tell them you're the publisher of the new book on the band." Tickets in hand, my daughter Emily and I headed off to Ottawa. I did what I was told. I announced to the security guards that we were the publishers of the new band biography, so it was essential we get into the auditorium along with the other press. Step right this way, they said. So we got to stand about five feet away from Dave, a position I held valiantly against the crushing onslaught of thousands of tank-topped 18-year-old women who were pressing forward and squeezing me to death. Those women are strong! I couldn't breathe. After an hour, Emily and I had to be crowd-surfed out to safety. My glasses were bent. On the way home I considered the fact that a life in CanLit had somehow brought me to that concert and was now returning me to Montreal, where I could savour the delicate and complex poetry of Eric Ormsby, one of Canada's greatest living poets, or the fiery tribulations of James Campbell in his relentless pursuit of hot sauce and abstract art. They were both ECW authors. I was embracing extremes.

If you decide to publish biographies of celebrities or rock bands you will soon be hearing from their lawyers. We heard from the Dave Matthews Band's lawyer, who tried to intimidate me into ceasing publication. ECW was forbidden, he said, to use the name of the band or any image of the band in our book. I reminded him that these were public figures, and that we were still living in a place that permitted free expression. Jack had his own lawyer problems. Every time he tried to produce a book related to a Hollywood movie or a celebrity, the lawyers were quick to pounce. Even nice old Jerry Seinfeld had a group of tough legal representatives who did not like the idea of our unauthorized biography. Usually these threats forced us to consult our own lawyers and to engage in various forms of consultation and negotiation, which always cost money. We had to play it safe. We worried that one of these Hollywood studios or some celebrity might actually sue us or try to get an injunction preventing us from selling an already-published book. What would we do then? We didn't like surprises, and we didn't like the odds. Fortunately, we knew about the kinds of insurance policies available to publishers—policies that would cover legal costs if we were sued for defamation, or libel, or violation of copyright. Better safe than sorry. We opted for a policy that would give us a million dollars' worth of coverage.

That was a good decision, especially when it came to our biography of Shania Twain. Our poetry editor, Michael Holmes, wrote it under the pseudonym Dallas Williams, mainly, I guess, because he did not want his reputation as a poet and editor sullied by this association with a big pop star. I had no problems with that. I had known Michael for years and thought highly of his poetry. He had come to Montreal to give readings to some of my classes and I had tried to support his work through course adoptions from time to time. I knew that Michael didn't like the idea of my signing poetry books or novels on my own. He thought that he should have full control of the list, while I thought that if a publisher couldn't make his own choices from time to time, what was it all about? Eventually we encouraged Michael to develop his own imprint—MisFit Books—within ECW so that he could segregate those titles that had received his editorial blessing. Despite my sense that he resented my support of various authors who didn't write to his aesthetic (even after he had his own imprint), I felt comfortable working with Michael and was convinced that he would find the right voice to make the Shania bio a success.

Things went just fine after the bio was published. Even though it cited the book as an example of the kind of biography that it would consider ineligible in the future, the Canada Council funded the title, which meant it would certainly break even. Sales were brisk both in Canada and the US. The only problem was that in fact we had not got there before anyone else did. One day, several months after the bio was published, I got a letter from Carolyn Swayze, the literary agent for Barbara Hager, the author of a book called *Honour Song: A Tribute*, which was a commentary on Twain's career, based on first-hand interviews that Hager had done with Twain. Swayze charged that Dallas Williams had used material from Hager's book without her permission, and that it was therefore a case of copyright infringement. I asked Michael about this and he assured me that his use of Hager's material fell within the fair usage rules, which meant that a writer could quote from another source so long as it was credited and only when that material was used to support a critical discussion. In fact, he pointed out, Hager's book was cited in his bibliography. It was no big deal. I decided that if I ignored Swayze's letter the issue would just go away. Was Hager really going to go out and sue us because one of our authors had used a few of her ideas and maybe even a few of her words without formal permission? Well, the answer was Yes. Hager found herself a lawyer and sued us for a fairly substantial amount of money, a sum that seemed ridiculous to us. But could we fight this? Would our copyright infringement insurance work? Would it cover our legal costs, not to mention a judgement against us, if we lost?

Our lawyers asked to see the insurance policy, which covered us up to $1,000,000. They went through it with a fine-tooth comb. Then came the good news. In fact it would cover us. We could go wild. I asked how much it would cost to fight the case to the limit and was told that it would probably consume the full million in legal costs along with a reserve for a judgement against us. How ridiculous was that? If it looked like we were heading for more than a million in total costs, we could just pull the plug with the lawyers somewhere around $750,000 in billable hours and hope that no judgement would award Hager more than a quarter million. Of course this was all insane. The first insanity was the amount that the lawyers would earn regardless of the outcome. What a great business they were in. They charged something like $500 per hour and got it, win or lose. By my calculation, they were telling us that they might have to work 1,500 hours on this, at $500 per hour. Ha ha! Meanwhile, the client, in this case us, lacking all expertise, was literally held hostage. Being a professor and a publisher was just so stupid. I should have been a lawyer. I would have no debt and I could go to good restaurants all the time. I could travel anywhere and probably even charge it to the business. Our own lawyers seemed like a happy crew. No mystery there. They were rolling in it. They said that because Hager lived in Vancouver the case would be heard there, in federal court, if we decided to fight it. I asked one more time: are you 100 percent sure we can spend a million dollars on this, and the insurance company will cover it all? They said Yes. They had consulted with the insurance company about the case and got the green light. I asked about our chances of winning. They said 50-50. (Were they going to say we only had a ten percent chance of winning when they knew we had an insurance policy for legal costs worth a million bucks?)

It didn't take Jack and I long to reach a decision. We would fight it, and, further, we would try to work the billing for the case so that Michael himself was not stuck with any costs. Why did we do this if our chances of winning were not that great? Maybe we could vindicate Michael, and ECW. Besides, it looked like a hell of a lot of fun. How often did you get to hire a team of top-drawer lawyers who toiled on the corporate floors of one of those big Toronto skyscrapers, knowing they would work for you at their outrageous fees while an insurance company that also charged outrageous fees would pay the obscene tab? I had always been fascinated by the process of litigation and had always wondered what magic these lawyers worked in order to charge those fees. This was like being given a winning lottery ticket. I could finally get involved in a law orgy at someone else's expense. And it might get even better, because if there really was a trial I would have to fly to Vancouver to appear in court, and the insurance company would pay for that too! A free trip out west! What could be better?

The wheels of the law turn slowly. The billable hours piled up. We were determined to fight this one out. The very reputation of our authors was at stake. No settlement could be reached. A trial date was set for September 1998. I was about to get my free trip. Michael and I met in Vancouver and talked with our lawyer out there. He seemed more nervous than the ones in Toronto. After all, he was the guy who was going to show up in court to defend us. I walked around Vancouver, hung out a bit with Michael, and finally showed up for the court date. Despite my protestations to the contrary, it was clear that small parts of Michael's book had in fact been based on Hager's research. It also seemed perfectly clear to me, in retrospect, that we should have just recognized this fact, apologized to Hager, and made a small payment to her by way of compensation and apology. But now it was too late for that.

The trial judge was a formidable, no-nonsense woman who looked down over her glasses at me as I testified. She could hardly hide her disdain. Our lawyer said it was not going well. But even if we lost, he assured us, there might still be some money left over to launch an appeal. I doubted it: we had already spent close to $600,000 of the insurance money, and we hadn't received a bill from our lawyers in at least ten days. Three months later, in December, the decision came down: we lost, and we would have to pay Hager $12,405 and the costs of her action. In addition, we would have to stop distributing the book. I tried to calculate the number of hours I had spent dealing with our lawyers on this case, along with the days I had spent in Vancouver during the trial. All for $12,405 in damages. Meanwhile, the final tally on the costs of our defence were almost in: close to the million dollars covered by the policy. The insurance company paid the bills and promptly cancelled our policy. No other insurance company would touch us. If we decided to get involved in lawsuits in the future, it would be at our own expense.

I don't know what kind of effect this had on Michael. Eventually his cover was blown and everyone knew that ECW's poetry editor had authored a bio of Shania Twain. Fewer knew that it had been the subject of a legal action that put Michael's own research methods in doubt. At the time, I didn't think this defeat had strained my relation with Michael. Later, I wondered if it had. Perhaps he felt that I hadn't gone far enough to defend him. Maybe he felt sullied by the whole affair. What became clear to me in the months that followed was that Michael had redoubled his efforts as editor, poet, and novelist, the roles in which he could most powerfully assert his creative individuality.

Although I didn't sense any direct tension between the Toronto and Montreal offices as a result of the Twain debacle, my longstanding doubts about the harmony between the two offices began to weigh on me. Jack had gradually rebuilt his staff over the years and they were intensely loyal to him. Because we had long ago decided that decisions about publishing individual titles would be taken independently, by me or Jack, there was little corporate unity. Of course I was happy when one of Jack's books clicked. And if one of mine did well he might write me one of his terse little notes: "Good work." But there was no team spirit bringing the offices together. On the contrary, there was a rivalry developing. Which office would sell more books? Which books looked better? How did our various sales teams see the titles?

In Montreal I had developed a relatively centralized model for book production and marketing. There were a few part-time staff members, along with Holly, and we would discuss the merits of a particular book idea, although the final decision was always left to me. Once a book entered the production queue it would be guided through the process by a production manager who handled all the titles. I liked this model because it meant that there was always one person who knew exactly how things stood on all the books in production. But in Toronto, which had a slightly bigger staff, books were handled from beginning to end by different people, depending on who took responsibility for the project or on whether they had been responsible for the acquisition. This meant that there was a lot more individual freedom in Toronto, and I know this was something Jack wanted to encourage. Whatever the model, the books got done, but it was clear that the company was fostering two different mentalities and two completely different sets of values when it came to the acquisition and production of the company's list. This is what I feared would be the outcome of Jack's decision, years earlier, to allow each of us the absolute right to sign titles without mutual consultation. We had grown the business, but in doing so we had also planted the seeds of a schism that now seemed to be emerging more clearly with every season. I never got the sense that the people in Toronto and Montreal were working to the same ends. There was very little sense of collectively sharing victories or examining defeats.

Ironically, Jack perceived this growing rift. He was always encouraging staff get togethers between the two offices, which we had for several years, but it seemed that each of these meetings only served to accentuate the differences between the offices and to underline how disunited we really were. At first I thought the problem could be solved if only Jack would abandon this idea of individuals developing and signing titles without some kind of corporate approval process. But he was hardened in his belief that this would deprive his staff of what they liked most about ECW—the freedom to pursue their individual ideas, and to turn them into books. I could see his point of view. On the other hand, it bred a feeling of separateness that bugged the hell out of me. I would call up the Toronto office to find out when someone would be receiving a cheque and be spoken to with coldness, as if I was a pain in the ass calling up to dun the company rather than one of the company's owners. Technically, the people in Toronto worked for me as well as Jack. But they had no loyalty to me. And why should they? They practically never saw me, I was not directly involved in their projects, and I was just a voice who called or e-mailed, asking for things.

Did Jack see the cracks widening as time went on? I'm sure he did. Every few years he would write me a letter expressing frustration at the way in which our roles were weighted. No matter how we adjusted things, he always seemed to be doing more. I know he resented this. I resented his growing lack of consultation, his refusal to address the rift that was developing through more than annual meetings of the two offices. Some days I felt he would just as soon be rid of me. He could be a wall of silence. But then we would discuss some potential deal and the old camaraderie would flow back. We had made this thing. It was almost the year 2000 and we had been in this for 25 years. The relationship had outlasted any other partnership in my life; it had far outlasted my first marriage. We were together in this in some kind of primal way that transcended day-to-day tensions, mainly because we had been so close to the edge so many times and had always come back, still together. But now I began to wonder how long this could be sustained.

One real irritant in our relationship was Paul Davies, who had now been typesetting and designing covers for both offices for many years. Although Paul was brilliant in many respects, he was also highly dependent on Jack, who had supported Paul and his eccentricities for years. To my surprise, he had even published Paul's poetry at a time when cash flow was particularly low, no doubt as a gesture of faith in Paul's work, and as a sign of his stature within the company. The two of them worked on countless books together. For my part, the relationship with Paul was always strained. There was lots of tension, particularly as I became more interested in developing trade titles that required other cover designers. I started to do this with the cover for the Melissa Etheridge bio, which came out in 1997. After that I began to work with a number of different designers. Paul was not happy about that. When Jack also began to turn to other designers, the writing was on the wall. Toward the end of 1999 Paul met with Jack to discuss the strains. We were still supporting Paul's operation, paying overhead, and maintaining a variety of computers and printers, among other expenses. Jack could see, as I did, that it no longer made sense to restrict ourselves to one designer, especially because the list was growing. Paul's involve-ment as a writer also became a point of contention. Although Jack had published a number of his small books, Paul wanted ECW to print all of his works together, in a collected edition. Jack balked at that, and Paul pulled back even more. Six months later, he was gone.

The year leading up to Paul's departure was a compounding series of stresses. The Shania trial had taken its toll, as had the increasingly strained relations between the two offices. For every successful title I published it seemed there was always another that lost money. I never began a day's work without feeling that somehow, somewhere, I was not pulling my weight. Despite our debt, Jack and I had made a conscious decision to grow the company, to sign more titles, to expand to the point where we would be recognized as a serious mid-sized company, even in the US. In order to do this I had to compartmentalize my brain and switch my different identities, often several times a day. Usually on Monday, Wednesday, and Friday mornings I was Professor Lecker, trying to stay focused on my classes and student needs. Then, briefly, I became editor Lecker, looking over articles for the journal and trying to pick out neat cover images for future issues. My mother had turned over the management of my father's estate to me, so I also became investor Lecker, trying to recover from the carnage of the tech bubble meltdown. I would sit there looking at graphs and reports, tortured by doubts about the competence of stock market analysts. Most afternoons I became publisher Lecker, and that's when things really began to heat up. There were no calm days. Agents called to hassle me. The attitude of the Toronto office staff bugged me. My conversations with Jack frustrated me. A screw-up on a cover or some page proofs would probably cause us to miss an important deadline. I felt ill-prepared for the upcoming sales conference in Chicago.

All of this was manageable if things at McGill were running smoothly, and most of the time they were. What made the job particularly enjoyable was the students. They were involved, passionate, and highly motivated. Almost always. But every once in a while things just crashed. In 1993 my routine had been disrupted by a student who kept coming to my office and accusing me of being P.K. Page. I could not convince him that I was not P.K. Page. I was afraid to show up during my office hours, knowing he'd be lying in wait. Then there was one particularly bad term: spring 1997, the same year I was trying to cope with the fallout from my writing about Quebec and right after I had started working on finance guru Brian Costello's book on managing your money (he was later charged with Ontario Securities Commission violations) and another about the women Jack Kerouac had loved.

The term started in a relatively normal fashion. I was offering two courses, one on the development of Canadian poetry and another on Alice Munro. The Munro class had about 40 students, most of whom were women. I think there were three or four guys in the whole group. Things were moving along nicely. Munro's fiction always got students involved. For one of their assignments they had to present a short paper on *Lives of Girls and Women,* or on a particular story we had been discussing. Each class would include one or two five-minute presentations. I was amazed by the range of reference in these little talks. Obviously the students had been strongly affected by Munro's work, and I was looking forward to making some connections among the various presentations. Then, one day, it was time for Steve to make his presentation. He had visited me in my office a few days earlier and asked if he was free to develop a "different" approach. I encouraged him to do so. "Surprise me," I said.

Now he was standing in front of the class. I could see the other two guys huddled in the back row, looking expectant. Steve began to give his talk. He disagreed, he said, with most of the women in the class who had portrayed Del Jordan as an innocent young woman whose actions were driven by her love of reading and art. He disagreed, he said, with the idea that Del's loss of virginity had nothing to do with her need for sex. No, he said, what Del really wanted was violent, brutal sex. "She wants to be fucked in the dirt like a dog!" is how Steve put it, gazing defiantly at the women while the other guys hunched in the back. Was this some kind of setup? What was he trying to do, and how could he come into my class and talk like that? I could see the women around me getting flushed and angry. Something was gonna blow. I said, "Steve, you can't say that here. I'm asking you to stop your talk." At this point several students started telling him they were insulted, that he should shut up. "No," Steve said. "I have constitutional rights to free speech. What right do you have to censor me?" He might have had a point, but there was no way I was going to allow the class to go down that road. Besides, I sensed that he had made the statement purely to provoke unrest. He continued talking. I cut him off. He slammed out of the room screaming "You'll hear about this!"

It was not a pleasant day. Soon after, Steve lodged one of those wonderful procedures that professors love: the grievance. This involves the laying of formal charges against the prof, the creation of a hearing committee, the time and energy of several faculty and student members. After weeks of meetings and hearings I was cleared of any wrongdoing. Unhappy with the result, Steve wrote me a note saying that his father was a powerful lawyer and that if I didn't print a full apology in the student newspaper within a week he was going to sue my ass. Apparently, I had defamed him and denied him his constitutional rights. For some reason, he seemed to think that I owned the *McGill Daily*, or that I could just send them a full-page apology to a single student, knowing that of course they would stop the presses to include my prostrations in their latest edition. I ignored his letter. He went away. But the whole affair killed the class, messed up the mood.

This was happening at the same time my poetry course was hitting a high point. The class had been compromised from time to time by the behaviour of one student, who became determined to irritate me after he unsuccessfully protested the grade I had assigned to his first essay. Neil showed up in my office hours, enraged with the "B" he had received on his analysis of *Seed Catalogue*, one of Robert Kroetsch's long poems.

It was definitely an "A," he pronounced. "Well," I said, "I don't think so, but you are entitled to have someone else read the paper and decide whether the grade is fair. Just take it down to the chairman's office and they will find another reader." Two weeks went by and the verdict came in: the grade was fair. Neil was even more enraged now. He showed up at every one of my office hours, demanding justice. Then he started coming to class with a big paper grocery bag filled with clementine oranges. Making lots of noise, he would pull an orange out of the bag, peel it slowly, and leave the peel in a pile on the table, around which the small group of students sat. Then he would pull out another and another, peeling and piling, peeling and piling, crinkling the paper bag. After four classes like this I said, "Neil, I don't mind you eating in the class, but could you work on one orange at a time, rather than on all of them at once? It's disrupting the discussion." He shot me a look of pure hatred. "No," he said. "Is there any rule that says I can't eat oranges the way I want?" Of course there wasn't, and I told him that. So he continued to peel and pile. I never saw him eat an orange. I couldn't wait for the end of the term.

In much better years, and especially as my interest in music broadened, the students were a huge help. I had always listened to a wide range of music, but at the same time I worried that I was gradually losing touch with what was happening now, just as I was concerned about not keeping up with contemporary Canadian poetry and fiction. Not keeping up was a sign of slowing down, I thought, sure proof that I was heading into that middle-aged state where your learning and willingness to hear and read new things begins to shut down. I was determined not to let that happen. I could see the inroads that hip-hop had made. I could see the effects that digitization and turntabling had on the kind of music my students were listening to every day. Yet I wasn't always sure where to start when it came to exploring new things or finding out what was hot. I decided to let the students be my teachers. Why not? There were hundreds of them plugged into all kinds of musical artists and trends.

In my big lecture class—Introduction to Canadian Literature—I started playing one cut from a CD at the beginning of every class. The only rule was that the CD had to be by a Canadian artist. The students jumped on this idea and started pelting me with CDs. I liked the music so much that it was hard for me to turn it off and get down to the lecture. Then I decided to let the students help me broaden my tastes even more. I would walk into a large lecture hall and ask 300 students: "What should I be listening to?" All kinds of hands would shoot up, and every year there would be a different consensus. One year was special. I posed the question and found at least 25 students recommending the same CD: *Further down the Spiral* by Nine Inch Nails. I ran out and bought the album and got sucked into Trent Reznor's decadent somnolence and hysteria, the wild primitiveness of that music. Just get in your car and crank up the cuts on that CD titled "The Art of Self Destruction," parts 1 and 2. Turn it up *loud*. There's nothing like it:

i am the voice inside your head
i am the lover in your bed
i am the sex that you provide
i am the hate you try to hide

I wanted to see Reznor perform live. Eventually I opened up the lecture to all kinds of music, asked the students to loan me CDs that I could burn. The Red Hot Chili Peppers, Beastie Boys, Lauryn Hill, Eminem, and Linkin Park:

I don't know what's worth fighting for
Or why I have to scream
I don't know why I instigate
And say what I don't mean
I don't know how I got this way
I'll never be alright
So, I'm breaking the habit
I'm breaking the habit
Tonight

I listened, and listened, and began to get some basic understanding of my students' fascination with hip-hop and rap. For many of them, it wasn't just something you heard; it was a way of life. I kept obsessing about certain groups. I couldn't get over the synthesis of musical forms in the Beastie Boys' *Ill Communication*, a classical flute piece segueing into the Boys' take on pleasure in "Flute Loop":

A little wine with my dinner so I'm in the grape ape
I feel like a winner when I make a mix tape
Because I get ill when I'm on the pause button
And I get my fill and you can't say nothing
More soul on this train than Don Cornelious
Got the mad subwoofer pumping bass for your anus

I saw a TV documentary about how the Chili Peppers recorded *Blood Sugar Sex Magik* (in order to make it happen they imprisoned themselves in a Hollywood mansion for many weeks and at one point brought in a church choir to help them get the right tone at the end of a song). They escaped only once—to a lumber yard where they bought 2 by 4s so they could hit the oil barrels they had collected in order to produce the special clanging drum effects in "Breaking the Girl." I ran out and got the album. Then I listened to it again and again and again. There was so much evidence of craftsmanship.

My range of reference broadened quickly. I wanted to keep those big classes active, moving the focus as often as I could. Whenever possible I would bring in writers, hoping their enthusiasm would spread to the class. Stuart Ross. David McGimpsey. Mary di Michele. Erin Mouré. I thought it was important for the students to see writers in action, to experience the fact that Canadian literature was alive and kicking and not just something you studied from a book. Still, I always worried about these readings. What if the students were bored, or offended in some way by the writer? Sometimes these visitors would surprise the class in the most delightful ways, like the time Stuart Ross told the class stories about some of the lines he discovered in various books he had been editing for a romance novel publisher:

She wrapped her arms around him and placed a hand on each buttock, male and female.

* * *

Large drops of rain began to fall, with spaces between them.

* * *

He tugged down her panties and kissed the valley between her breasts.

One of the most stressful readings I planned had to be the visit by Michael Turner. We were studying his wonderful punkoid long poem, *Hard Core Logo*, and I had been playing the *Hard Core Logo* "Tribute" CD in class, with all its great punk cuts. We had also watched Bruce MacDonald's terrific film version of *Hard Core Logo*, to the students' general delight. Why not ask Michael if he would find some way to make it to Montreal and drop in on the class?

I got in touch with Michael. By sheer coincidence he would be flying to Toronto from Vancouver for a meeting about his upcoming novel, *The Pornographer's Poem*. He would see if he could extend the trip to accommodate my class. Maybe he could even set up another reading in the city, which he did, at the Jailhouse Rock Café, a local club. So it was really going to happen—Michael Turner in my class! The day before the lecture I picked him up at the airport and drove him to his hotel, which was under siege by renovation teams who had gutted most of the building. Sawdust floated in the air. Wires jutted from walls. Michael hardly seemed to notice. I took him home for a drink. As I was scurrying around looking for a corkscrew and wine I heard Michael talking with Mary in the next room, spinning stories about how his ancestors were violent unruly Cossacks. I introduced Michael to five-year-old Claire. "Hey Claire," he says. "Nice to meet you." When the babysitter arrived, Michael was introduced. This tall stranger, dressed in black, a shock of black hair splayed over his forehead, locked eyes with the babysitter, smiled, and said, "Hi. You'll be looking after me tonight."

I was definitely feeling nervous. What direction would Michael's quirky sense of humour take when he got in front of my students the next day? It had been a good semester and I wanted it to end well. All of a sudden I realized that the man in my living room was the author of *The Pornographer's Poem*. He could say anything. He could *do* anything! He claimed to have written many pornographic novels under various pseudonyms. Renovation didn't bother him, he made up stories about his Cossack heritage, he had an intense dark look about him, and he was very comfortable with the babysitter, who was the same age as my students. I skittered around the kitchen. I found the corkscrew.

But Michael didn't want wine. He said he would like vodka on *one* rock with some freshly cracked black pepper over the top. Of course. He sipped at the drink. I think he just asked for vodka with black pepper because it sounded like the kind of drink a person with Cossack bloodlines would demand. He was only pretending to drink it. I asked Michael if he would allow me to interview him for an article I hoped to write on his work. But even as I said the word "interview" I was struck by the absurdity of the idea. Turner would make it all up. He would say whatever came into his head. Well-researched questions would be pointless. And after all, I could make him up just as easily as he could make himself up. He didn't even seem to care if I made him up! I suspected it would make him happy. This was all speculation. I told myself to sit back, relax, and take in the show. The class tomorrow would work out just fine. Michael was no fool. He wasn't there to embarrass me.

I tried to relax but still there was something nagging at me. Although I had never seen the film, I wanted to show the class a clip from the production of *American Whiskey Bar* that had recently been broadcast by City TV in Toronto. Michael had graciously arranged for me to get a video copy, and the night before he arrived I had screened it at home. What did I see? A curious mix of dialogues and fantasy clips about sex, rape, homophobia, racial stereotyping, cynicism, corporatism, and pornography. In other words, just a typical Toronto art movie. Not really. At one point in the film, two women exchange notes about their sexual fantasies. One of them recounts her experiences of having intercourse with and fellating the best endowed black man you could ever imagine. Her description of the event is graphic. While Michael was pretending to drink his vodka I was thinking about the film. I knew that at some point I would have to ask Michael what clip he wanted me to show to the class, since we obviously didn't have time to show the whole thing. So I took the plunge and asked. Without the slightest flicker of hesitation he responded: "I want you to cue it up to the beginning of the dialogue between the two women talking about sex with the black guy."

How was I supposed to sit back and relax when the next day, in front of hundreds of students, I would be pressing the button that would expose them to the glories of this woman's sexual adventures with her big imagined black stud? In fact, I had begun to worry about this the night before, when I first saw the film. If I told Michael I didn't want to show the film because it was too risqué he would think I was some kind of prude. But if I showed the clip the class would go crazy. I imagined hordes of outraged students—many of them black—rising up from their seats, booing and hissing as they left my politically incorrect lecture just a few days before I was set to wind up one of the most stress-free terms I'd ever had. Their parents would call me and say I was corrupting their children. The university would investigate. I was so worried about mass protest that I called up a trusted former student and put the question to her:

"Okay, so you're sitting in the big lecture hall and I introduce Michael Turner and then he says he is going to show a clip from *American Whiskey Bar* and then the film comes on and it is two women talking about a big black penis and fellatio."

"Yeah, so?" she says. "I mean, get with it. Last year we were forced to watch *100 Days of Sodom and Gomorrah* and write an essay on its pornographic merits. You want to show a five minute clip with a woman just *talking* about a blow job? Big *fucking* deal."

Big fucking deal. This was the mantra running in my head as Michael and I left the house to head downtown for his reading. The evening is still present to me. The Jailhouse Rock Café is a long dark space with a bar at the far end. We walk the length of the room, down to the bar. Michael buys me a beer. From here I can see that the stage for the reading has been set up in an alcove near the front door. There is a table with some candles on it. Behind the table is a film screen. I look around the room. I think I see one or two of my students but it's too dark to tell for sure. The crowd swells. Michael is introduced. He gets up behind the table, lights the candles, and tells us that he is going to show a clip of an old silent porno film. He's always wondered what those silent porno performers were saying and thinking when they did their thing, and he was going to give them the film voices they were never able to have. He starts reading poetry—or maybe it is actually an excerpt from *The Pornographer's Poem*. There are the candles, the crowd, Michael reading, and behind him the unfolding bodies, caresses, various penetrations, silent gasps of pleasure. Then there is a short frenzy and the man in the film ejaculates. His partner looks happy. Michael stops reading. Some of the candles have blown out. Strong applause. Michael blends back into the crowd. People shake his hand.

The next morning I pick him up to take him to the lecture. I am about to bring into my class a man who is obviously obsessed with pornography. It didn't add up until last night, but of course now it's too late to stop the show. He has been spotted by several students who want him to sign their books. He walks into the lecture hall. I finally get him seated in the front row. Now I'm ready to spring him on the class. I have no choice. "For an end-of-term surprise," I say cringing into the mike, "we're very fortunate to have with us today someone whose work you've been studying—the author of *Hard Core Logo*, Michael Turner!" There is a sharp intake of breath, a couple of squeals and shrieks, and then the whole class breaks into spontaneous applause. Michael gets up at the front and talks about his work. He talks about his fascination with pornography. He says we are going to look at a little clip from *American Whiskey Bar*. I look around the lecture hall, studying the faces in the bleachers. What will they do when they see this? I press the button, the lights go dim, the clip rolls. I wait. There are no screams. No protestations. No outrage. No one seems the least bit fazed. The clip ends. The students applaud raucously. It's over. I thank Michael for being with us and turn off the mike. Dozens of students run up to speak with him. No one complains about the film. Ever.

Turner's visit was the last event I had planned for my class in what turned out to be an incredibly busy term. However, some relief was in sight. I would be on sabbatical the following year. For most profs that meant a good rest, the chance to travel, complete a scholarly work, and catch up on reading. It meant some of that to me, but there was no sabbatical from the press. I was supposed to be writing a book on contemporary Canadian fiction. Although I had been teaching the subject for two years now, as a way of preparing to write, I had nothing much to show in the way of real progress and little hope of actually completing a book during my leave. Instead, it seemed that I would be working on a number of ECW titles that were coming into focus: celebrity biographies of Gwyneth Paltrow, Claire Danes, Neve Campbell, and Tom Green (from the beautiful to the ridiculous) along with a serious biography of Dennis Wilson, the Beach Boys' misunderstood drummer, and a book about rave culture in North America. I was also deeply involved in the design of *Sex Carnival*, a new book by Montreal journalist Bill Brownstein. It was an account of his various romps through the sex capitals of the world, funded in part by ECW's advance. Bill had a wonderful time attending the porno Oscars in Las Vegas, stopping in at the Playboy mansion in L.A., and signing up for a crash course on fellatio offered by a woman who had a dishwasher full of dildos. He had been spending his nights at clubs where swingers, fetishists, porn stars, lap dancers, and naked coiffeurs burned up the evening. When he returned to Montreal from one of these escapades (he had flown to New York to visit a restaurant run by a dominatrix who whipped her customers) I told him enough was enough. I wanted in. So we flew off to Amsterdam to retrace Bill's extensive research in the Red Light district. Now I understood more about the power of publishing. My author was obviously famous! People called out to him from clubs and doorways. He would pause from time to time, introducing me to some bouncer who looked mean as hell, until Bill held out his hand. Then the bouncer would grin and start up a happy chat with Bill, his obviously long-lost friend. When the book came out we launched it in a Montreal bar where drinks were served by people dressed up in S & M garb.

I thought about working on all those commercial titles, each of which had different demands in terms of editing, design, and production, and then I thought about the authors I was supposed to be reading and writing about: Russell Smith, Ann-Marie MacDonald, Yann Martel, Lynn

Crosbie, Andrew Pyper, Douglas Coupland. Sometimes, in my dreams, the face of MacDonald would merge with Paltrow's, or I would start thinking about Smith and end up with Tom Green. I'd focus on Crosbie's incredible take on Paul Bernardo in *Paul's Case* and then get disrupted by memories of Beach Boys music and my teenage love life. There was a disconnect there, a conflict in obligations that I didn't know how to resolve. But I knew one thing: ECW was growing, and even though the expenses kept mounting, Jack and I had resolved to stay the course, increase production, put the company on the mid-sized publishing map. It was risky. It had always been risky. It was a new millennium. Things would get better. And that dream kept us going full tilt until the biggest crash of all came, two years down the road.

CHAPTER NINE

I wasn't too worried about physically making it into the new millennium, although I did stock up on water and wine, just in case. My sabbatical was in full swing. I was supposed to be writing a book on contemporary Canadian novelists, a group that had been widely ignored by Canadian critics, many of whom were still preoccupied with writers who had emerged during the previous generation. However, the project was not going well. It was one thing to increase my exposure to new Canadian fiction through my courses, as I had been doing for a number of years. It was quite another to find the time to sit down and organize my thoughts in a way that could produce a scholarly study. Besides, I had become increasingly wary of academic publication. Although the same scholarly journals continued to publish articles, and while new books appeared from time to time, it was clear that the whole CanCrit machine was slowing down, gasping for something that would revive it. There were new CanLit profs out there, for sure, but nobody was really shaking things up or making it interesting. A sense of complacency had set in, which was only accentuated by the gradual reduction of publishing venues that had taken place over the last 10 or 15 years.

In many ways, ECW's movement away from academic publishing was symptomatic of what was happening on a national scale as publishers began to realize that there was no real market for this material. Sure, libraries would buy it and there were still some grants to cover costs, but there was no way anybody was going to make a living doing this; the youthful idealism that had once led many to believe they could support themselves in this way had long vanished. Ironically, the various government programs that had been established to support Canadian criticism ended up producing an industry that was reluctant to take chances or break into new territory. With ECW's departure, the field was controlled by a few university presses that would never publish a book of criticism unless it was backed by a grant, or by the occasional small publisher—like Cormorant or the Porcupine's Quill—who would risk a book of criticism from time to time, often with dire results. Here was an industry that had really started rolling in the 1970s, gathered tremendous momentum in the 1980s, began to fall off in the 1990s, and was just about dead after 2000.

I can already hear the objections, especially from those who did manage to publish a scholarly book or get their article out in one of the few respected journals in the field. All I can say to them is that they are either too young to remember what it was like when there was real energy out there—people quarrelling about issues as if they mattered and others willing to rock the boat—or that they are too old to remember the days when there was a sense of community, a shared sense of purpose, even idealism, about the national implications of literary-critical acts. You can't sustain that energy or sense of community in the absence of challenge and dissent, and by the turn of the century there was precious little of that. Nor can you sustain it if there aren't enough venues competing for good minds. When the publication avenues get cut off, as they did during the 1990s, the result is going to be stagnation, creeping conservatism, and a general sense that this is not the place to be in criticism at this time.

ECW's pullback from criticism, which reflected a more widespread degeneration in the CanCrit industry, left me feeling isolated when it came to the Professor Lecker side of me. Even if I wrote this book on contemporary Canadian fiction, who would publish it? Who would read it? Why should I sit in front of a computer screen for months writing something that would appeal to so few people? Wasn't this the story of my academic career? I had spent decades writing things that only a handful of people read, and never with much pleasure. When the Dr. Delicious in me dreamed of publishing a different kind of book—one that might even earn a few laughs from time to time—I realized that it would still be hard to find a publisher, mainly because books about publishing and CanLit just didn't sell. What Canadian publishing company would want to publish the story of another Canadian publishing company? At one point I approached Martha Sharpe, the publisher at House of Anansi Press, with the idea of doing this book. Martha was a former student of mine, and she had published my last book, *Making It Real*, so I figured this was the logical home for my next one, even though Martha had already turned down my monograph on Dennis Lee's *Civil Elegies*. I guess the writing was on the wall. Once upon a time Anansi was a press that was willing to take some chances, go out on a limb to support different kinds of Canadian writing—the writing that the big-name publishers would never touch. But it had become a bottom-line press like most of the others, withdrawing from CanCrit and memoirs because the sales just weren't there. So Martha passed. If Anansi was so out of the CanCrit game, who would be left to carry the flag?

Questions like that became even more pertinent a few years later, for reasons that will soon become apparent. In the meantime, back at my desk, where I was supposed to be thinking about novelists like Yann Martel and Russell Smith and Lynn Crosbie, I was thinking about all of the exciting movement that was taking place at ECW. Jack and I had returned to our discussion about company growth a few times and, despite the swelling debt, the mood was cautiously buoyant. My idea, which I think Jack came to share, was that a publishing company like ECW was not going to become a recognized trade publisher by moving forward slowly, season by season. No, the idea was that you had to take more aggressive action to put yourself on the map. Yes, that kind of action—which involved publishing more high-risk trade titles—would involve more money. However, if the plan worked we could be looking at substantially higher revenues in, say, a year, when the revenue from our expanded trade list started rolling in.

We knew the risks, but we decided to take the plunge. One of the first things that happened as a result of this decision was that I moved ECW Montreal to larger offices. Jack had a pretty good space in Toronto, but I was operating out of small, cramped quarters not too far from McGill and it was clear to me that with the increased production and new staff that would be required, it was time to find a bigger place. I looked around and found a nice spot on the top floor of a distinguished old downtown brownstone. The landlord agreed to paint and put down new carpets. Jack and I discussed the costs that would be involved in the move—new furniture, new computers, lots of new stuff. Given the cost of office space in downtown Montreal, this one seemed reasonable, so we decided to make the move.

By May of 2000 I was into the new office. It was bigger, more professional. The process of signing an increased number of new titles was well under way, and this meant it was also necessary to hire additional staff. With a production and office manager, a PR person, and a number of other part-time employees as well as the occasional intern, the new office quickly became a busy place. I liked the feeling of being there, but it also made me anxious, mainly because every time I walked through the doors and looked around at the staff, I was reminded of just how many books would have to be sold to pay for this kind of expansion.

And although Jack had supported my desire to find the new office, I knew he was worried about costs. Soon after we moved he came to Montreal to check out our new digs. Money was on his mind. At one point he reached into his briefcase and pulled out a wad of cheques about five inches thick. "These are the cheques we've written since the beginning of the year," he said, waving the pile in the air.

Why was he doing this? To show me how much my extravagances had cost? To make me aware of how we were bleeding cash? To make me think twice about my surroundings, which seemed luxurious in comparison with the previous ones? I didn't know. What I did know was that if we didn't get our shit together, or that if I didn't get *my* shit together, something bad was going to happen. Jack's visit only emphasized the growing rift I felt between Toronto and Montreal. There was no sense that we would come at our publications from a common angle, test each other's decisions through dialogue. On the contrary, I started to get the feeling that the Toronto office was increasingly removed from our pub-lishing program in Montreal. There was just no sense of unity between the offices, and often my staff would complain that they were not consulted about various decisions being made about the direction and promotion of the company in general. I didn't really have a strong relationship with anyone working in the Toronto office, and the rise of e-mail meant that most communications were written, rather than verbal, another factor that isolated each office by keeping the level of human interaction to a minimum.

Although we had been publishing trade books for close to a decade at this point, I don't think the harsh realities of the industry had really set in. Many authors imagine that once their book is published thousands of copies will be sold. They are often surprised when they don't see their books in Indigo, or Chapters, or Barnes and Noble. Do they think these chains buy every title that is published? Do they know that often each chain store will order two or three measly copies, just to try them out? The business of deciding how many copies to print of every title is very tough, especially for small and mid-sized publishers, because a bad decision can have enormous consequences. The truth of the matter is that unless you are very good (and lucky) at acquiring titles you will be fortunate to break even, and you will generally be happy when a book sells in the range of 10,000 copies. You might even be relatively happy if the book sells 5,000 copies, assuming that production costs are not too high. Often, even if you sign a title that you think is original and promising in terms of sales, you might find on publication that another publisher has a similar book on its list, and that could wipe out your own sales, or cut them in half. You could be thrilled when a big buyer like Barnes and Noble expressed faith in a certain title by placing a large advance order. But then you went crazy worrying about how many copies to print in the face of that order. If you underprinted, you couldn't fill the order. Barnes and Noble would not be happy. Maybe they would see you as an amateur, and hold back on future orders. However, if you printed enough to satisfy the order, you might find that in fact Barnes and Noble was wrong, the book actually wasn't going to sell, and in a few months the bookseller would be returning thousands of copies that would lie in your warehouse, unsold. Yet the bills for printing and production were still there, sitting on your desk. Conversely, you could have a title that had sold modestly until some news item suddenly drew attention to it. Bang! A big order would come in. This could be just a flash in the pan. It probably was. But what if it wasn't? Nobody knew. Should you reprint? How many thousands? And if you reprinted, how soon could the job be done? You could reprint, only to find that by the time the books came off the press the sudden interest in them had vanished, although the bills connected with printing them were all too present. Which reminded you: would the printer even *do* the reprint, since so many of their bills remained unpaid?

It wasn't just the anxieties caused by dealing with the chains and wholesalers and printers that gave me daily stress. There were all kinds of other anxieties connected with each title. The very decision to sign a title was always huge. I tried to get my employees, most of whom were in their twenties, involved in the decision-making process, but I sometimes felt that they would see the titles in a different way if they were actually paying the bills, or had their houses on the line. An idea could seem cool and original, but when you actually had to put it out there it could either make it, or just die. One of our employees suggested we do a biography of Shaggy, the popular reggae singer. It sounded good to me. No one had ever touched that story, and the man was so popular. Yes, I said, let's do it! The book bombed. Another author persuaded me that there would be a huge market for a book that surveyed "jam bands," which were essentially rock bands that improvised their music on stage and had cultish followings across Canada and the US. I was convinced that those followers would buy the first book ever on all those bands. The book bombed. I was enticed by a book proposal for teens—a novel about video games, the plot of which revealed secrets about winning those games. What a selling point, I thought. The book bombed.

Bomb. Bomb. Bomb. And those were only *my* bombs. Jack had them too. Each failure ate into the bottom line and meant that the books that did succeed had to do really well. Because we were essentially living from hand to mouth, with lots of loan payments to make, there was very little room for error. A larger, more established publisher could rely on steady revenues from its backlist in order to offset the losses caused by failed titles, and even the big publishers had plenty of those. And if they had huge backlists with titles that kept selling year after year they could absorb those losses. Also, they didn't have to worry about getting their reprint numbers right. When it came to *The Catcher in the Rye*, the publisher—Little, Brown—knew exactly how many copies would sell in a given year. And that same title had been selling strongly for 50 years. So what if they were off by 5,000 copies? It was peanuts. I thought of that in comparison with one of my best-selling titles—the story of the Dave Matthews Band. How long would that one be popular? A couple of years at best? Meanwhile, other ECW titles could have an even shorter backlist life. A book of poetry might sell a few hundred copies when it came out, and then maybe a few dozen copies a year. It was almost more expensive to warehouse it than to sell it. The possibilities of mass pulpings loomed large.

The pressure involved in publishing any title only began with the contract signing and was never limited to the end result—actual sales. Every step in the process of getting the book into the stores was fraught. Who would design the cover and the text? What kind of look would be best? (Individual egos were always embroiled in these questions.) What kind of artwork or photos would be in the book? Who would collect them? How much would it cost? Who would do the editing? What if the book needed a total rewrite but the author was a prima donna? We would work on the covers long in advance because they had to be shown to the sales reps at the conferences that took place twice yearly. Often, I'd show up at the conferences and show Jack my covers. We were copublishers, but if this was the first time he was seeing a cover his own company was publishing, there was a problem. By the same token, I was seeing many of his covers for the first time. I always worried about how the sales reps would react to these covers, which were often the product of hours of discussion, image-searching, design, and redesign. Sometimes they would express mild enthusiasm, but more often than not I got the feeling they thought the covers were entirely predictable, and how could they not be, since so many of the books were celebrity biographies with headshots for covers? What the reps really wanted to hear about was advertising and marketing. What kind of money were we going to put into promoting this title? What kind of campaigns would we be launching? Sometimes we were able to say we had a few thousand dollars to spend on a tour, or an ad, or a publicist (and sometimes we really did spend it), but more often than not the truth was that we could ill afford to pay for publicity. We did it anyhow, partly to convince the distributor and sales team that we supported them, and partly because we could never decide whether this kind of limited advertising boosted sales.

Despite the pressures attached to the selection and production of every title, I almost always enjoyed the process of seeing a manuscript become a book. It was inevitably a cooperative process among a team of people involving choices about style, font, image, layout, and the general look and feel of the package. I loved the way you could tease the design, move images around, and work with different typefaces, all part of the complicated process involved in making each book distinctive and appealing. Every time a shiny new book came back from the printer it was like opening a present. I felt happy. I would hold each one, admiring it from different angles, my new baby. I imagined the truck loaded with boxes of this brand new title heading off to the warehouse, where it would quickly be dispatched to all the stores that had placed their orders. In this brief fantasy moment, the birth of the book, all seemed well with the world. I had made this object. *We* had made this object. We were a team. We were united. The book would bail us out. Jack and I would recover some of the old-time fun because there would be money, and less debt, and he wouldn't have to come to Montreal waving a pile a cheques.

This feeling would last a minute or so. Sometimes less. Then I would open the book and look at it more critically. Like most publishers, I would spot a typo right away. Who proofread this book, anyhow? I could feel the irritation rising. The space below the text block was just a little too high. I had bugged the designer about that again and again. Why couldn't she get it right? I checked the index, flipping from one of its page references to the actual page in the book: wrong! How did the index get fucked up like that? Who was supposed to have checked that index? I couldn't do it all. Why did every single book seem to have some flaw? (Answer: this is book publishing.) I would close the book, telling myself that it didn't matter. No one but me would notice. Had I ever received a letter of complaint because the page numbers in an index were off? Nope. So, chill, I told myself. Just chill.

But then there was the matter of the cover. It was glossy. My choice. I had made the decision for glossy against the desire of the younger staff members, who thought glossy was uncool. Matte is where it's at, they kept telling me. And you know, damnit, they were right. If only I had gone with matte, this cover would have been so much more restrained. Probably would have sold a lot more copies. Damn. But then again, the sales reps had told me to watch out for matte covers because they scratched so easily and always showed fingerprints. "Would you buy a greasy book?" one of them asked me. No, I thought, imagining the cover of one of my pristine new titles contaminated by some kind of human smudge, a collage of oily fingerprints from the hundreds of fans who would be fondling it. God, people were disgusting. Always emitting some kind of effluvium, sweating out oils and who knew what else from their heads and hands and various body parts. They should be dried out before they slicked up my books with their fluids. What could be done? Ruminations such as these inevitably compromised the joy I felt in holding each new book. And in fact, I could see my own greasy fingerprints on the cover, already—a glossy cover at that! Christ, I was the publisher, and I was the most contaminated one of all!

Too bad. There was nothing I could do about my grease level and besides, there were books to be sold, contracts to sign. I had decided that one niche we should explore in a much more aggressive way was celebrity biographies with colour photo sections. This decision introduced a lot of contradiction to my life. A few years back, I would leave McGill for the ECW office and find myself working on a biography of Michael Ondaatje or Leonard Cohen. That was an easy bridge to cross. But now I was leaving McGill to find myself immersed in heated debates about books on Gwyneth Paltrow, Jennifer Lopez, and Neve Campbell. I wanted to print that picture of Campbell sitting on the billiard table in a skin-tight minidress, surrounded by billiard balls and holding an upright pool cue. Several women on the staff objected. I kept the picture in. Campbell's mother wrote me a letter, pleading with me not to violate her daughter's privacy. I tried to talk her down, to explain that the book was respectful and non-intrusive, to no avail. Meanwhile, it was time to choose the photo for the Lopez cover. Yeah, let's go for that sexy cleavage shot I said. Not much office resistance to that decision, I thought, but who knew what they were saying behind my back? Pervert. Anyhow, even when the book was published, no one objected to the cleavage. Apparently, cleavage is J. Lo's middle name. No, what they objected to was her hairstyle on the cover. That was last year, people wrote to say. I could see that these books just couldn't be pumped out fast enough to accommodate the chameleon personalities of these various stars. Only the tabloids and *People* could keep up with their hair colour from day to day. I was fighting a losing battle. Still, sales weren't bad. The real problem was the cost of permissions for all those photos, and the added costs of printing books with full-colour sections. Very expensive.

At one point most of my publishing efforts were going into these celebrity biographies and into the Secret series, which was a lot more respectable. I would find myself sitting at a table next to the designer of our biography of Tom Green, looking down at the cover image, a picture of Green sucking on a cow's udder. Then it was time for more serious matters: a history of Christian rock & roll. Talk about a niche market! The author of this history was a well-known music teacher and journalist who was an authority on Christian rock. He assured me that there were millions of young Christians out there, dying for a history like this. It had never been done. He was absolutely right, my research showed. This one was going to take off. Wrong. Can you figure out what the problem was? This was a book by a Christian for Christians. What I learned, to my astonishment, is that Christian books will not be bought by the big chains unless they have been supplied by special Christian distributors who put their imprimatur on the title. Of course, I should have known this. But now it was too late. ECW had built up no relations with those Christian distributors. Hell, I couldn't even imagine how to speak to them. Besides, I was Jewish. How would I pitch them on this title? Was there a correct form of address? Did one have to sound kind of pious and reverential? Were priests involved? That would be pushing it, for sure, but still, someone out there was going to judge whether my title was wholesome enough for Christian consumption. They could blacklist it, just like that. Poof. End of title. To his credit, the author worked hard to get the book accepted by the Christian censors, but I guess they had some questions about his publisher, given those celebrity biographies, J. Lo's cleavage, and a little legal problem involving Shania Twain. Besides, they also learned that we were developing a line of books on Wicca and witchcraft. ECW was the antichrist. Everything Christian Wanting.

Ah, Wicca. Somewhere along the line Jack and I had been reading about companies that were sold for a song because they were going bankrupt. It seemed natural, as we explored our growth mode, to think about swooping in on some distressed publishing company and scooping up their inventory at rock-bottom prices. The very thought that we could ever have succeeded in such a venture is testimony to the delusional state we had reached. But that didn't stop us from licking our chops over the demise of Carroll Publishing, a New Jersey-based company that specialized in books about Wicca, witchcraft, gambling, and spirituality. Although they were going belly up, Jack and I decided we would head down to the bankruptcy auction in April 2000 to see if we just might acquire some damaged goods, which included the rights to more than 1,500 backlist contracts and 130 unpublished manuscripts. If we got the rights, bought the contracts, then we could issue new books for cheap. The auction was taking place in Secaucus, New Jersey, the delights of which I had never experienced. Jack and I drove around the place looking for our motel. "Jesus," I said, "there's so much garbage on the road. Maybe a garbage truck overturned." Jack knew better. He had been there before. "No," he said, "it's just New Jersey." We found our motel and went out to dinner at a restaurant that must have been owned by Tony Soprano.

Just in case we made an offer, a deposit was required. A Soprano-size deposit. Jack took another advance on his credit card, had a certified cheque issued for $25,000 US, and off we went to the auction. It was pretty clear to us immediately, in looking through Carroll's list, that many of their winning titles were books about gambling or books about Wicca and witchcraft. When it came to witchcraft, Carroll only had one major competitor at the time—Llewelyn—and it looked like we could do something with those titles. Give the more successful ones new covers, maybe put out a whole Wicca/witchcraft line. Our hopes didn't last long. As soon as the bidding opened there was an offer made that far exceeded anything we could afford. A few minutes later the company was sold for a few million dollars. Why had we bothered to come? Clearly there was a reason. We had come in order to learn that Wicca and witchcraft and gambling sell, and although we didn't snag Carroll, I returned to Montreal determined to start my own line of Wicca and witchcraft titles (Jack followed up on the gambling end). It didn't take long to get the word out, and before long I had signed contracts with several Wiccans, including a number of people who told me straight out that they were witches. They were almost always very nice, but I knew that if I messed up on their book they were going to cast a spell that would probably result in truly bad luck, disaster, or death. (I remembered the fate of the child-hero in Roald Dahl's *The Witches*. He was turned into a mouse by the grand high witch, who subjected him to a magic potion called Delayed Action Mouse-Maker.) This was a publishing problem I had not foreseen, and I had no idea how to protect myself against those potentially evil spells. Worse, many of the witches had witch agents. I tried to be especially nice to them.

While I was thinking about the witches, I was keeping an eye on

Russell Crowe. I hoped he became even more famous than he was, because I had just commissioned a biography, which would be pseudonymously written by one of my students, who decided to write the whole book from Crowe's point of view. Very odd, but effective, I thought. Back in 1993 we had set up overseas English distribution with a London-based company called Turnstone, and later we signed on with Wakefield Press, a distributor in Australia. The Australian connection boosted our sales a bit, and it kicked in more actively when we had a title, like the Crowe bio, that was more directly connected with the Australian market. In England, we had built up a strong distribution relationship with Turnstone, even though we did not have many trade titles in the early years. By 2000 Turnaround was selling a good number of books, and we tried to work with them to expand our marketing efforts in the UK. Claire Thompson, who was managing Turnaround, was always perfectly calm when it came to our wide range of titles. Give her a Wicca title one day and Russell Crowe the next. It was fine. She would do her best to make it work.

Although our overseas distribution seemed to be healthy, there were problems emerging with LPC, our US distributor. For small and mid-sized publishing companies that don't have their own distribution facilities, the solvency of their external distributor is crucial, especially because the distributor is sometimes attached to a sales team. The team gets the orders and the distributor fills them, collecting payment from the stores. Then, usually about three or four months after they do their initial billing, the distributor sends the amount to the publisher, minus their fee and charges for books returned by the stores. This arrangement works fine if the distributor has adequate cash flow and the returns are not huge. It works even better if the distributor has some cash reserves, because the bookstores don't always remit their own payments to the distributor within three or four months, so sometimes the distributor, who is in a contractual arrangement with the publisher, has to cut a cheque even if they haven't yet received their own cheque for bookstore sales (to avoid this situation some distributors only pay the publisher when they themselves get paid). The publisher has no way of collecting directly from the stores and so is entirely dependent for its income on regular payments from the distributor. And if the distributor and the sales team are part of the same company, then the relationship becomes even more crucial because if the sales and distribution company is distressed, sales will fall and payments will slow down and dry up. When the publisher faces lower sales and delayed payments it will have to deal with its own credit issues. Even a month of delayed payments can have a crucial impact on the publisher's ability to maintain its business, particularly for publishers that are carrying high debt loads or that have a lot of outstanding bills. Typically US and Canadian distributors represent a number of small and medium-sized publishing companies. Although it might seem that there would be all kinds of distribution companies, in fact there are only a handful that can offer true distribution (and sales) from coast to coast. Because there are so few distributors, financial problems at any one of them can have a profound effect on multiple publishers.

Our relationship with LPC Group (which originally stood for Login Publishers Consortium) had begun with the k.d. lang biography in 1992. It took a few years for our relationship with LPC to get off the ground, but by 1997, with the increase in our trade list, they had become a crucial source of revenue. We relied on their sales force, waited anxiously for our monthly payments, and built up the relationship to the point that we were consulting with them about potential titles. When David Wilk bought our original distributor, InBook, he kept many of the young staff members, which gave the company an edgy, alternative presence among American distributors. Wilk did not always make his payments religiously, but in the first few years he was generally on time. We might have to bug him a bit to send the money. Sometimes we would even have to wait a few extra weeks, but the cheques came through. And the sales team was certainly working. LPC was selling thousands of copies of some of our titles, with advance orders that made us believe this trade publishing business could expand. Even better, Wilk seemed to be developing a business model with tremendous potential. LPC had become the biggest American distributor of independent comics publishers into mainstream bookstores. He represented the cream of the crop when it came to graphic novels and alternative comics— companies like Top Shelf, Dark Horse, Tokyo Pop, Drawn and Quarterly, Oni, Highwater Books, Alternative Comics, Humanoids, Cross-Gen, and Ait-Planet Lar. It was partly on the strength of the LPC connection that we had decided to expand ECW, even though many of our titles seemed conservative, given LPC's lineup. But Wilk encouraged us. It was a nice fit. We would grow together.

That scenario was fine so long as LPC remained in good shape. However, early in 2000, we started to notice some warning signs. Cheques were coming in more slowly. Wilk was harder to reach by e-mail and phone. A few staff members had been let go. The sales conferences were downsized and no longer held in Chicago hotels but at cheesy highway motels near Milford, Connecticut, where LPC had its original home. Then we learned that the Chicago office would be closed and operations would return to Milford. Future sales conferences would be held there. We made one frantic trip to those offices in fall 2000. We met up at Newark airport, rented a car, and bolted up the highway to Milford, where we made a quick presentation and then scrambled back to the airport, racing to catch our flights. This was no way to engage in a meaningful dialogue about our titles, and besides, there was hardly anyone to listen to us. At its high point the LPC sales conference included at least 20 reps who met with publishers over a two-day period; the energy was palpable. But now we were racing to a meeting in a narrow office in Milford and there were three people sitting around the table, looking distracted and bored.

We left wondering what the whole trip had accomplished. Six months later, in March, we were scheduled to appear at another sales conference. This time we were determined not to spend that kind of money again, so we decided to drive down, Jack from Toronto and me from Montreal. We would meet at a motel the night before the conference and then finish the journey together. The drive took about seven hours. Why was I doing this? I tried to reassure myself that this was good for ECW: we were saving oodles of money by avoiding those two airfares. Finally we rolled into Milford. It was Monday, March 12. There were three LPC representatives sitting at the table. David Wilk himself was absent. The national sales director, whose name I had never heard before, sat in front of me with his head propped on his hand. He was gazing at the ceiling and looking miserable. Couldn't have cared less who we were. The other two offered muted comments about our upcoming titles. Their minds were clearly elsewhere. Where the hell was Wilk? How could we be asked to come all the way down here and speak to three people who didn't seem to give a damn? Did they know something we didn't?

We left the LPC offices and headed down the interstate. Jack turned on the radio, looking for sports scores. That was a bad thing to do. The stock market was crashing and burning, with the Dow suffering its worst loss in 11 months. I was worried about my few investments. Maybe Jack was worried about his, too. He was reserved, driving, silent. It was raining. The sense of some kind of impending crisis at LPC was only accentuated by the stock market slide and the futility of this whole trip, the two of us heading along the highway, 25 years after we had started out on this publishing trip. I felt a profound sense of unity with Jack. Whatever happened, we would stick it out. We were survivors. But I also felt a profound sense of loneliness. I couldn't really share my emotions, my isolation, my fear. He so seldom opened up. He would get back to Toronto and I would get back to Montreal and we would follow our separate paths within the company that had put us together in this car, on this highway in New Jersey, on this gray winter day, listening to news flashes about just how much money was being lost by investors from coast to coast. A million. A billion. Billions. It felt apocalyptic.

Nothing happened right away. The LPC cheques arrived sporadically. There weren't too many people answering the LPC phone, but Wilk assured us he was working on big plans. Don't worry, he said. I wasn't able to let go of my concerns entirely, but I couldn't keep them front and centre all the time, mainly because there were way too many books in production that demanded my immediate attention. There were the titles in our new Wicca lineup. There was *Down the Tube*, Bill Brownstein's second book, describing his experience of channel surfing and watching TV without interruption for one full week. Of course there was the biography of Russell Crowe, and a book on Elvis Presley's Jewish roots—*Schmelvis: King of Jerusalem*. I was also gearing up for my fall courses—the introduction to Canadian literature that would enroll about 200 students, and another devoted to Michael Ondaatje. My head was full of Ondaatje's poetry, some of it so beautiful and haunting, like the closing lines of *Tin Roof*:

> I wanted poetry to be walnuts
> in their green cases
> but now it is the sea
> and we let it drown us,
> and we fly to it released
> by giant catapults
> of pain loneliness deceit and vanity.

The problem was that just as soon as I started hearing the music in those lines, their almost unutterable sadness and their longing confrontation with the despair of writing, I got static flowing in from all sides—witches arguing with me about cover designs, angry missives from the pretentious New York agent for the *Schmelvis* book and his pompous Montreal author, the photo costs for a colour spread in the new biography of Sarah Jessica Parker, and the proposals for new books sitting on my desk: an account of America's first, but secret, nuclear disaster; the life story of an extreme martial arts fighter; a huge guide to "pagan traditions online"; the reprint we were going to do of *King Jammy's* (the story of a legendary Jamaican reggae producer); and a book called *Born to the Mob: The True-Life Story of the Only Man to Work for Five of New York's Mafia Families.*

I would look at those titles and wonder who I was. The title of Michael Turner's song kept popping up: "Who the Hell Do You Think You Are?" How could I possibly have become the person who woke up thinking about "The Cinnamon Peeler" and went to sleep fretting about Schmelvis? Talk about deceit. I didn't care about Sarah Jessica Parker. I didn't give a damn about Wicca. I had no personal interest in many of the books I was publishing. So why do it? It wasn't hard for me to answer that question. The constant need for cash translated into the need for titles that would sell. Too much debt. My house still on the line. If extreme martial arts and wrestling sold, I would sell them. I had become a pub-lishing pimp. And I would spend my afternoons pimping a stranger and stranger array of titles. Then my double life would pull me back to the other side: the poetry I was teaching, the intellectual challenges posed by so many young Canadian fiction writers, and *Essays on Canadian Writing* itself, which continued to rumble on and remind me that there were still people out there who were concerned about Canadian art, postcolonial theory, representations of gender, shifting ideas about history, and versions of postmodernism. This was the world I knew. This was the world I could share with my students. But every time I talked with them I felt like a bit of a fake. How genuinely interested could their professor be in this subject, or this essay, or this grade, if somewhere in his head he was thinking about the saleability of yet another trade book? I could feel an old longing. Just the desire to be in that unprofitable world of CanLit, doing books for a small community, knowing the players, feeling secure in my professional role. Yet those days were gone. Or I thought they were gone. The community I had once idealized was missing in action. The CanCrit industry was impoverished, in decline. And yet, in the midst of this loss, there were some constants: the students, eager and interested as ever; the writers, going from strength to strength, every day.

To be sure, the signals were confused. Which world did I belong in? Was it possible to bridge the two? Was the jumpiness and alienation I felt part of some kind of annual cycle that corresponded to the beginning of the academic year when all the pressures associated with teaching start running full force? No sooner had classes started in September 2001 than everything was sundered, wrenched in multiple directions by the horror of 9/11. Like everyone around me I watched the images, mesmerized, unable even to fathom a coherent response. I was in shock. I had no tools to make sense of this, but I knew I was about to witness some kind of seismic shift in the world I had known. What I was seeing would not go away. Wherever I turned I saw the pictures, the planes, the billowing black smoke, the sense of a gray darkness settling over a city that to me had always symbolized vibrancy and life. In fact, Mary and I had been planning a trip to New York on October 11. We planned to stay at The Marriott, World Trade Center. Destroyed. That made the tragedy feel even closer. This was happening in a city that was an hour's flight away. It was not on the other side of the world. It was here. A week later my *New Yorker* magazine arrived. The cover: pure black.

How do you walk into a class and talk about anything in the face of such loss? The business of talking about poems or narrative devices seemed so pointless. Yet, that was my job. I didn't know what to do. Carry on with the scheduled material? Cancel classes? Hide? McGill decided that lectures would continue as usual. In retrospect, it was a wise decision. I entered my classes on Wednesday, September 12, with no idea what would happen or how many students would be in the room. It was full. I looked around. I couldn't read the students' faces, didn't know what they were feeling. I just stood there for a few minutes, and then said: "Does anyone want to talk about what happened?" There was a brief pause, a silence, and then one woman broke down and started sobbing. She was American, her family was in New York, and she didn't know if they were all okay. Yet here she was in class. It was her refuge. I tried to reassure her. The other students helped. We got a discussion going. There were tears, and fear. Everybody remembers a point in their life when they become aware of their mortality. That probably has a lot more to do with becoming an adult than reaching the voting age or getting a driver's licence. I remembered my students in Maine and how I had tried to get them interested in fiction about the war in Vietnam. I had tried to convey the pointless loss that war involved, death after death. It meant nothing to them. That was a war fought in another time, by other people, in another place. It didn't touch them. But this time, in that classroom at McGill in September 2001, things were very different. The students understood, perhaps for the first time, that death could come at any moment, that it was happy to take people of all age groups and colours and social status, and that it could appear, tangibly, out of the sky, on a bright September morning.

The whole term was shaded by 9/11. We were carrying a weight.

The mood was so down. And where would it all lead? To Afghanistan? To other terrorist attacks? To Canada? I tried to keep my mind on work, to concentrate on the existing structures of my week as a way of providing focus and direction. One way I had tried to link my two lives as a publisher and professor was to offer a course called "The Material Construction of Canadian Literature." It was about the ways in which economic and financial considerations, along with government policies, contributed to the formation of literary taste. It was also about the ways in which these forces favoured certain genres and forms of writing over others. Canadian literature had always been studied in an aesthetic vacuum, as if money and market forces had nothing to do with literary selection or value. Look at any history of Canadian literature and you will see how little is said about money, credit lines, bank accounts, grants, tax refunds, and so on.

One reason academics tend to bypass these material concerns is that many are still in denial, caught up in the idealistic view that literature and money are not related, or that talk about profit and loss has little to do with literary reputations, or excellence. Although it's a badge of their pride that they would never dream of trying to make a profit from literature outside the academic market, it's the material comforts of the industry of scholarship, of tenure, of sabbaticals and campus celebrity that they often crave. In truth, they've become cynical and corrupted by their own profit system—the spoils of academic life. My experience had taught me that literary history had everything to do with money. I knew that some books went to bigger publishers because they had money, and that an author's reputation could be made by that publisher spending money. I knew that some books were ineligible for funding by the Canada Council, and that as a result publishers who needed grants would stay away from those kinds of books. I knew that if you were a publisher in Newfoundland you stood a better chance of getting more money from the Canada Council than if you were a publisher in Toronto, because the council awarded bonus dollars to publishers that were in the more remote regions of the country. We should have started ECW in Nunavut.

I tried to acquaint the students with the evolution of funding programs for Canadian publishers, including the Book Publishing Industry Development Program, those offered by provincial arts councils, and the assistance provided to scholarly publications through the Aid to Scholarly Publications Program. I also showed them just how much it cost to make a book and what the publisher retained after the bookstore and distributor and sales team took their cuts. Then I subtracted the payment to the author, overhead costs, and advertising fees. The bottom line: you couldn't make much money unless you sold 5,000 copies, and even that was iffy. In Canada, unless you were one of the few wealthy multinational publishers, you needed grants just to break even. And that was before you considered the fact that about 25 percent of your books would eventually be returned.

No, it was not a pretty picture. Nor were the games that Canadian publishers had to play in order to get those grants, crafting their applications and the very descriptions of their books through strategies that would make the granting agency enthusiastic and supportive. The students were surprised. Some of them saw my approach as cynical, of course. Students in literature live in an idealized realm of the finished book, the novel or short story or collection of poems that moves them and presents intellectual challenges. They want to talk about ideas, structure, image. But the story of how those books became required reading is linked to the culture that produced them. The history of Canadian literature after the Massey Commission is largely the history of how economic policies and forms of government intervention created a vibrant literary culture, but one founded on the idea that literature and subsidy go hand in hand. Critics were eager to "historicize" literary works, to talk about the way they were the products of certain historical moments and values, but they seldom talked about the material conditions that made the physical act of book publication a reality. Because good arguments are often about money, and because Canadian critics did not pay much attention to the material aspects of literary production in Canada, there weren't many arguments to give things zip. How would Canadian literary history have differed if there were no grants, no tax credits, no government guarantees of bank loans to publishers, no support for scholarly books? The answer is simple: Canadian literature as we know it would not exist. That fact is worthy of study.

Finally, mercifully, the fall 2001 term was over. Teaching a course on the material construction of Canadian literature had done nothing to ease my concerns about the material construction of ECW Press, which remained shaky. For one thing, revenues for all publishers were down in the aftermath of 9/11. People were staying away from bookstores, and publishers had become increasingly cautious about signing new titles, wondering, naturally, what kind of books would sell in a post-trauma world. ECW experienced falling orders, coupled with problems collecting from our two main distributors—LPC in the US and General Distribution in Canada. About 70 percent of our revenue came through those two sources. We entered 2002 with a sense of growing trepidation. We knew that both distributors were having problems. We discussed the possibility of jumping ship but Jack felt loyal to David Wilk and especially to Jack Stoddart, the man who had turned General into the largest distribution company in the country. Stoddart was facing some major problems. Chief among these was the relationship between General and the Chapters/Indigo chain, which had become increasingly powerful and arrogant as it squeezed out the small independent stores and began to take control of the book industry in Canada.

Chapters and Indigo control about two-thirds of book sales in Canada. They use the leverage provided by this market dominance to obtain higher discounts from publishers, a tactic that inevitably eats into the publishers' bottom line. In addition, Chapters/Indigo shows little in the way of allegiance to small publishers. They might stock their titles, but they are also quick to return books by the hundreds. All of this activity is a threat to publishers and writers, but it also traps the distributor, who loses money when books are returned, yet who must rely on Chapters/Indigo for the majority of its revenue. If the chain is slow to pay, the publishers don't receive their money from the distributor, who is inevitably caught in the middle. To make matters worse, in Canada, Chapters/Indigo tried to bypass companies like General by setting up its own distribution company. It wanted to profit from selling books under terms that squeezed the publishers, and then it wanted to squeeze publishers further by disempowering their distributors, leaving them no place to turn. By eliminating the independent bookstores and imposing even harsher financial terms on small and medium-sized Canadian publishers, Chapters/Indigo contributed to the ongoing destruction of literary expression in Canada. Sales and sales volume became the arbiter of taste. There was less and less room for the eccentric and the experimental, and much less room for poetry or literary critique, which is crucial to any self-respecting culture.

The evolution of ECW's publishing program is emblematic of what happens to a relatively small press when it has to adapt to the kind of market created by the large chains. It starts to think about titles that will sell in volume and to bypass those titles that won't. It might continue to publish poetry and other marginal genres, but only so long as there's a grant that will make breakeven possible. Gradually, it places more emphasis on celebrity biographies or books about television series because more people will buy those than books about Gwendolyn

MacEwen, or poetry by Stuart Ross. In one respect, it's only good business: make a product that sells. On the other hand, we are talking about the cultural life of a country. How impoverished does that cultural life become when excentric or esoteric voices don't get heard?

The decline of CanCrit was the ironic result of the introduction of programs designed to support Canadian companies that were publishing primary material (novels, short stories, poetry); those very programs worked against the production of secondary materials related to the literature itself. The rise of Canadian literature was paralleled by the fall of Canadian criticism. The more ECW got squeezed by cash flow problems, the more determined it became to publish books that would qualify for as many grants as possible. Jack was always thinking about the grant criteria, looking for the project that would be funded by the Canada Council, the Ontario Arts Council, or a federal government program (preferably all of them), one that also qualified for an Ontario tax credit. He felt that, all things being equal, it was better to find a Canadian writer. I argued that this would restrict the publishing program and confine us strictly to those projects that were eligible for funding. Wouldn't we achieve the same end by focusing on trade titles that would sell in large numbers, even if the book didn't get the tax credit or the grant? I had come to the point at which I believed that some kind of global market-ability was the means of ensuring the survival of unique titles that could stand on their own. No, Jack responded, why go for the speculative title that might or might not get international sales when the grant was assured, unless of course you were talking about a wrestling book, which would almost always garner enough sales to break even or return a profit. Somewhere along the line, in adapting to the unforgiving demands of the trade publishing jungle, both of us surrendered our founding belief in the value of Canadian criticism. We had long ago abandoned the relation between our publishing program and the idea of cultural sovereignty.

Even though ECW had adapted its list over the years to accom-modate the increasing dominance of the chains, there was nothing it could do to stop the nuclear bomb that was about to drop on the Canadian publishing industry in 2002. General's payments started coming more slowly, then they came sporadically, then they just stopped. Everybody knew that Jack Stoddart was in trouble, but few suspected how bad that trouble was. We talked about getting our books out of the General warehouse, finding a new distributor who would make the payments on time, but this presented a strategic timing problem. What if we pulled the books and then Stoddart found the money he needed? After all, he was reported to be in deep talks with several banks. He certainly wouldn't be putting us first on his payment list, since we had jumped ship. And if we did jump ship, assuming we could find another Canadian distributor, it would be months before we saw any money from the new outfit, so the outcome would in some ways be the same as if we stuck around with General, hoping for the best. As the months wore on the warning signs became more urgent. Finally, in December of 2001, we wrote to Stoddart and told him we would be pulling out and transferring our stock to a new distributor after six months, the notice time required by our contract. But it was too little, too late. In early April, our US distributor, LPC Group, announced that it was filing for bankruptcy. Then, just three weeks later, Stoddart dropped the second bomb: General would also be filing for bankruptcy protection. None of the publishers would be getting any money, and, worse, their books would be locked in the General warehouse as security for the preferred creditors (aka the banks). This meant that it would be very difficult to transfer ECW's inventory to our new distributor. Some publishers, realizing the situation, were hiring trucks to race to the General warehouse to rescue whatever books they could before the padlocks snapped shut on the doors. Others understood, immediately, that the end of their business was at hand. This was a national crisis. About 70 publishers were affected by General's failure. For a great many of those publishers the effects continue to be felt today. For us, the end of General and LPC meant the loss of almost $400,000 in revenue. When that was added to our other loans and payables, including the money we had loaned to the company over the years, we had debts totalling close to $1,000,000. It was game over for us.

Jack and I were in shock. It wasn't as if we hadn't seen this coming. But receiving the official confirmation was still a staggering blow. We had no idea how we could carry on without that General money. Even if we got a bit of a settlement out of the bankruptcy process, it would be a small amount, far down the road. How would we pay our employees, keep up the loan payments, deal with the printers, stay on top of the day-to-day expenses that allowed the company to run? We were already massively in debt. No one would lend us another penny. What were the options? Fire everyone, reduce the list, wait for some grant money to come in, and hope our own creditors would give us a bit of breathing space. We could do that, but it would be tantamount to dismantling the company, and that certainly wouldn't pay the bills. I found it hard to talk to Jack about this. At a certain point he just seemed to withdraw into a protective shell.

There was no light on the horizon, just a daily scramble to survive. Now there were no sources of revenue except a few grants, and of them only the Canada Council grant was due anytime soon. Besides, it would only be a drop in the bucket when it came to the bills sitting on our desks. I don't know what was going on in Jack's head but he went even more silent. When we did speak he seemed angry and resentful. I had no idea why, but it was persistent. My response was to back off and look for my own shell. We were both desperate. Jack felt that the only way to deal with the issue was to sell the company to someone who would assume the debt. That was the only way we could come out of this without surrendering our houses and who knew what else. I couldn't imagine selling the company at bargain basement prices, not after all those years. I tried to convince Jack that we should follow plan "B": fire all the employees, close the offices, go back to where we had started—the two of us in a small room. Eventually the grants would arrive and we could start to make a comeback. Anything other than abandon the fight at this moment of crisis. But Jack was determined to find a buyer. He looked around, made multiple inquiries, came up empty-handed. I could feel him simmering, pulling back. He'd bottled up his rage; he was a muffled bomb. Maybe he was having some kind of breakdown. Whatever he was feeling, he was clearly unable to share it with me. And in some ways, I even felt like the object of his suppressed rage. I thought this was a time to join forces, to support each other, talk it through. But Jack was in no mood. And then, just when it looked like a buyer would never materialize, one did.

The name of the interested party was Stewart House, a company run by Ken Thomson, who had started up a distribution unit within McClelland & Stewart and then spun off his own company from that. The company had its head offices in Toronto, and another office in Indianapolis, Indiana, which was run by Ken Proctor. Stewart House had made some money selling series like the Time Passages Commemorative Yearbook, the Visual Bible, and the Klutz and Baby Genius series. A perfect match for ECW. Thompson wanted to expand his book business and he was circling companies blown away by the demise of General like a barracuda. In fact, he had already made a deal to buy Quarry Press, which was run by Bob Hilderley, the guy I had stood next to at our first Book Expo display. Hilderley had done a number of deals with Jack, and I think they had a good working relationship, but I didn't find him very responsive. Now Stewart House had come along to save his hide and he was in bed with Thomson and Proctor. I think he saw himself as their key to further expansion through acquisition. He would find companies on the verge of collapse and deliver them to Thomson. Meanwhile, Thomson himself struck me as a pure operator. He had no investment in literature and no real sense of ECW's history. He was primarily interested in our celebrity books and in our music and sports titles. I could tell from the moment I met him that he thought the idea of an office in Montreal was a waste of money. It wouldn't be long until he shut me down. Although Hilderley was brokering this deal, he never spoke to me. In fact, he didn't even bother to respond to the numerous e-mails I sent him with questions about the deal. And then there was Ken Proctor, the guy from Indianapolis who was in the process of moving to Toronto so he could help Thomson expand the business. He seemed nice enough, but his orientation, like Thomson's, was all about book as product. I guess he was thinking about the packaging principles on their toy lines when he suggested that we abandon the idea of individual covers for each of our books and come up with a single design template so that we could save design fees. The same would apply to the text design of the books: one model would do just fine.

This kind of talk made me nervous, especially because what Stewart House wanted to do was redefine the way we managed acquisition and production. For example, if I acquired a book in Montreal but it was a music book, production might be handled by the Toronto office, which would be in charge of music titles. That made no sense to me, since I would lose control of the title I had brought into the company and be prevented from applying my vision of the book to the production process. By the same token, Jack might sign up a sports book, but it would be edited in Montreal. I knew nothing about sports.

Meanwhile, the deal had not been consummated. Thomson met with Jack a few times in Toronto and then he took the next step toward acquisition, which involved sending in an accountant to do some due diligence and check out our expenses and revenues and to make some projections concerning future profits. Naturally he found that it was uneconomical to have two offices; he also found that Toronto's titles were selling better than Montreal's. I could see where this was going. I could also see that within this new corporate structure, if it came to pass, that I would be the odd man out. Thomson was already corresponding exclusively with Jack, although Thomson was a terrible communicator who seldom responded to messages or respected meeting times. Proctor had various strategies up his sleeve; he was staying mum. Hilderley was talking to Jack about how things would be run. I saw the power shift and I saw Hilderley's maneuvering. I didn't like what I saw.

None of the tensions produced by the new relationship with Stewart House helped the 27-year relationship I had with Jack. In fact, it made things worse. Jack retreated even further, if that was possible. As he put it, this was the new order, someone else was about to take over the company, and he was about to become an employee, someone who did as he was told. Although no formal agreement had yet been signed, Stewart House agreed to start paying our bills and to take over our distribution in Canada. Getting those cheques out of Stewart House was like pulling teeth. Employees were not getting paid. Visa bills were running late. The rent cheque for the Montreal office did not arrive on time. No one was happy about the rate of payment or about the impending shake-up. Meanwhile, Stewart House had a legal agreement drafted. They would assume our debts and pay us a modest amount as goodwill over a five-year period. We had nowhere to go. After a bit of negotiation, we told them the agreement was okay and asked them to send us the final copies for our signature. It was the end.

I couldn't stand this new order. I had a conversation with Proctor in which I asked him directly about the future of the Montreal office. "You definitely have nothing to worry about for at least six months," he said. And after that? There was no response. Jack and I were supposed to continue as publishers, but all decisions would have to be approved by Thompson, in consultation with Proctor and Hilderley. Well, I thought, this is the way things are going to work now, so I'd better earn my bread and butter. I sent off a number of proposals for new titles, with profit and loss sheets, but never heard back from anyone. Things were apparently moving forward, but in reality things were on hold. However, the bills were being paid, even if they were being paid slowly, and that kept us alive. It wasn't a question of whether I was going to be able to do interesting or creative books anymore. It was only a question of hanging on with this crew so that I could hold onto my house and not run into personal bankruptcy. The funny thing was that Stewart House had no interest in *Essays on Canadian Writing*, which had always broken even or made a slight profit, due to its success in obtaining grants. They were content to see it just plod along, so long as it was self-supporting. So if I wanted to find any semblance of my former life in this new structure, it would reside in the journal, which took me back 25 years. However, there was little consolation in that. I had long ago realized that the journal was not going to save us financially. For me, it was an intellectual pursuit, something I was doing to link my publishing and professorial lives. At the same time my involvement with the journal also reinforced the distance between me and Jack, who had long ago lost interest in *Essays*, believing that it had become too jargon-ridden and theoretical in its orientation. And of course I now had to think about the perception of Stewart House when it came to running the journal. They would know that I was spending time on this venture when I should really have been turning out big sellers on sports, or music, or popular culture. That knowledge would only encourage them to dump me as soon as they could.

It was May 2002, and I was under a cloud. Yet I carried on. I hadn't yet signed any deal with Stewart House, even though we had all agreed to a draft version of the agreement. So long as that agreement remained unsigned, I was technically a co-owner of ECW Press. Every day I hoped that something would get in the way of that agreement. I tried to reason with Jack about this, to convince him that we were about to get into bed with people who had no sensitivity to books, with a company that sold Bible guides in plastic packages and games called Klutz. I didn't believe they were going to pay us the money they said they would over the coming years. We would be surrendering our business to a company that would itself go bankrupt, and we would have no way of coming back, since we would no longer be a corporate entity. Jack remained closed. He said there was no way out. Our fate was sealed.

The next month, spiritually apart but physically together, we participated in another Book Expo. We were working with a new American distributor, the Independent Publishers Group, a highly respected sales and distribution company operating out of Chicago. We had signed on with them prior to the collapse of LPC, but it would still be months until we saw any revenue from the new arrangement. Stewart House had no distribution setup in the US and finding a distributor to replace LPC could only help ECW's bottom line, even if we were swallowed up. Our agreement with Stewart House allowed for some kind of bonus to us if we hit certain sales targets, so there was still an incentive to increase revenues.

Well, this was strange. It was June 2002, and we were supposed to be signing off on our ownership of ECW any day, but still the final agreement had not been provided by Stewart House. I had my own ideas about why the agreement hadn't come: Stewart House knew they couldn't afford to live up to the deal. In fact, I speculated, they couldn't even pay the lawyer's fees to set up the deal. They were obviously running out of cash, fast. To me, this meant it was even more important not to sign with them. And besides, we had taken the first step toward recovery; we had found a new American distributor. Again I pleaded with Jack not to sign the deal with Stewart House. But he remained determined to go ahead because he didn't think we could recover. We had no cash, no hope of sales money for at least eight months, and huge expenses. He thought we would be pushed into bankruptcy and lose our houses.

June came and went. New book ideas were stalled. Stewart House couldn't seem to decide how it wanted to proceed, or what the acquisition process should be. Communications were spotty and inconclusive. I went to Toronto to present my titles to the Canadian Manda Group, our national sales team. We had signed on with Manda in 2000 and had our first season with them in 2001. Their commitment and energy had always been impressive. We made our presentation and told them it would be our last. They wished us luck with Stewart House. I think it was the saddest moment of my publishing life. Jack and I headed back to ECW's Toronto office for a meeting with Bob Hilderley. Maybe at this meeting we would get a better sense of how the process would work. That meeting turned out to make me even more suspicious about Stewart House's plans. At one point, Hilderley got up and went over to Jack and whispered something in his ear. Whatever he said, it was not meant for me. The exclusion hurt me, pissed me off. Who was this guy, anyway, whispering to my partner?

I went back to Montreal feeling grim. There was only one little light on the horizon. Back in the spring a call had come into the ECW offices. In many ways it was the call I had been waiting for for years. It was Fodor's, in New York. The big travel book publishing company. They had noticed the Secret series and were wondering if we might consider selling it to them. I was out of town when the initial call came in, but when I returned I started talking to their editor about the possibilities. They liked the profile of the series and they liked its look. We went back and forth with numbers for a month or so, and then, in August, they came up with an offer. It was a substantial amount of money, certainly enough to help us stay afloat and pay off some debts in the coming months. I could tell that Jack was buoyed by the possibility of this sale. I could hardly believe this was happening. At the same time, two other rays of hope appeared. Jack had signed Neil Peart, the drummer for Rush, to write the story of a motorcycle road trip he undertook to recover from the depression he sank into following his wife's death. Advance orders for this title were surging. Jack knew he had a major winner in his pocket. However, he didn't mention those orders to Stewart House. Maybe Jack was coming back. Then, the Book Publishing Industry Development Program of the Department of Canadian Heritage figured out a way to advance publishers their grant money as a way of compensating them for General's demise.

To its credit, the DCH worked quickly, and soon those publishers who were still alive had their cheques in hand. In the few months following the collapse of General, four crucial things had happened: our US distributor started to get orders, it looked like we were going to sell the Secret series for a considerable bit of cash, Jack had a massively winning title on his hands, and the government had come through with some emergency relief. All of a sudden, we could see a way to operate until the end of the year. By early August, Stewart House had still not sent us the agreement to sign. What was wrong with them? I didn't care. I was happy something was wrong with them. Jack called. He began the conversation with these words: "Don't gloat." Gloat? As if I had won some kind of battle? I had, but the battle wasn't with Jack. I didn't feel like I had triumphed over him. I felt like ECW had triumphed over Stewart House, which was ready to take us down the tubes with them. Jack said he was now ready to tell them we wanted out. And because we hadn't signed anything, there was nothing they could do about it. However, exiting the arrangement did pose problems. For one thing, Stewart House had been paying our bills for a few months now. They had kept us alive. For another thing, they had our inventory. If we walked away from the deal they would certainly try to keep that inventory as a form of payment for their investment in ECW. That would mean another huge blow to us. Probably close to another $160,000. Was it worth an additional loss like that to retain the company? With prospects looking favourable, we decided to take the plunge. We backed out of the deal. By September of 2002 we were our own masters again. And what happened to Stewart House? A few months later they filed for bankruptcy. We had survived the company that was supposed to rescue us.

Yes, we were our own masters again, but of a very fragile house. We were beginning to see some revenue from American sales and we had found a new Canadian distributor—Jaguar Books—but their policy was to pay the publisher when the bookstore paid them. Given the increasingly slow payments being made by Chapters/Indigo, we knew that it would be even longer until we saw some of that money. So the fall was a stressful season. Although the General collapse had long since faded from the news spotlight, the effects remained with us every day. And not all the relief we had planned on materialized. For one thing, the deal with Fodor's went flat. I had no idea, when I was negotiating with them, that they expected part of the purchase price to be used toward buying out the contracts of the numerous authors who had written books in the series. Fodor's did not pay royalties on any of their titles. They wanted our books, but only if the authors would agree to relinquish their royalty arrangements with us and accept a flat fee, the standard at Fodor's. Soon, to my surprise, I was facing an author revolt. The Secret authors who had signed with ECW did not want to go to Fodor's. They liked, as one author put it, the "cozy" feel of working with ECW, and they feared that Fodor's would treat them like hired help. Also, because the increased sales that would undoubtedly have resulted from a Fodor purchase would have no effect on them in the absence of a royalty arrangement, there was no particular incentive for them to make the switch. Yes, they were willing to cancel their contracts for a fee, but after I tried to negotiate an appropriate fee with each of the authors, I realized that, given those costs, ECW didn't really stand to make that much from the deal in the end. So, we let it go.

The death of the Secret deal sharpened our awareness of how careful we had to be with expenses, and of how crucial it was to produce winning titles. Jack had a huge success with *Ghost Rider*, the Neil Peart story. It is no exaggeration to say that the publication of that title saved the company. And it was a tough number to follow. Every title we did was being scrutinized for its sales or loss potential. In Montreal I was developing a number of new books that I thought would do well—two restaurant guides to Montreal, as well as books about wrestling and extreme martial arts. It was difficult to deal with the authors during this period. Inevitably their payments would be late. I tried to explain that we were trying to cope with the fallout from the General situation, and I tried to be honest in confessing that we had almost lost the company. Some authors were understanding, and some had zero sympathy. You owe a million dollars and almost died? Not my problem.

Things went on, but they did not go on. I knew that the past year had taken a tremendous toll on both ECW offices, and the discussions about how we would be rearranged after the Stewart House takeover had caused people to get territorial, to protect the sense of worth they saw in their camp. Inevitably, the discussion within the company turned toward the profitability of each office. Given Jack's track record with *Ghost Rider*, it was difficult for Montreal to claim any victories in the profit department. For this crucial year, he owned the winning title. It might go the other way in a different year, and it had, but that's not what counted now, when we were engaged in a daily fight for survival. I got the sense of increasing competition between the two offices. They were on a different trajectory. We weren't speaking much. A collision was at hand.

Somehow, I made it through the school year. By the spring of 2003 I was exhausted. The ongoing difficulties at ECW had taken their toll, as had the demands of two big courses on Canadian literature that were just coming to an end. One was a lecture class with close to 200 students—Introduction to Canadian Literature—another was also large—70 students in a class on the contemporary Canadian novel. It was inconceivable to me that I had actually devoted myself so completely to those courses, given the meltdown at ECW over the past 12 months. I was an experienced teacher, true, but I had never found it easy to just walk into a classroom without extensive preparation. I'd spend a lot of time worrying about every class, thinking about where the discussion should go, the points I wanted to make. I couldn't stand it when the students got that glazed look in their eyes.

The introductory course always reminded me of my past days in CanLit, mainly because it was so sweeping in its coverage. It began with nineteenth-century travel narratives, focused in on Canadian poetry since 1945, and then switched to an equally broad-based consideration of fiction. I was lecturing on figures such as A.J.M. Smith, Irving Layton, Raymond Souster, Gwendolyn MacEwen, Dennis Lee, bpNichol, and Michael Ondaatje. I found that in various lectures I kept coming back to the way these poets saw their country, how they struggled with problems in language and form to develop new ways of speaking that were not tied to the traditions of other countries. The challenges they faced when it came to the relationship between language and nation still seemed real to me, after so many years. I could see that same issue repeating itself in the fiction—always the problem of finding a voice appropriate to a particular time and place. In the fiction course I was drawn to texts that seemed to be about the making of identity, how we find out who we are and the challenges that such finding involves. The stories of Alice Munro. Ann-Marie MacDonald's *The Way the Crow Flies*. Lynn Crosbie's brilliant exploration, in *Paul's Case*, of how identity is constructed. Her use of Barthes's *S/Z* brought me right back to my early days as a graduate student at York, when I was preoccupied with Barthes and his complete rethinking of the interpretive act. A book about one of Canada's most notorious murderers made me nostalgic. Strange.

No matter which of these writers you read, it was clear that this thing called "self" was slippery, something you could rarely get to know. At the end of the term, as soon as the grades had been submitted, I would have access to the evaluation forms that the students completed every year, just to get a sense of how they liked the course, and of how I had done. I always approached these evaluations optimistically, believing they would demonstrate some consistency in my methods, or proof that when I stood at the front of those classes or lecture halls I was who I thought I was. But the evaluation forms offered little help, mainly because they made it clear that there were so many versions of me. I'm looking through the forms now:

- "Generally very enjoyable."
- "Too much emphasis on poetry."
- "He really knew a broad amount of knowledge."
- "He was good and knowledegable."
- "Too many novels."
- "Lecker was on top of his shit."
- "Fire Robert Lecker for the good of McGill's integrity."
- "It's very difficult to be lectured to at 9:30 a.m."
- "Nice ass!"
- "Tells good stories."
- "Terrible. Boring."
- "Sincere and clear."
- "More modulation in the tone would be helpful."
- "Great lectures!"
- "I didn't find myself to be as engaged as I would have liked."
- "Too much background information."
- "A two year old with any scrap of intelligence could have done the same thing as bpNichol."
- "Friendly and approachable."
- "Neat and organized."
- "A bit too much literary bull-shit. If I hear too much about the limits of language I fall asleep."
- "A little dry."
- "Lecker's voice is too quiet."
- "Very clear."
- "Went way too much into detail on things, like the author's life."
- "Seems like he had a lot to tell us."

Yes, I had a lot to tell them. But Professor Lecker could be somewhat subdued and overly preoccupied with structure. Lecker must be the one who is neat, organized, and quiet. Sometimes Lecker would let Dr. Delicious into the classroom, just to liven things up. Delicious would tell stories and remind them how fortunate they were to be at McGill, which had refused to admit him as a student. He would confess to being the oldest person at the Linkin Park concert, but he could see they were not impressed. Even Dr. Delicious was getting on. He needed release. Linkin Park cheered him up. All that screaming. In fact, whenever he blasted the music in the car, Dr. Delicious was happy. Sometimes Professor Lecker would join him and they would both be briefly happy. The Beastie Boys. The Killers. Interpol. I listened to them again and again, cranking it louder and louder, a true wall of sound protecting me.

But most of the time the wall was down. And now the students were gone. It was time to confront what was going on with the business that had been a source of happiness and anxiety for so many years. Things were getting worse. The bankruptcy of General and LPC, followed by the pressures of dealing with Stewart House, had left big scars. I felt more and more distant from Jack and the Toronto office. When I complained to him that I was being left out of the loop he responded curtly: "There is no loop." That may have been true, but for whatever reasons I could feel the alienation expanding. I never got a call from anyone in Toronto asking me what I thought we should do about a particular problem, or how we should approach a specific advertising campaign. On the day I met with Jack and Bob Hilderley in the Toronto office, Bob said one thing I thought was true: "You guys are essentially running two separate businesses." That's really what it had come to, the result of our decision, years earlier, to pursue acquisitions independent of each other. Gradually, the separation of our acquisition decisions had created a rift in company culture as differing staff ideologies began to align themselves with each of us. Of course, the physical distance separating the two offices played a part in reinforcing the company's dualistic culture, but it was more importantly the result of years of independence on the part of myself and Jack. There was no way, given the company's history, that those two solitudes were going to be reconciled. Jack believed I was being overly sensitive to what I saw as my exclusion from the decision-making processes in Toronto. I believed that he was being too quick to bypass my concerns in favour of backing his staff.

By the time we got down to Book Expo 2003 in Los Angeles at the end of May there was a lot of tension in the air. I was sitting in our display booth next to Jack, but I might as well have been alone. I wished the silence and distance would just go away and that we could somehow get back on track together, find a way out. But it was not to be. I was brooding over an e-mail I had just received about a company action that was being undertaken in Toronto, again without my knowledge or participation. Jack grabbed the paper out of my hand, telling me I had to "get over" this idea that I was being excluded. Something in me snapped. I started yelling. I don't know what I was yelling about. It wasn't just that moment. It was years of feeling inside but outside, years of being in a partnership that made me feel alone, years of Jack's cryptic silences, his suppressed resentment and anger over who knew what, the fact that I had to live two lives in order to make a living, the fact that my job at McGill made it impossible for me to devote the same time to the business as he did, the fact that I had a nine-year old child and I needed time to be a father. It all came roaring out.

Right after Book Expo, Mary flew down to meet me in L.A. Our plan was to take a five-day vacation in Napa. We had a good time, but I was completely distracted by the blowout I'd had with Jack. So distracted that when we finally checked out of our hotel I managed to leave most of my clothes in the room. Jack and I spent the rest of the summer in retreat from each other. The next time we met was at the Word on the Street literary festival in Toronto at the end of September. We had decided to get the staff from both offices together, not only to participate in Word on the Street but also for a meeting in which we would all discuss the future of the company. That meeting was a disaster. With all of the staff in one room, the differences between the offices were immediately apparent. Jack took it upon himself to chair the meeting. We sat there listening, but it was clear that we were not united. When we got back to Montreal, several of my employees commented on our body language at the meeting: "You and Jack were obviously in conflict," one said. And another added, "You guys were on different planets."

About two weeks later, in the middle of October, Jack came to Montreal. We went out to dinner. I hadn't seen him alone, face to face, since our fight back in May. I told him that if it would save the business I would consider getting out. He said he believed that if we cut out the Montreal office and all of the expenses associated with it that eventually the cost-cuts would create a more efficient and profitable company. He was probably right. Besides, how could we go on this way? I had a drink. I had more drinks. I got drunk. I was so angry with him, and I loved him. I staggered out of the restaurant, went home, and crashed.

The next morning I just hung around, feeling resentful, rejected, sad. I had no idea how my life would change if I went through with this. Once it was done, there would be no turning back. I thought our buy-sell agreement. Under the terms of that agreement, either partner could offer to buy the other out. The partner who received the offer could then turn around and force the other one to sell at exactly the same price he had offered. This was a conventional mechanism used to ensure that buyout offers were fair. Jack made me a basic offer. I could have turned around and made him accept that same offer. Then he would have had to sell to me. But he knew that would mean I would have to move to Toronto, since that's where all the grant money was, not to mention the banks, accountant, and lawyers. There was no way I could do that, not with the money I owed and my job at McGill. It would be suicide. And besides, the people in the Toronto office would all have quit. It didn't take me long to understand that I had no choice but to accept Jack's offer.

Over the next few weeks we worked through a basic agreement, outlining the terms of the sale. If Jack ran the business effectively and stayed solvent, I might see my massive personal debt disappear in about three years. That was no small thing. And then on top of that I would get a reasonable amount of cash for what I had put in. Would I be happier when all that happened, if it did? I had no way of knowing. However, there was no turning back. On the strength of the draft agreement Jack and I had drawn up I told the Montreal employees we were closing up shop in November, in just a few weeks. There was shock and disbelief. After that announcement, I could hardly walk into the office again. And when I did go in I was receiving angry calls from my authors, many of whose contracts were being cancelled by Jack, the starkest illustration yet of how little faith he placed in some of my ideas. There was no sense protesting. I had to let go.

Less than a month later, everyone in ECW's Montreal office was gone. I handed back my keys. The academic term was over, the students off on vacation, the grades turned in. December was always a month of transition for me. I savoured the brief period of respite that followed the end of classes and the lull before winter started in earnest. Briefly, the wind would die down, the sails would slacken, and I could drift. The campus went eerily quiet. McGill was like a set that had lost its actors. There was a winding down. And then, just a month later, the whole place would be populated again. All the energy would surge back. I would be walking into other classrooms, somewhere on this campus, to talk about Canadian literature again. There would be novels and poems and short stories, new students to meet, ideas to discuss, lectures to be prepared. Then, in three months, it would end once more. There was a constancy and excitement in that ritual, a rhythm to every term. On this quiet December day, classes over, I wondered where I should go. What I should do. Something big was missing. I knew what it was.

A month flew by. It was a new year. 2004. Jack had been completing the production of a few titles I had signed up for ECW a year or so before I left. My last surviving title was a book called *WrestleCrap: The Very Worst of Pro Wrestling*. Apparently it did quite well. The most recent ECW catalogue says it is "The #1 selling wrestling book on Amazon.com for over 6 months. Over 20,000 copies sold." A claim to fame? How did I get there from the first book Jack and I published almost 30 years earlier—a collection of essays on Hugh Hood? Just last week I looked through the most recent ECW catalogue in depth. The company had redefined the meaning of ECW. Now, according to the catalogue, it stood for "Entertainment, Culture, Writing." There was a whole page devoted to new wrestling books. Other titles included a guide to help real estate agents protect their deals, a book on how to cope with the boss from hell, an easy low-carb cookbook, and a biography of Michael Moore next to a book about Stephen Harper.

Well, wrestling sells and Michael Moore will sell and I suppose the company will make money. And the funny thing is, I can't fault them for publishing any of those titles. It's a business, there are bills to pay, and this is what it takes. But I also can't help feeling the cynicism behind it, the same cynicism that got me publishing books about wrestling, or Wicca, or Jennifer Lopez. In Canada you can pursue the noble path of publishing good poetry and fiction (ECW still does that); however, if you really want to survive you are going to have to embrace the desires of a much wider audience. The wrestling fans, the TV series fans, people desperate to make money or lose weight.

The history of Canadian publishing is littered with the corpses of companies that pursued the good cause of Canadian literature, only to find that the market simply couldn't sustain them, even with all the grants and incentives in place. ECW published more books about Canadian literature than any other company, but at what cost? Our involvement with CanCrit went from ebullience to exhaustion in 20 quick years. There are still a number of excellent small presses out there that have weathered the storm and avoided the wrestling books and celebrity biographies. I don't know how long they will last. And, in the end, I'm not completely convinced that publishing Canadian poetry or criticism or fiction is a higher calling than publishing books about Björk or a travel guide called *Secret San Diego*. It's all literature. Each book has its readers. There's no reason to believe that a book about Archibald Lampman or Margaret Atwood is of more intellectual value than a book about dieting or business. In fact, if literary theory has taught us anything, it's that these are all just texts, ready for the taking. The only problem is that we've been brought up to believe that some texts are better than others, mainly by teachers who would like to convince us that they hold the keys to some kind of cultural literacy or heritage we can learn to share. Once upon a time we thought that Canadian literature represented this heritage and that Canadian criticism could allow us to find it, but today, who knows? Maybe a book about about wrestling or *The West Wing* or dining out in Montreal tells us a lot about the culture that produced it, but just in a different way than a book of literary criticism. To believe otherwise is simply to reinforce an artificial distinction between high and low culture that holds no credibility today. Why should a poem have more status than a restaurant review? Why is a novel a higher form of writing than a well-written travel guide? They are just different kinds of texts and their value lies in what we make of them.

That would be the argument, anyhow. It would be the way I would explain so many of the publishing decisions I made, and ECW's gradual abandonment of Canadian criticism in favour of more commercial titles. Not to mention my persistent desire to avoid personal bankruptcy. I can even believe that argument half the time, usually when I'm not in class. The only problem is that when I am in class, as Professor Lecker and sometimes as Dr. Delicious, I keep getting this sense that in fact literature is indeed a higher form and that I am lucky to be professionally involved in such a rich and ambiguous force. I can talk about Dennis Lee's amazing concept of cadence and its relation to national identity. I can look at Robin Blaser's "Image-Nation" series and try to imagine the nation through his eyes. I can get wrapped up in the unbelievably complex mysteries that seems to course through every story by Alice Munro. I can talk with 70 students about a novel in which a man wakes up one morning to find out he is a woman. How would that feel? Or I can try to explain the incredible polyphony behind George Elliott Clarke's *Whylah Falls*, the blues meeting T.S. Eliot in rural Nova Scotia, years ago.

* * *

A little more than a year after I left ECW I attended an academic conference on Poetics and Popular Culture at the University of Western Ontario. The conference was being held in honour of Frank Davey, who was retiring that year. It was a big gathering of CanLit profs and graduate students, the largest I had seen in years. I was a little nervous about my paper, which was entitled "It Doesn't Taste Like Anything at All: Five Reasons Why Canadian Criticism Has Lost Its Flavour." My main argument was that Canadian criticism had lost its edginess, that there were few dissidents out there, and that even if there were, the industry had evolved to the point that there were practically no outlets for their work. The literature had grown but the criticism was stalled, a victim of general complacency. I was ready for a little debate, perhaps some heated discussion. When I showed up at the conference room to present my paper I was surprised. It was a large hall. And there was a good-sized audience, given that it was a Sunday morning. Sparks might actually fly. The three panelists each gave their papers. After five minutes of questions the moderator took the microphone to say we had run out of time. Sorry, the next event was a hand. Everyone left the room. I felt a little bereft. No debate?

I thought back over the last few days at this conference. Not much had changed. There were some old faces and some new ones but not much had changed. I ran into George Bowering and he teased me about how I had dragged him off to a hospital when I got stung by a bee in Tahiti. (George thought I was being silly, but I'm allergic to their sting.) We were on some CanLit boondoggle. At the conference banquet George stood up, hugged Frank, and said he loved him. People got drunk. Christian Bök did a funny voice performance and David Bentley told me it was not poetry. This was normal. I ran into people who asked me how ECW was doing. I told them it had been more than a year since I'd left. I saw Barbara Godard and Aritha van Herk and Robert Hogg. The first Canadian poet I ever wrote about was Daphne Marlatt. She was there, along with Fred Wah and Roy Miki. I sat next to Brian Henderson and Susan Warwick, who were in my graduate class on Margaret Laurence, taught by Clara Thomas. I tried to remember the year. There were several young poets around who took themselves very seriously. They informed me that there was indeed dissidence out there, recently, mainly because of them.

I was determined to go to as many conference sessions as I could bear. It had the old feel. People gave papers and then there were a few questions and then the session ran out of time. Most of the papers didn't excite me, but every once in a while there would be a jolt of energy, someone who was exploring something new. I was ready to make my move. I would run up to them after the session, introduce myself, talk about a possible book. I could make it happen. Then I remembered where I was, what had changed, and what hadn't. I wasn't a publisher. I was a professor. I was home. The subject was Canadian literature. We were still doing it. For life.

Index

Véhicule Press

www.vehiculepress.com